THE COLLAGE HANDBOOK

THE
COLLAGE
HANDBOOK

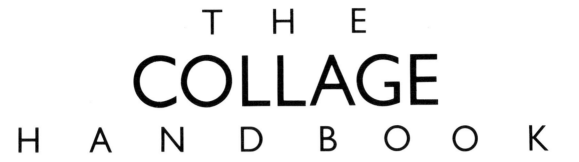

John and Joan Digby

with 123 illustrations, 20 in color

Thames and Hudson

© 1985 Thames and Hudson Ltd, London

First published in the USA in 1985
by Thames and Hudson Inc., 500 Fifth Avenue,
New York, New York 10110

Library of Congress Catalog Card Number 84-
52179

Printed and bound in Spain
D. L. TO: 831-1985

Contents

Preface

This book is about collage in current practice. By definition, the term collage derives from the pasted paper compositions, *papiers collés*, of the cubists, but the medium already had a long history before it had a name. Although paper and paste were its first materials, pasted compositions of fabrics and diverse organic substances as well as paper evolved historically centuries before the cubists intruded cane, wire and oil cloth into their paper compositions.

In order to reflect accurately the scope and genesis of the medium, the term collage as we have used it in this book refers broadly to a pasted picture. By this definition the photomontage, a composite picture made from photographs, is one species of collage, and indeed many artists working with photographic sources or combining photographs with other media often refer to their work as collage. So do many painters working in mixed media and sculptors who see their three-dimensional assemblages of diverse objects as belonging essentially to the collage tradition.

While photomontage, mixed media painting, and assemblage all require separate studies to record fully their materials and methods, we have included some work that extends in these directions as a reflection of collage in the fullest sense employed by practising artists. Although the term collage in contemporary usage resists strict definition according to its materials, by far the greatest number of collagists we have encountered are still engaged in making pasted compositions from paper.

Contemporary collage is most deeply connected, we believe, with the long process of culture that has brought paper to its present state. The medium evolved with the chemistry of paper-making, flourished with industrial technology and in due course also became subject to the frailties of mass-produced paper. The most recent connection between collage and paper emphasizes values of permanence and survival of both the material and the art. This ecological trend is a profoundly important new direction for collage and one that continues to illustrate the abiding link between collage and popular thought.

From its roots in folk art, collage has always been a democratic medium widely practised without special training; and even in its history among trained artists collage has always reflected the people and derived its strength from the immediate reality of ordinary materials in daily use. Only recently have people become aware that the material world can use up its resources and burn itself out. Conservation, in all its manifestations, is an optimistic retaliation against the threat of extinction and one that has entered the mainstream of collage both as a political idea and as a scientific concern with the permanence of paper and adhesives. For this reason we have emphasized the connections between collage and technology devoted to conservation.

Thus the book is about contemporary collagists and about contemporary materials that look ahead to the future and to the survival of collage. It is intended for all readers, from artists to collectors, who might be interested in the current practice of collage. Since the medium has its own democratic history, we have endeavored to continue this tradition by presenting the widest possible cross-section of collagists, not simply the well-known. Our discovery has been that there are a great many more contemporary collagists than a single work could hope to contain. This selection, therefore, is offered as representative but by no means comprehensive.

We approach the work of practising collagists through an introduction on the history of collage and two chapters on materials. In this way the book can also be used as a text or a handbook. Although we present models of archival techniques, we have deliberately avoided writing a manual of collage with specific instructions on "how to make" art or how to imitate collages that already exist. Both are contrary to our notion of creativity.

We have, on the other hand, emphasized the working procedures of collagists in this book, intending them to provoke experimentation, to trigger suggestions, and to provide the basis for solving entirely different problems. Collage has always been a medium that encourages free association, and insofar as this book is a collage manual it is deliberately structured to work by free association rather than imitation.

Writing the book has introduced us to a great number of remarkably kind and original people. In our talks with them, the conversation has often come round to a particular material or experimental method, and sometimes we have been able to say, "so-and-so has tried that; why don't you contact him or her." Finally, we have been able to gather all these techniques, materials, and people together so that the information might be shared.

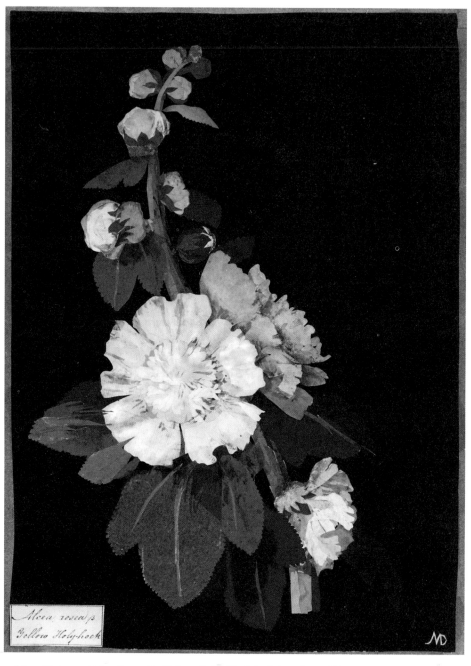

1 Mary Delany: *Althea Rosea B, Yellow Holly Hock* (1782). $13\frac{7}{8} \times 9\frac{7}{8}$ in. Reproduced by Permission of the Trustees of the British Museum

CHAPTER ONE

A Short History of Collage

From its first manufacture in the Orient, paper was regarded as a sacred, ceremonial material, as the earliest known collages reveal. These were made by twelfth-century Japanese calligraphers who copied poems on collaged sheets, "pasted up from a number of irregularly shaped pieces of delicately tinted papers."[1] The poem itself was embellished with patterns of flowers, birds, and stars cut out from gold and silver papers.

Thus collage began as an ornamentation of text. Later the book as ornamental artifact played a major role in the history of collage. As early as the thirteenth century, Persian bookbinders employed surface leather patterns in decorating precious texts. The art reached its pinnacle in the fifteenth and sixteenth centuries, after which it shifted to a tradition of paper cutting.

From the first, collage followed the trade routes of paper and the eastern influences moving west. In Western Europe cutout emblematic devices, coats of arms, even decorative hunt scenes were pasted into conventional books of heraldry and genealogy from 1600. This technique, employing parchment and silk in addition to painted papers, had a more general vogue in eighteenth-century family albums, which popularized the silhouette among its pasted pictures. Among the most elegant of silhouettes are the botanically accurate paper collages of flowers by Mary Delany (1700–88). Pictorial collage within the context of the private book continues today in the folk art montage of family scrap books.

Decorative ornament exclusive of paper entered the folk tradition very early and is another aspect of collage with a long inherited history. In the sixteenth century feather decoration, brought from Mexico to Europe, inspired conscious imitation. Straw portraits and butterfly wing collages later became popular in a secular tradition, while the embellishment of icons, saints' pictures, and reliquaries with filigree, gems, gold brocade, and the like entered religious folk art in baroque Central Europe and Russia. Both the secular and the religious traditions persisted. They came together in the eighteenth century with the first cards that celebrated St. Valentine's Day, which led to the nineteenth-century vogue of greeting cards adorned with cameos, cupids, and gilded or hand-colored paper lace.

The Victorian period is epitomized by its memorabilia: caskets, dried flower and hair assemblages, *découpage* screens and walls ornamented with composite mementos. Of these, the folding screen of Hans Christian Andersen (1808–75) is the best known. Its vast montage of landscapes, buildings, historical portraits, miniature genre scenes, and imagery borrowed from the history of art mesmerizes the viewer with shifts of imagined space. It has the magnitude of a Last Judgment, and in a special, almost ironic way, its nostalgic view of the past can be read as a judgment on the technology of its own period. For the paper of Andersen's age carried in its acidic chemistry the seeds of inevitable destruction.

From the nineteenth century, collage is linked to mass production and ephemeral waste paper. Indeed, collage is chiefly a medium of the last eighty years, a by-product of modernity, and the history of twentieth-century collage until the 1970s has shown its deepest connections with disposable culture and all its paradoxical implications. It has responded with mixed affections to information, fragmentation, war, propaganda and technology, and also to commerce and its junk.

The earliest collages of Picasso (1881–1973) and Braque (1882–1963) were made between 1912 and 1914. Their planes of wallpaper, oil cloth, and cane introduced the surfaces of common material textures that became the contextual reference of modern collage. Picasso was the first to use commercial objects – labels, calling cards, matchbox covers, and tobacco wrappings. On the table among the suggestions of guitars and wine, they organized a constant frame of daily reference that followers of cubism and the collage tradition of *matière* study continued to pursue. They placed the viewer clearly in the café where the most prominent connection with ordinary life, the newspaper, was a dominant recurring image, forcing the viewer away from nostalgia to face the modern world.

Picasso and Braque made these pictures of pasted paper, *papiers collés*, which defined the term collage in the tension that led to the First World War, and from that point forward typography gained political significance for collage. Fernand Léger (1881–1955), fighting on the Argonne front, made collages directly on lids of ammunition boxes, later citing his war experience as a decisive influence that shook him out of abstraction and back to reality.[2]

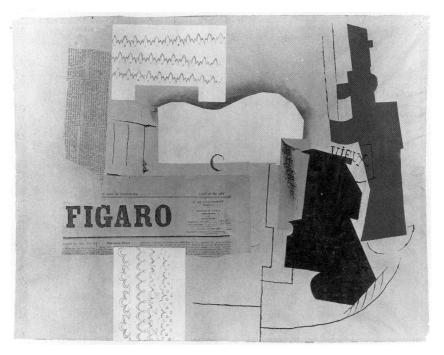

2 Pablo Picasso: *Bottle of Vieux Marc, Glass, Guitar and Newspaper* (1913). $18\frac{3}{8} \times 24\frac{5}{8}$ in. Tate Gallery, London.

The demand for an affirmative material connection between art and reality came, also in the war years, from the futurists. Umberto Boccioni (1882–1916), whose *Technical Manifesto of Futurist Sculpture* called for composite forms to be made in metal, glass, cement, cardboard, electric light and all the material expressions of a new dynamism, also extended his confronting posture into collage. Into his paintings he thrust newspaper sheets reporting the war and printed matter proselytizing his aesthetics.

Futurism's verbal dynamism exploded in the "typomontages" of Filippo Tomaso Marinetti (1876–1944). His early manifesto, *L'Immaginazione senza fili e le parole in libertà (Wireless Imagination and Free Words)*, of 1913, expressed the unconstrained energy of the liberated typeface. Herta Wescher has interpreted his random shapes, shattered syntax, and simulated noises as "an attempt to reproduce the hallucinatory experiences of soldiers in the front lines."³ Carlo Carrà (1881–1916) and Gino Severini (1883–1966) pursued the violent energy in typographically profuse collages. Even material reality – the ticket stubs, labels, photographs, postage stamps that rested on cubist still-life planes – was charged with a restless energy that the artists associated with the dynamism of the machine age.

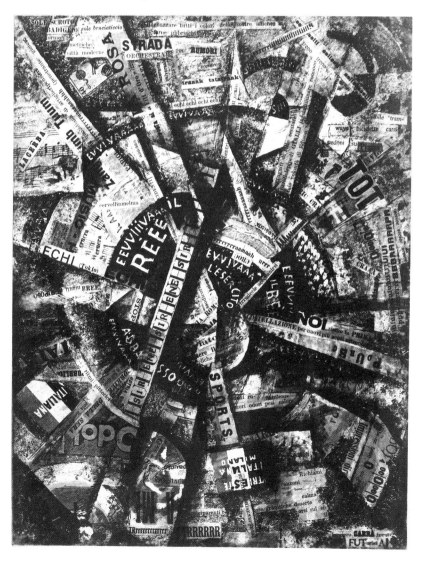

3 Carlo Carrà:
Interventionist Manifesto
(1914). $11\frac{7}{8} \times 15\frac{1}{8}$ in.
Gianni Mattioli
Collection, Milan.

Closer to the saturated colors of Sonia Delaunay than the subdued materials of Picasso and Braque, the futurists also pursued the textural implications of abstract form and color. Giacomo Balla (1871–1958) in particular made collages from colored papers and foils articulating powerful shapes in abstract motion. Progressively, futurism stripped the utilitarian frame of reference, exposing the plastic and architectonic potential of the material fragments.

The connection fostered by the futurists between collage and poetry was shared by the early Russians, possibly under the impetus of Marinetti's visit to Russia in 1910. The Russian "Zaum" poets exploring non-rational word innovations came inevitably, under the futurists' influence, to typographical invention mingled with collage. Handwritten copies of books, often using collage jackets and illustrations, circulated in limited editions. In Russia, furthermore, poetry extended naturally to performance. Granovsky, who worked in book collage, also designed for the theater. Natalia Gontcharova (1881–1962) and Alexander Sakharov (1886–1963) made elaborate collage sets and costumes for Diaghilev ballets, similar to the Picasso collaborations for *Parade*. Picasso's radical dissections of space, along with his free integration of material objects, constituted a second tension field in Russian constructivist aesthetics.

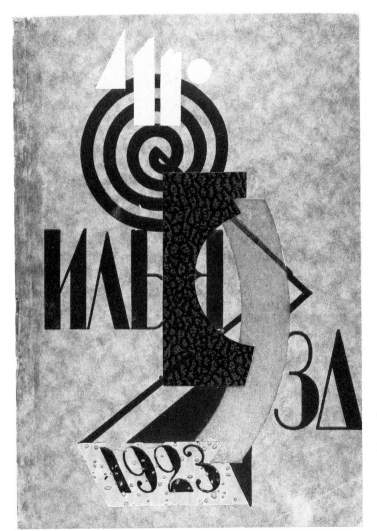

4 N. Granovsky: Collage cover of Il'yazd Zdanevich, *Le Dantyu as a Beacon* (Paris, 1923). $7\frac{5}{8} \times 5\frac{1}{4}$ in. The British Library Board.

The "Suprematist" style of Kasimir Malevich (1878–1935) evolved as a reductive, nonfigurative distillation which he described as "cubistic-futuristic." His paintings and collages expressed this in elemental squares and visual blasphemies that paved the way for dada. His collage sets and costumes for Kruchonykh's futurist opera, *Victory over the Sun* (1913), brought to the stage a walking "square" followed by robotic actors costumed in hardboard and wire assemblages.

Even more dramatically than Malevich, Vladimir E. Tatlin (1885–1953) was inspired by the wire strings that Picasso had used in his early musical reliefs. In 1913 Tatlin visited Picasso in Paris. Unlike many Russians who made the pilgrimage to Paris and stayed, Tatlin returned to Russia and, after a period of found-object construction, began in 1915 to fill rooms with "counter-relief" wire arcs that sparked the first real connection between Russian constructivism and mechanical engineering.

All the diverse sources of the Russian aesthetic were unified by a continuing dialectic of *poetry*, *performance* and, from Tatlin onward, *propaganda*. If cubism and futurism fostered a particular combination of intellectual and material revolution, they were timely influences that fed into the mainstream of political reality.

With the Bolshevik Revolution collage exploded into a popular force, used in posters, pageants and photomontages that carried the message of the Revolution to public squares. There is a certain irony in the *avant garde* emerging as spokesmen in a folk idiom, but not in the context of Russia, where the roots of collage go back to the icon. Natalia Gontcharova's costumes for the Diaghilev/Stravinsky *Liturgie* – never performed – were constructed of wood and metal with silver and gold papers, in the fashion of religious icons. Other collage designers for the theater employed both the legends and the iconography of Russian folk art. Among the Jewish artists too the folk idiom was strong. Issachar Rybak (1894–1965), Marc Chagall (b. 1887) and El Lissitzky (1890–1941) all designed collages for magazines, books and theater, making use of Hebrew inscriptions and Yiddish tales integrated with the visual theories of cubism and suprematism.

Thus, without abandoning Russian folk traditions, collage became a vital medium for imagining the future and the new society. And in the revolutionary period it was full of the visual paradoxes to be expected of a sensibility in transition. The cubist influence encouraged the use of nostalgic materials such as wallpapers, fabrics, and lace, at the same time that it offered the example of materials from the machine age. Both cubism and futurism set further examples in a fractioning of space and time consistent with the new physics epitomized by Einstein's Relativity Theory.

El Lissitzky's "proun" works, particularly, apply constructivist principles to physical interpretations of pictorial space, and his emphasis on color as the purest state of matter charged with energy implies the engineering of a new vision. Lissitzky contributed his vision to Marxist utilitarianism along with constructivists such as Tatlin and Rodchenko (1891–1956).

But other artists, among them the brothers Anton Pevsner (1886–1962) and Naum Gabo (1890–1977), were concerned to maintain the independence of art from politics. Both continued to work on problems related to space and time, using the kinetic and plastic materials of the age. By the end of the Revolution, constructivist

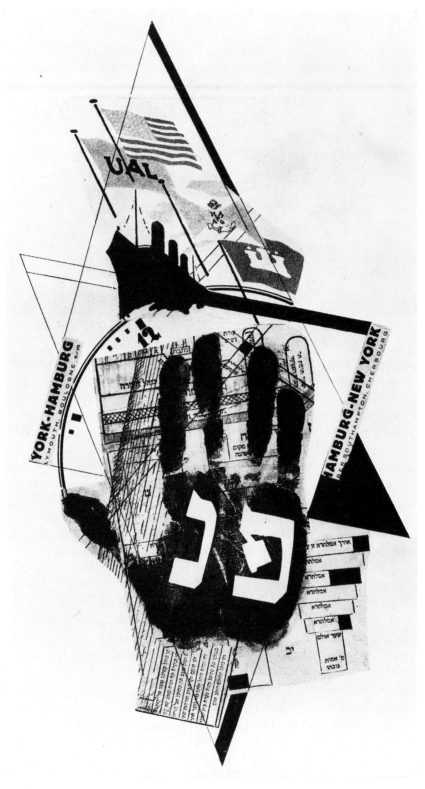

5 El Lissitzky: Illustration to Ilya Ehrenburg, "The Boat Ticket", from *Six Tales with an Easy Ending* (Moscow, 1922). S. Lissitzky Collection, Novosibirsk.

collage was divided into two camps, one concerned chiefly with politics, the other with a kind of literal materialism. They were to go their separate ways in the same manner as the dadaist camps.

Dada's posture was vehemently ANTI – beginning with its radical stand against the First World War. Its logic was impeccable. War derives from civilization, from its luxuries, its goods and hence its art, as marketable perfection and beauty. To be antiwar, according to their logic, implied a refutation of the whole contingent chain, and so they asserted themselves to be anti-beauty, art, goods, luxury, and civilization as a way of bringing war to its knees. Though theirs was a rational stand, reason was unacceptable to them because of its use in justifying war. Therefore, they expelled logic and gave themselves a meaningless name that exploded in revolt. They were writers denying the moral value and efficacy of words; they were artists attacking art. Their uncompromising stand against war forced them to undermine their own professions and cast themselves as public enemies.

In February 1916, one small group of these artists, writers and poets founded the Cabaret Voltaire in Zurich. They were Hugo Ball (1886–1927), Tristan Tzara (1896–1963), Marcel Janco (b. 1895), Hans (Jean) Arp (1887–1966), and Richard Huelsenbeck (1892–1974). They sang, danced, banged on drums and staged mimetic performances protesting against war and society. Unlike the cubists, who spread planes of newspapers to arouse reality at the breakfast table, the dadaists used newspapers like voodoo dolls into which they could stick pins. Better than that, they cut them up and, according to Tzara's directions, put the isolated words into a paper bag and made poems from the random order that emerged. In this way they denied both the logic of sentences and the unpleasant reality of news.

Denial led the dadaists to perpetual inversions that refuted utility and art. At the New York Armory Show of 1913, Marcel Duchamp (1887–1968) aroused provocation by his outrageous "ready-mades." He dared to turn a latrine upside down and call it *Fountain* (1913). In collage, too, he made minimal alterations of paper surfaces, titled them and called them art in order to shock. Duchamp settled in New York in 1915. From that distance he could afford a more detached sense of humor than the entrenched Europeans surrounded by war. New York dada, with its object transformations, was literally a movement of name-calling. Francis Picabia (1879–1953), a refugee from cubism, stressed even further the title of a work as its unconscious dimension of ingenuity. His mechanical images, often called portraits, became his calling card. Picabia's camera "Portrait of Alfred Stieglitz" (1915) is suggestive, too, of the role that photography was to play in dada and later in surrealism.

The American, Man Ray (1890–1976), a figure on the cusp of both movements, lent his name to photograms ("Rayographs") made by placing objects between a light source and sensitive paper. The intrusive object was also a staple of his collaged surfaces; furniture parts, knobs, and the like were employed as *trompe l'oeil* enquiries into planes of reality. His collages, which began as cubist patchworks of paper and fabric, became progressively more abstract and light-sensitive. In the *Revolving Doors* album (1926), he built up layers of transparent architect's curves in luminous colored papers and silk.

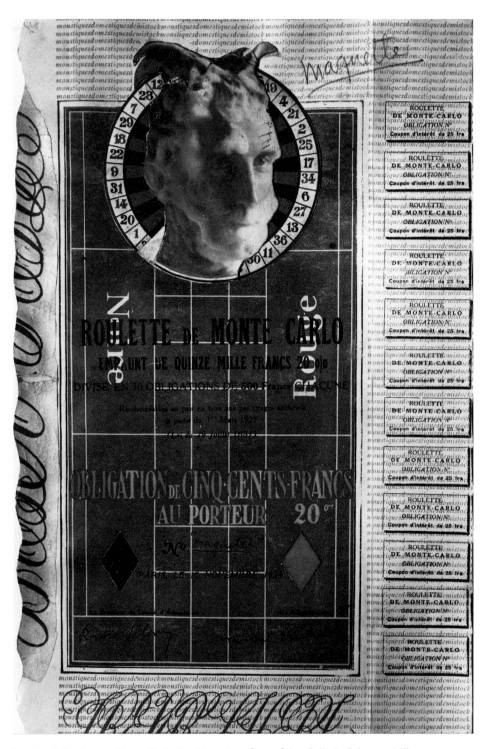

6 Marcel Duchamp: *Monte Carlo Bond* (1924). $12\frac{3}{8} \times 7\frac{5}{8}$ in. Galleria Schwarz, Milan.

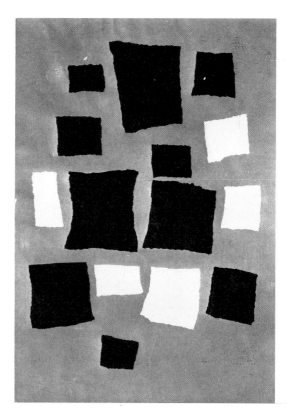

7 Jean Arp: *Collage with Squares Arranged According to the Laws of Chance* (1916–17). 19⅛ × 13⅝ in. The Museum of Modern Art, New York.

Ray's shift from cubistic materials and planes to free-floating shapes has a parallel in the work of Arp. His early collages, too, were sharp-edged constructions in fabric and printed paper. The use of cloth constituted for him an important dimension of dada revolt that can easily be misinterpreted as a cubist remnant or overshadowed by the more overt outrages of dada. Arp turned to fabrics in protest against traditional paint and painting's mimetic imitation of the world. Many current collagists reiterate Arp's position, but through the politics of feminism they have come to emphasize fabric as a feminine vehicle of attack against the traditional media of male-dominated art. The sexual association was not consciously a part of dada, though the attack on the mainstream was. The cubist Sonia Delaunay (1885–1979), who at one time ran a collage boutique in Paris, was certainly a feminine influence in the use of tailors' swatch books. But tailoring materials were widely employed even by male cubists, futurists and constructivists before Ray and Arp converted fabric to dadaist ends. If cloth symbolized for them an attack against traditional representation and art media, its use had become associated with the mainstream of collage from early on.

In Arp's case the abandonment of patterned fabrics is generally attributed to the influence of his wife, Sophie Taeuber, who was ironically a teacher of embroidery and weaving. Together they worked on collages that grew into chance geometries gradually restricted in color to gray, blue, black, and white. The strong element of play in Arp's work can be construed as political only in the broadest sense. In defiance against the adult world that was busy at slaughter, he and the Zurich club struck the childish posture of a naughty gang absorbed in games and making toys that deflected attention from the brutal seriousness of war.

At the same time, closer to the center of action, Club Dada in Berlin confronted the war with direct propaganda in an outpouring of collages, assemblages, and photomontages. Raoul Hausmann (1886–1971), in his manifesto *Synthetische Cine der Malerei*, again made reference to child's play, regarding the dadaists as rejuvenators of dolls, toys, and the scraps of reality.[4] Hausmann, Hannah Höch (1889–1978), George Grosz (1893–1959), Johannes Baader (1876–1955), and John Heartfield (Helmut Herzfelde, 1891–1968) emphasized in their proliferation and distortion of images a thorough disgust with political affairs. Their materials were taken from contemporary magazines, newspapers, and other photographic sources. Typically, they filled an entire spatial field with disturbing figures in chaotic urban and war scenes. Typographical cries of DADA, ANTI, and satiric slogans emerged as self-reflections and eruptions of protest. Their image-making, only a few decades later than the Victorian montages of passive memorabilia, illustrated the degree to which the war had obliterated the past and made nostalgia impossible for them. Even the shapes of these dada collages frequently suggested the cogs and springs of machinery that could only anticipate further peril.

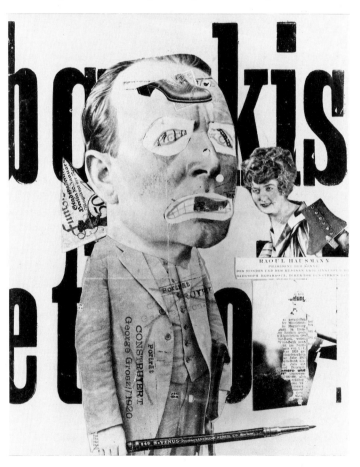

8 Raoul Hausmann: *The Art Critic* (1919–20). $12\frac{1}{2} \times 10$ in. Tate Gallery, London.

John Heartfield met the peril head-on in his attack against the Weimar Republic and the rise of Hitler. Earlier he had used his training in a Berlin film company to make dadaist photomontages and illustrations for the Malik-Verlag, a press founded with his brother, Wieland Herzfelde, during the First World War. His images, montaged from books, newspapers, and magazines, were themselves frequently returned to their sources by publication in the media. His particular genius was to make composite images, however bizarre or satiric, appear to be a photographic documentation of reality. Thus an X-ray of "Adolphe the Superman" (1932) exposed the gold and junk on which he fed; and a family swallowing machine parts – reminiscent of Gillray cartoons against the Napoleonic War – documented the simple truth that there was no more butter (*Hurrah, die Butter ist Alle!* 1935).[5] By means of W. Reissman's complex photography, and with refined touches of airbrush, Heartfield's work arrived at a unified, uncompromising image that, like an X-ray, saw through the world caught by the camera.

That collage, a medium of surface planes, could explore subsurfaces of reality was an idea Picabia had raised in his attribution of titles to the unconscious. Dada was to generate two superheroes who, between them, divided the issue: Kurt Schwitters (1887–1948), the masterbuilder of material surfaces, and Max Ernst (1891–1976), the archimago of dreams.

Kurt Schwitters trained for dada in the army and the factory. In the first he jammed the cogs of the machine, disorganizing files to make impossible the tracking of deserters; in the second he discovered the cog as an abstract symbol of the human spirit. In 1917 Schwitters went to Berlin to join Club Dada and was promptly rejected by Huelsenbeck, whose name he twisted into a derogatory pun on the word "husks," *huelsendadaists*. For Schwitters, a man of the wheel, the *real* dada (of Tzara and Arp) was a movement of abstraction; and yet, paradoxically, Schwitters' abstractions were made of husks. In 1919 he began to compose pictures of gathered scraps. To describe them he coined the term *merz*, from the fragment of a newspaper advertisement for the Kom*merz*iel-Privat Bank which he had pasted into one of his collages. Underlying the syllable was Schwitters' real business with the products of commerce. His appropriation of commercial refuse for art was unlike the gatherings of other dadaists, who used the stuff in protest. He was not merely attracted to surfaces, textures, the patina and color value of worn papers; he saw them as potentially contributing to a unified aesthetic. "I value sense and nonsense alike," he commented.[6] Though his favoring of nonsense was calculated to assert his allegiance to dada, the real emphasis of the statement falls on the first two words: *I value*. Whereas dada had set itself up to deny and destroy values, Schwitters reaffirmed them: the aesthetic value of particular fragments, and, even more profoundly, the value of unity that comes with deliberate composition.

From his refuse Schwitters composed with a clear purpose of artistic unity. The most flamboyant expressions of this were his *Merzbau*s. In 1923 he began a ten-year Jungian transformation of his house into the *Kathedrale des erotischen Elends* (Cathedral of Erotic Misery). After it was destroyed in the Second World War, he began another in Norway, and finally one at Ambleside, England, which remained incomplete at his death. The compulsion to create these buildings can be linked to a

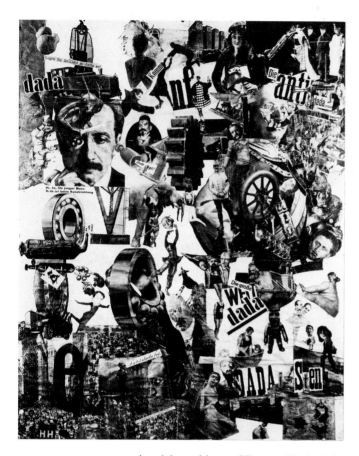

9 Hannah Höch: *Cut with the Cake Knife* (1919). $44\frac{7}{8} \times 35\frac{1}{4}$ in. Nationalgalerie, Staatliche Museen Preussischer Kulturbesitz, Berlin.

romantic vision akin to Horace Walpole's eighteenth-century transformation of Strawberry Hill into a place of spiritual longing. For Schwitters, who dreamt of a *Gesamtkunstwerk*, a union of all the arts, these buildings manifested his belief in the spiritual environment of modernity and its products.

Constructivism and *de stijl* also played into his fertile imagination. As early as 1919 he had begun publishing a magazine in collaboration with Arp, El Lissitzky, Piet Mondrian (1872–1944), and Van Doesburg (Christiaan E. M. Kupper, 1883–1931). Van Doesburg later used the title, "La Matière dénaturalisée" (Matter Denatured), for one of his own collages, a title which could be regarded as thematic in Schwitters' work.

Schwitters' dealings with the matter of commerce were at times extremely pragmatic. In the twenties he worked with Lissitzky for a time in advertising, promoting modern typography and progressive design that emphasized geometry and simplicity. In his private transformations, the reduction and denaturing of material went even further. His collages, which have had the most enduring influence of all his work, pared the matter to its essential harmony of dimensions bound in unity. Schwitters' choice was also, in part, a conscious record of his intimate life. The scraps came from his immediate surroundings in Germany, Norway, England – his records, letters, stamps and associations that connected his remnants with scraps of the world at large.

There is no collagist alive today who can bring together discarded papers gathered from the street and wastebin without evoking references to Schwitters. His signature

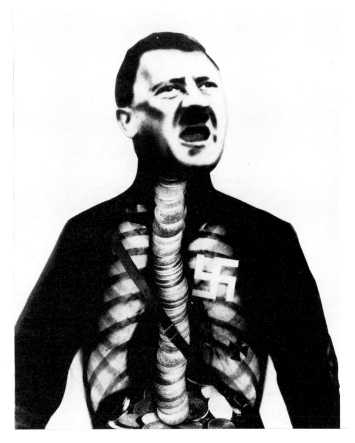

10 John Heartfield: *Adolf the Superman Swallows Gold and Talks Tin* (17 July 1932). Photomontage enlarged and posted up over Berlin in August 1932.

has stamped these materials of commerce with aesthetic value; his choice and order of them have validated collage as a medium of modernity comparable to painting.

While Schwitters gained approval for its ephemera, a second affirmation of collage's instinctive methods came from the surrealists. Virtually all the art movements early in the century had used collage to cultivate alogical, unpremeditated encounters among wildly disparate images. André Breton's *Manifeste du surréalisme* of 1924 finally connected their impulse with Freud and called for an automatic poetry and art that would reveal what Freud described in theory – an absolute reality of unconscious mind and uncensored emotions that lay below the threshold of reason. Collage was the perfect vehicle, a *tabula rasa* that simply received the readymade images as they presented themselves in free association.

Surrealism itself was a receptacle for free-floating artists who had been through other movements and were ready to go beyond. Picasso, Arp, Hausmann, Archipenko, Picabia, Duchamp and a host of others gravitated to Paris and surrealism. But above all, the history of collage was affected most deeply by the impact of Max Ernst.

It is fitting that Ernst came to collage through a chance encounter. He was at the time already involved with Johannes Theodor Baargeld (Alfred Grünewald, 1891–1927) in the Cologne dada group, and he had exhibited fantasy paintings at Der Sturm gallery in Berlin. One day in 1919 Ernst happened on an illustrated catalog of scientific instruments so profuse, improbable, and contradictory that they

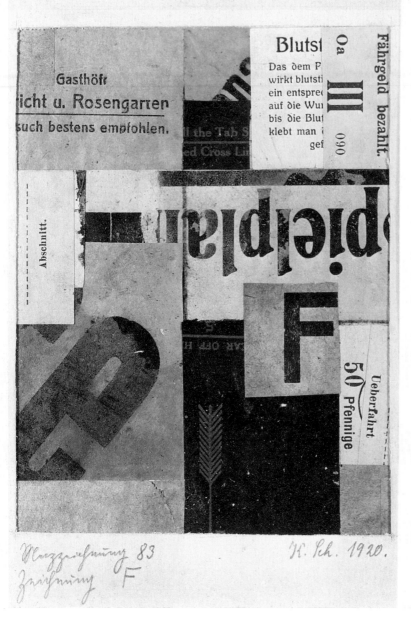

11　Kurt Schwitters: *Merz 83 Drawing F* (1920). $5\frac{3}{4} \times 4\frac{1}{2}$ in. The Museum of
Modern Art, New York (Katherine S. Dreier Bequest).

raised hallucinatory visions. Taking the plates and transforming them with paint and
pencils, he revealed the world that they presented to his inner eye.

Mechanical images, even catalogs, had been used before. But in his narrative
imagination, Ernst invested them with a totally new and visionary potential for
collage, untouched by art with a capital A. In truth, Ernst liberated collage from art,
from its concerns with plastic and visual planes, and turned it into a theater of the
irrational.

His materials – paper and paint, fabrics and photographs – recapitulated the
whole history of collage, like a patient's narrative leading the psychiatrist up to the

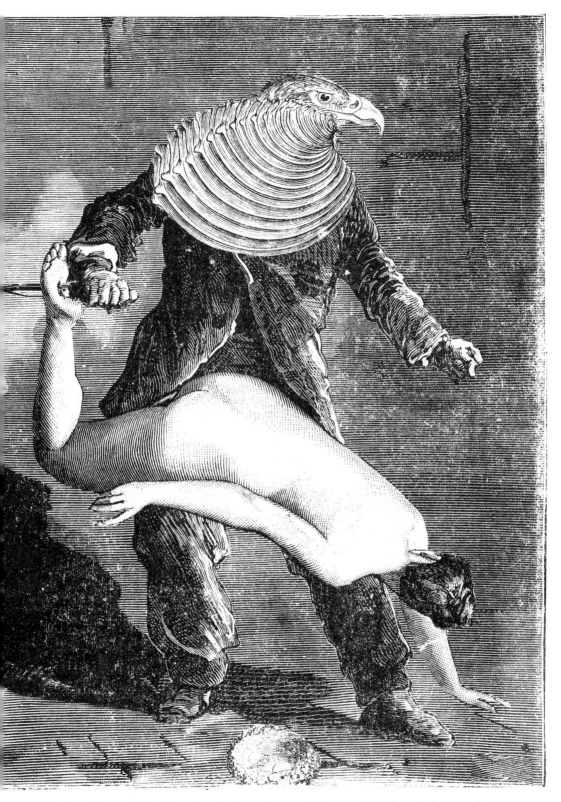

12　Max Ernst: Plate 25 from *Une Semaine de Bonté* Volume 4 (Paris, 1934). The Museum of Modern Art, New York (Louis E. Stern).

ultimate revelation. Ernst's revelation was that *"ce n'est pas la colle qui fait le collage"* (it isn't the paste that makes the collage), and from the moment he disclosed it he was free to go beyond.

Above all, Ernst understood the liberating value of the narrative itself. He published four books of collages – collage novels – constructed from engravings found in cheap romances and catalogs: *Les Malheurs des immortelles* (1922), *La Femme 100 têtes* (1929), *Rêve d'une petite fille qui voulut entrer au Carmel* (1930), and *Une Semaine de bonté, ou Les Sept éléments capitaux* (1934).

His frightful visions of women in their private chambers ravaged by bird men, of fanged lions, vampire confidants and bound figures drowning in an ornate world invite our own disturbances to come alive. They are, like a technique he also invented, *frottages*, rubbings of sensibility. Ernst conjured them from Victorian and Edwardian images which became, in his vision, universal archetypes. At about the time when dada had filled its frame of vision with current horrors taken from newspapers and magazines – as if to argue the total annihilation of the past – Ernst recovered the past as the psychological *locus* of dreams.

Even years after their first publication, Ernst's collage novels remain popular and are reprinted regularly, for they have a permanent ability to disturb, haunt, and tease us with glimpses of our own erotic imaginations caught dreaming. Ernst is still a father-figure in contemporary collage. To his countless followers he has suggested the engraving as a quintessential medium of veiled allusion. Just as we associate the name of Schwitters with used papers, so it is impossible to look at Victorian illustrations without thinking of Ernst. Indeed it might be said that engravings found it necessary to invent Max Ernst.

Other surrealists of the Paris group that included Ernst drew their free associations from different materials. André Masson (b. 1896) did automatic drawing with strong references to biological life, which he emphasized by introducing real feathers, leaves, shells, bones, pebbles, and sand. Valentine Hugo (1887–1967), a great ballet enthusiast, made visionary portraits in painting, woodcut, and photography by collaging them with sequins, paper lace, and other ephemera she associated with dance. Salvador Dalí (b. 1904) also began to overlay painting surfaces with the fantasy intrusion of symbolic objects. Joan Miró (1893–1983) worked with even greater diversity. He composed *Spanish Dancers* out of common building materials. He applied free drawing and paint to collaged patterns of cut paper, and invented his own lyrical dreams in everything from assembled photographs to three-dimensional constructions – the other favorite medium of the surrealists.

One could go on counting the artists who experimented with surrealism like sheep going over a fence that leads eventually to one's own private dreams. As a movement, surrealism opened the fence to subjectivity and was, in that sense, to borrow the contemporary artist Esteban Vicente's perception, the last great movement of ideas in twentieth-century art. It emanated from Paris and became a diaspora, spreading as far as Chile, where the group Mandragora was founded in 1938. Surrealism took root particularly well in climates threatened by repression.

In Czechoslovakia, the birthplace of Kafka, surrealist collage with a strong satiric element flourished in the work of Adolf Hoffmeister (1902–73), Jindrich Štyrsky (1899–1942), Toyen (Marie Cernisova, b. 1902), Vincenc Makovsky (1900–66), Zdeněk Rykr (1900–40), and Karel Teige (1900–51). These artists and the influence of surrealism are still important today in the political climate of Czechoslovakia. The original Prague group was driven underground by Hitler's *Kulturkampf* in 1938.

That same year the Belgian surrealist E. L. T. Mesens (1903–71) moved to London from Brussels and opened the London Gallery. In England he promoted the movement which attracted, among others, Edward Burra (1905–76), Sir Roland Penrose (1900–84), Eileen Agar (b. 1901), Conroy Maddox (b. 1920), and Jacques B. Brunius (1906–67), the French film director who worked for the BBC. More

13 André Masson: *The Blood of Birds* (1956). $29\frac{1}{2} \times 29\frac{1}{2}$ in. Musée National d'Art Moderne, Paris.

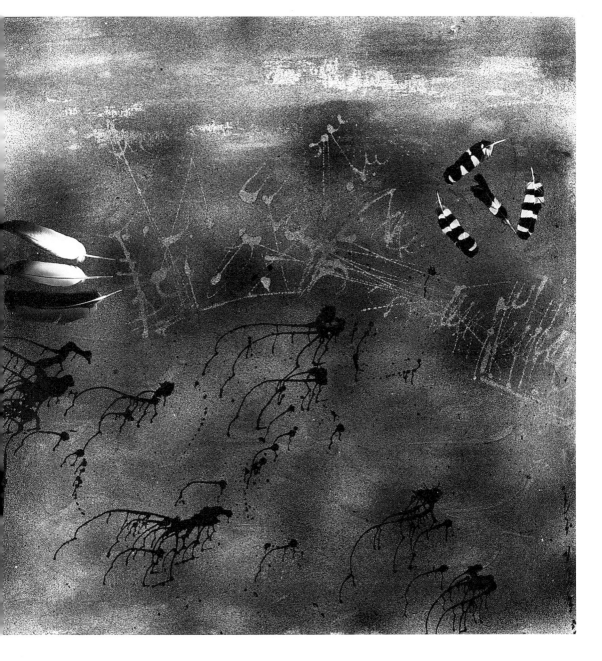

recently, Terry Gilliam's graphic contributions to *Monty Python's Flying Circus* have made the BBC a latter-day guardian of surrealism in Britain. Gilliam (b. 1940) is an American, but his fantasies are European, and his revival of the Victorian line engraving perpetuates the comic spirit of Ernst.

The Ernst influence on American surrealism probably made its first impact on New York artist Joseph Cornell (1903–72). In 1930 he saw *La Femme 100 têtes* and decided to try his hand at collage. Though his debt to Ernst is apparent in his early pieces, he soon developed his own personal style. In recent years Cornell has gained increasing importance as an influence on contemporary American collage. He has come to stand for the isolated American, emotionally connected with Europe. Cornell's boxes, fusions of collage and surrealist objects, are icons of his vision. Some house his passion for French literature and art. The influence of Gérard de Nerval, Lautréamont and Baudelaire permanently conditioned his sensitivity to evocative images of the voyage and the chance encounter. He built palaces and hotels, penny arcades of the Medici family, habitats for exotic birds, archaic charts and maps of the stars. Cornell lived, quite appropriately, on Utopia Parkway in Queens, New York. He never traveled, but in his soap bubbles and shifting sand boxes he found his way into a magical world far from the urgent city.

Urgency itself was changing the city in ways that Cornell deeply regretted. He found his boxes and gathered his scraps in the shops and streets of New York, which he looked upon as a warehouse of ephemera lost among the skyscrapers. Once he wrote a scenario for a stereoscopic film that was set in Central Park late in the nineteenth century.[7] It was about a photographer for whom the common world had turned to vision. In later collages Cornell used the photograph more and more as a backdrop for displaced visions. His haunting figures, dolls, angels, and children borrowed from the history of art, are time travelers through all the lost ages between the Renaissance and our own. They are allegories of innocence that speak of childhood memory, but also of the darker side of loss and longing.

Cornell's work hinted at modernity only in its mysterious imagery, of springs, clocks and coins turned back to toys. It certainly was made without explicit reference, even in the period of the Second World War that was bringing European modern art to America. The rise of Hitler forced many artists to flee their native countries and find refuge in the United States. The surrealists Ernst, Breton, Duchamp, Tanguy, and Masson were all in New York by 1942. So were immigrants from other European artistic traditions, Chagall, Grosz, Huelsenbeck, Mondrian, and perhaps most decisive for the future of American collage, the refugees of the Bauhaus, László Moholy-Nagy (1875–1946) and Josef Albers (1888–1976).

Both were protégés and later teachers in the school founded by Walter Gropius (1883–1969) on the ideals of a purely functional art responsive to industrialization. The Bauhaus training emphasized the study and handling of materials. In this respect it was an extension of the constructivist direction taken by Gabo and Pevsner and particularly by Pavel Mansurov (1896–?), who had made educational reliefs of bark, roots and diverse natural materials to express the organic origins of artistic form. In his term as director of the Bauhaus, Johannes Ittens (1888–1967) engaged students in the manipulation of tactile materials and in spontaneous compositions

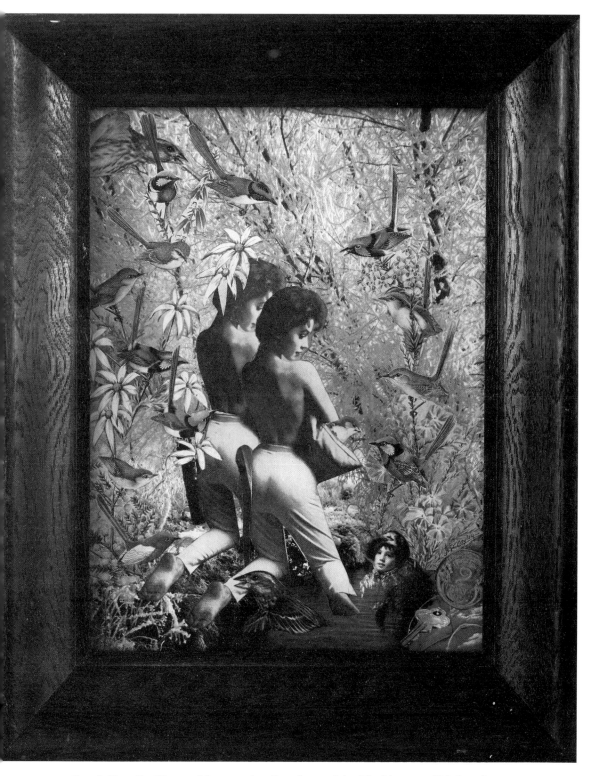

14 Joseph Cornell: *Allegory of Innocence* (1956). $15\frac{1}{4} \times 12\frac{1}{4}$ in. The Museum of Modern Art, New York.

generated by the feelings they aroused. Both Albers and Moholy-Nagy succeeded Ittens, and when they came to the United States, they brought with them his methods. Moholy-Nagy gave impetus to photomontage as well as to the collage treatment of materials. In collage the more prominent influence was Albers, as a teacher at Black Mountain College and Yale University, and also by the extended impact of his writings.

Connected with his theoretical work on color, his practical cultivation of *matière* study helped to promote the abstract collage in America. Dissatisfied with paint pigment as an accurate medium for studying color, Albers encouraged his students to compose directly with materials, particularly colored papers and autumn leaves. Their *matière* studies of crumpled, torn and manipulated shapes served Albers as proof of the relativity of color, while it provided American collage with materials that came to be regarded for their own sake as personal and pure. Many of the collagists directly influenced by Albers show a greater interest in the textural value of found materials than in their color relationships. And while Albers brought Color-Aid paper into wide use among collagists, the fluid treatment of them was often more closely related to Matisse cutouts than to Albers' *Homage to the Square*.

Whether from Albers or Matisse, Ernst or Schwitters, collagists took what they needed and assimilated disparate theories into personal expression. Abstraction gathered strength in the 1940s. In the year of Schwitters' death, 1948, Charmion von Wiegand (1900–83) helped to arrange an exhibition of his work in New York which stimulated an awareness of collage as an intimate structured gathering. Von Wiegand, who in the early 1930s was a news correspondent for the Hearst newspapers in Moscow, became a close personal friend of Mondrian in 1943. She followed his geometric compositions for a time and later became president of the American Abstract Artists (AAA). For several decades, under the influence of Oriental thought, her abstractions bore the delicate calligraphic traces of Chinese characters and ornamentation.

Also in 1948, Ronnie Elliott (1910–82) was an exhibitor in the first New York collage show at the Museum of Modern Art. Like Charmion von Wiegand, Elliott was moved to abstraction both by the found materials of Western culture epitomized by Schwitters and by Oriental fabric remnants. During the Second World War her husband, who was a news correspondent in China, sent her rags from Yunnan province which she was determined to use as compassionate statements about poverty and waste. Bleached and handpainted, they became the personal fabric of her collages. Prior to her death in 1982, the influence of African masks and textiles drew her into a new sphere of collage expression. Like Charmion von Wiegand she sought a fusion of east and west, and in abstraction a "universal expression" that would "merge the contributions of all past cultures and . . . create a world tradition in art."[8]

The collective pursuit of universals through emotive expression came to be called abstract expressionism. As a movement of style it crested in the wake of surrealism. Surrealism had liberated the unconscious to pursue its own direction, and the abstract expressionists, with their emphasis on impulse and nonconformity, simply agreed to go their separate ways. Many of them, including Robert Motherwell (b.

1915), William Baziotes (1912–63), and Ad Reinhardt (1913–67), found collage a medium conducive to their unpremeditated methods. Conrad Marca-Relli (b. 1913), for example, cultivated the speed and automation of collage worked in cut canvas. New York painter Theodoros Stamos (b. 1922) remembers how he came to collage with no formal idea in mind, but from the materials and the color themselves, mainly tissues, corrugated board, and the crinkled papers in which seedlings came wrapped. His found papers drew him away from the large canvases that were characteristic of his format and gave him a new scale of dimension. During the 1960s he made collages between sessions of painting, conscious of their difference but maintaining the equal importance of collage as a medium. The edges particularly were different in collage from those in painting, and he emphasized the torn edges, setting forms against each other on variously surfaced papers which he sometimes painted. "The ideas came from the surfaces," he recalls, and only later developed an allusive attachment to the natural world, sometimes expressed in the title alone.

For many collagists since, the medium has remained quite simply – to borrow Stamos' definition – "tissues and other things glued down." Collagists who refer to color, form, edge, surface texture, and particularly the freedom of direct, impulsive contact with tangible materials illustrate the permanent impact of abstract expressionism.

Motherwell is still prolific in collage. So too are Fritz Bultman, Leo Manso, Robert Goodnough, Esteban Vicente, Claude Bentley and a great number of younger contemporaries motivated by the spontaneous impulse toward abstraction. The nonrepresentational collagist – with or without reference to expressionism – has an essential perception of material stripped to qualitative purity.

This does not always mean that the material is stripped of all imprint. Many contemporaries, both abstract and figurative, use paper deliberately with reference to data and particularity in the vast industrial waste-heap of culture. In doing so, they bring forward the traditions begun by cubism, futurism and dadaism, which announced almost simultaneously – if from different perspectives – the centrality of the newspaper to the modern world. Newsprint has been historically a most versatile and recurrent source of cut-up texts and collage images. This runs the gamut from the expressionist abstractions of Ad Reinhardt to the humanist fantasy portraits shaped from newspaper by Arthur G. Dove (1880–1946) and Jean Dubuffet (b. 1901).

Many collagists have acquired their imprinted papers from another medium of communication, the street poster, tearing fragments off walls and even imitating the character of effaced originals in their *affiches lacérés* compositions. The Italian Mimo Rotella (b. 1918) is best known for this method, though it has been practised with variation by many artists. British collagist Gwyther Irwin has made large landscapes from the monochromatic reverse side of torn posters, entirely transforming the meaning of his source papers.

Collage as a metamorphosis of scrap has proliferated in economies based on disposable paper and a barrage of communication. At present this is nowhere more noticeable than in the United States, which probably produces more books, magazines, seductive wrappers and obsolescent merchandise than any other country. Its economy has made it a watershed of collage – with some ambivalence. While its profusion has occasionally generated an apotheosis of junk, the glut has driven some American collagists (like William Dole) to European paper sources, looking for the more exquisite remains of a more lasting society. In all there has been a certain unrest, a need to isolate and make something out of the tidal wave of words, images and information that is simply being discarded.

Even in the folk culture of America there has been an impulse to salvage something from the wreck. This is sometimes economic, as in the houses of rural Appalachia where the tradition of collaging walls with magazines, newspapers, and burlap flour sacks developed over the first three decades of the present century. The women recycled the disposable materials to keep the houses insulated and clean, but also to make them beautiful. They placed photographs strategically, saved the newspaper color supplements for special holiday decorations and made conscious patterns of image and print that gave ornamental structure to their rooms.[9] Although the tradition, developed out of poverty and ingenuity, was abandoned when people could afford commercial wallpaper, it dramatizes much more profoundly than scrapbooks, pattern pictures, and *découpage* – also folk traditions of salvage – the connection between collage and economics in the industrial world.

Collage as folk craft continues in art education. There are numerous books on how to make collages, books written for children and for adults with a creative urge to decorate their walls. The do-it-yourself craft tradition of collage believes in "mass"-creativity just as it believes in mass-production. It implies that collage is the normal behavior of practical people who do not like to see things go to waste. It emphasizes recycling the materials of daily life and, indeed, turning the dross into something beautiful.

This same desire to rescue and transform the disposable materials of society is one of the strongest impulses in contemporary collage. Nowadays, largely without reference to the historical movements from which these motives derive, collagists pursue their private reclamations. They are alternately driven by the taste for matter and an impatience with the material world. From its cast-offs they rescue their intimate selves, gathering fragments of reality into unity, like the gathering of Osiris from his scattered remains.

Some collagists still cry "dada" against the culture itself, angry at the scattering, the economics, the signs of waste and war. An affirmative counter-politics establishes different values: conservation instead of waste, craftsmanship instead of mass-production, and permanence instead of decay and inevitable destruction. These philosophical values have had a radical impact on recent collage. Derived in a certain sense from *matière* study, the new collage seeks not merely to retrieve and preserve discarded materials by the methods of the archivist, but also to make material, particularly handmade paper, for the express purpose of collage.

The awakening of this sensibility is best epitomized by Anne Ryan (1889–1954), who has been described as "a Victorian lady and an abstract artist."[10] Her collages, as reflections of herself, bridge the two worlds without conflict. They are formal abstractions of paper and fabric that nevertheless seem as personal as old family portraits in their oval frames. She began them, with no purpose in mind, at the age of fifty-eight. Seeing an exhibition of Schwitters simply drove her to compose. But before completing the first dozen pieces, she had already abandoned his kind of printed scrap papers. She required materials emptied of all content but their own precise values of color and surface. This led her first to paint her cloths and papers. Finally she came upon the handmade papers of Douglas Howell.[11] Their mottled colors and suggestive grains represented an aesthetic close to her own art, and she brought it progressively closer, even providing Howell with linen fabrics for his papermaking. At first, because of their expense, she used the Howell papers sparingly as mounts, inviting her collages to be read in their setting. Later, when she had more money, she was able to collage directly with the Howell papers, which became a principal material in some of her strongest pieces.

Anne Ryan worked for only six years, and yet among contemporary American collagists she is one of the most frequently cited influences, particularly with reference to the lyrical value she extended to the use of handmade paper. In the present climate of collage, handmade paper has come to be sought not only for its aesthetic value but for its quality as an enduring material. The fragility and impermanence of paper, which once positively aroused the sensibility of the collagist, have at this stage of the art become a challenge to overcome.

The new *matière* study is based on an aesthetic of permanence. It has turned many collagists to the technology of paper and its conservation. They take steps to preserve their found papers. They seek out and deliberately manufacture papers of archival quality as the conscious foundation of their art. Privately and quietly, without the writing of new manifestos, collage has taken an important ecological turn, attaching itself emphatically to the post-industrial goal of survival.

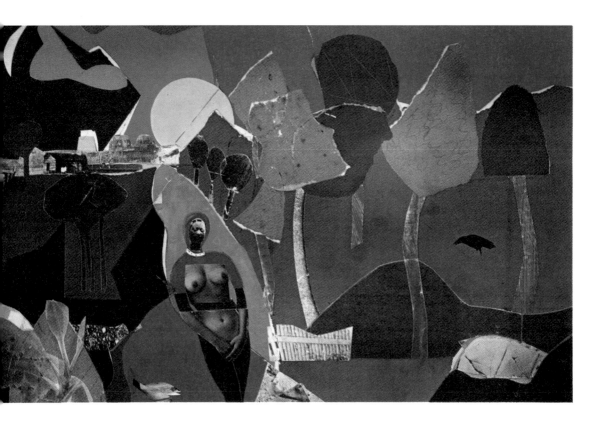

I Romare Bearden: *Memories* (1970). Paper collage on board, $14 \times 19\frac{3}{4}$ in. Courtesy C. W. Post College, Long Island University, New York.

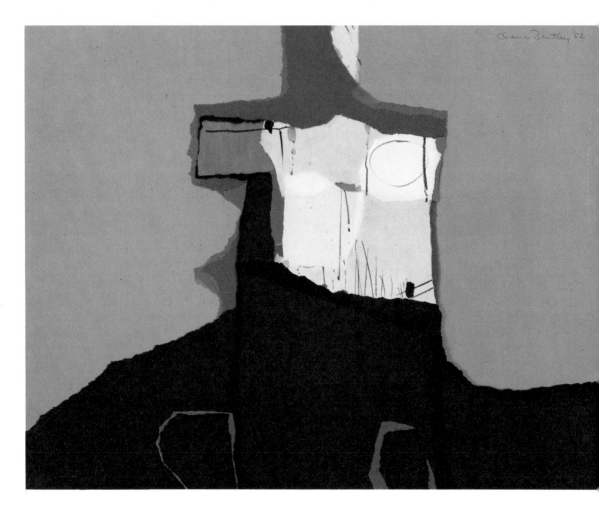

II Claude Bentley: *Dream of a High Place* (n.d.). Paper and adhesive, $19\frac{1}{2} \times 25\frac{1}{2}$ in.

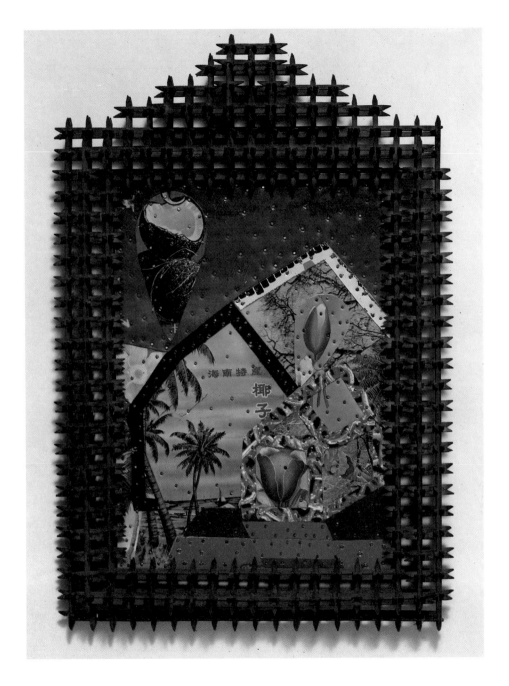

III Tony Berlant: *Hawaiian Village* (1981). Metal collage on plywood with brads in a tramp art frame, $14\frac{1}{2} \times 21\frac{1}{2}$ in. Courtesy Xavier Fourcade Gallery, New York.

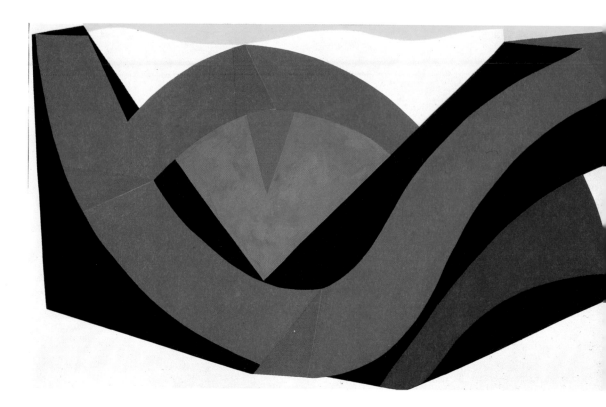

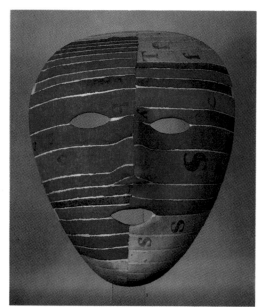

IV Fritz Bultman: *Blue Wave II* (1982). Paper collage, 48 × 80 i

V Robert Courtright: *Blue and White Mask with Letters* (1981). Papier mâché, magazine print, and acrylic, 7 × 5¾ × 3½ in. Courtesy Andrew Crispo Gallery, New York.

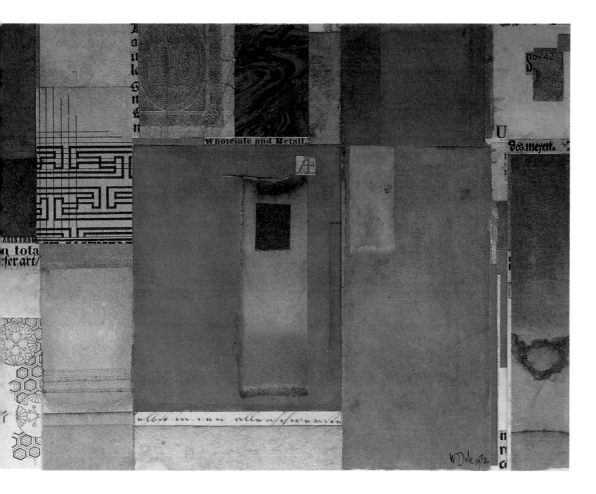

VI William Dole: *Improve Every Shining Hour* (1972). Paper collage with watercolor paint, $9\frac{3}{8} \times 6\frac{3}{4}$ in. Collection Mr. and Mrs. Richard Feld.

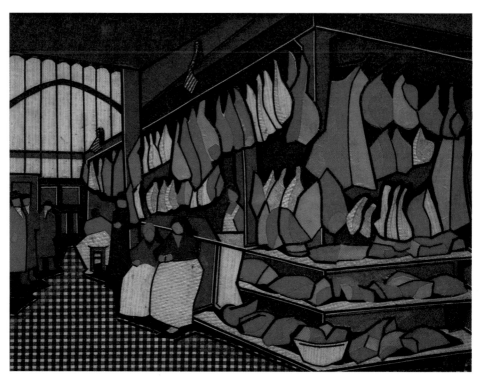

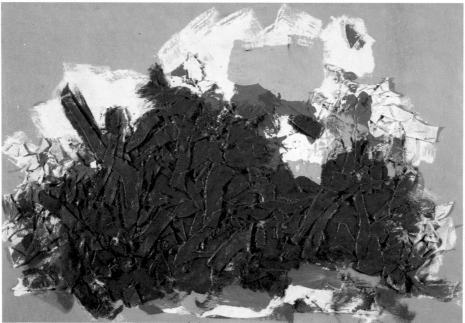

VII Estelle Ginsburg: *Charcuterie* (1969). Paper collage, 10 × 13 in. Collection of the artist.

VIII Robert Goodnough: *Collage Painting #5* (1981). Painted canvas on wood, 16 × 24 in. Courtesy André Emmerich Gallery, New York.

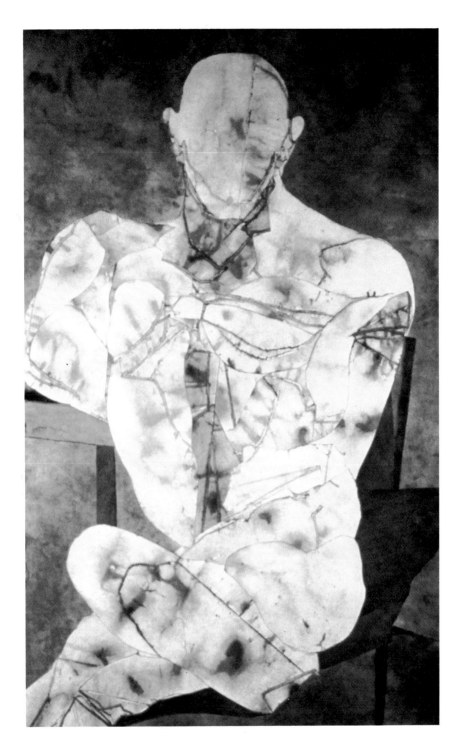

IX Nancy Grossman: *Cloud Figure Seated* (1976). Aniline dye soaked paper collage, $61\frac{1}{8} \times 37$ in.

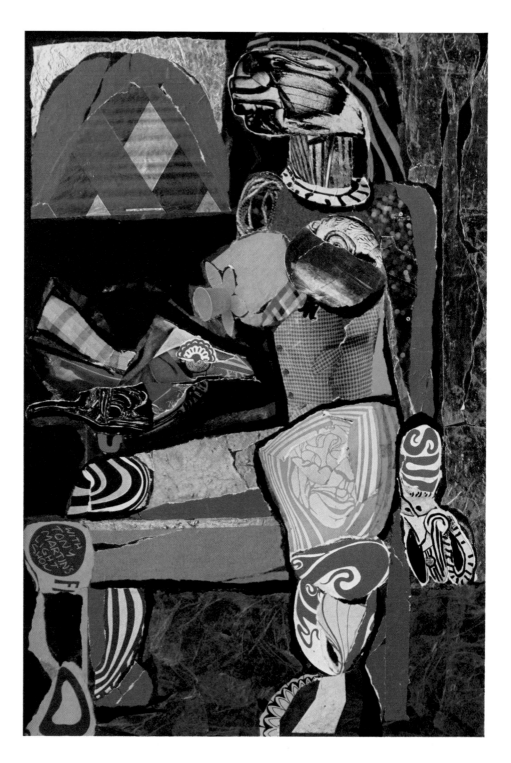

X Satish Gujral: *Paper Collage* (1964–68).

CHAPTER TWO

Paper: The Fiber of Collage

In the year AD 105, Ts'ai Lun announced the invention of paper to the Emperor of China. In one sense he was also proclaiming the birth of collage. For the essence of collage is an exuberant response to the use of paper. In 1982 Robert Rauschenberg went to the People's Republic of China to work at the oldest paper mill in the world at Jing Xiam, Anhui province, where paper has been hand-made for fifteen centuries. He completed an extensive series of collages which brought the medium full circle back to its roots.

Like Rauschenberg, many contemporary collagists have been directly inspired by paper, the material and the process of its creation. From an historical point of view, collage is inseparable from the development of papermaking, the trade routes that brought it to the West, and the technology that brought it into the twentieth century.

Simply speaking, paper consists of cellulose fibers, inert carbohydrates that are the chief components of plant cell walls. The earliest papers were made from the fibers of barks and the filaments of plants and grasses such as mulberry and hemp. The softened pulp mixed with water was probably poured from vats into molds and dried in the sun. By 700 sizing was developed as a means of improving paper for writing and printing. Sizing coated the matted fibers with a hard surface that could be rendered smooth enough by burnishing to prevent ink from feathering. Wheat starch, rice flour, and lichen glue were among the earliest materials used.

From China, papermaking spread to Korea and Japan by 600, and though the Japanese had no written language until the third century, they were the first to accomplish printing on paper in 770. Chinese prisoners of war conveyed the secret art to Samarkand (now in the Soviet province of Uzbek) in the eighth century. From there the trade route of the caravans brought paper to Baghdad and Damascus in the same century, to Egypt by 900 and to Morocco in 1100.

Arab papermakers modified Chinese methods and materials. Most notably, the Arabs turned to rags fermented in wood ashes and lime as a source of pulp. The lime and wood ash treatment deposited an alkaline residue in the papers, improving their permanence and strength. This lime treatment was to be revived centuries later by conservators, papermakers, and artists anxious to reclaim paper from the modern technology that had filled it with destructive acid.

When the Moors conquered Spain in 711, paper made its entry into Europe. From Spain it spread to Italy. The mill at Fabriano, Italy, began its manufacture in 1260 and adopted the first known European watermark in 1282. By the fourteenth century gelatin size, made from the horns, hooves, and hides of animals, came into use. And by the same century paper was manufactured in France and Germany. It spread rapidly to Flanders (1405), Poland (1491), and England (1495), its production linked inextricably with the revolutionary advent of the printed book.

Paradoxically, the destruction of paper came about with progress and the technology that made mass production possible. The discovery of chlorine in 1774 by Karl Wilhelm Scheele led to its use in bleaching rags for paper. A strong oxidizing agent, chlorine in contact with moisture forms hypochlorous acid, which is damaging to cellulose. Acid was already a problem. From the mid-seventeenth century, papermakers had begun using alum to encourage fiber bonding and set the gelatin size. Alum is acidic, but the destructive effects implicit in its acidity were not known to eighteenth-century papermakers, who saw its value in preventing bacteria and mold formation in the gelatin and increasing resistance of the size to ink penetration. Nineteenth-century manufacturers displaced gelatin altogether, shifting to alum in combination with rosin to form a water-repellent size, which unfortunately liberates sulfuric acid in the chemical reaction. Thus rag papers progressively declined in durability, so that by 1829 the publisher John Murray lamented that a Bible only thirteen years old was "crumbling literally to dust."[1] Probably more than any other development, the use of alum-rosin size contributed to the deterioration of paper as a factor of nineteenth-century life.

The introduction after 1860 of groundwood papers also had negative effects. Unpurified woodpulp contains noncellulose materials such as lignin, which breaks down into acidic compounds when exposed to light and air. Thus, by the mid-nineteenth century the same technology which expanded book production and decreased the cost of paper generated brittle sheets of short life expectancy. While groundwood papers (such as newsprint) are inherently unstable, it was later discovered that carefully made chemical wood papers, especially if they are buffered, can have quite a long life.

The breakthrough came in 1901 when Edwin Sutermeister, a paper chemist in Maine, revived the use of calcium carbonate to produce an alkaline wood pulp paper of greater permanence and strength, though it was not until 1960 that this was developed on an industrial basis through the efforts of W. J. Barrow, working in Virginia.

In more recent years, many commercial papermakers have adopted lines of paper that are neutral or alkaline and use nonacid size. The reaction against commerce has also played a certain role, reviving significant interest in handmade and even homemade paper. While this is often part of a greater ecological consciousness, there is no doubt that technology has assisted the quest for paper permanence. The development of polymer chemistry has indeed supported the production of synthetic size, adhesives, and paint media that have become beneficial staples of contemporary collage.

CHAPTER THREE

Treatment of Papers; Adhesives; Tools

Since papers and pastes are the essence of collage, it is extremely important to consider these materials in some detail. Much of the paper manufactured today, including paper of a very high grade, is machine-made on a Fourdrinier paper machine. But artists working with paper have a much greater variety of textures and tones available to them in mold-made and handmade papers. Mold-made papers are formed on a machine by a slowly rotating cylindrical mold. Handmade papers are also made with molds, but these are rectangular and the papers are formed by a vatman dipping the mold into a slurry of pulp. Some of these papers bear the mark of thin lines on their surface. These are "laid" papers and get their name from the thin wires that run at right angles to the widely spaced chain lines on the mold screen. "Wove" paper, formed by a fine wire, cloth, or synthetic mesh, is smooth and without surface markings – unless the paper has a watermark. "Laid" and "wove" papers each have their special characteristics.

Appearance is a matter of personal taste. Whatever choices the collagist makes, these should be governed by a basic concern with the stability and permanence of the paper itself.

The greatest enemies to paper are light, which can cause discoloration and fading, water, heat, mold growth, and acid. A certain elementary protection of all paper can be achieved by keeping collages and collage materials away from direct exposure to light and in a temperate, dry storage area. Extremes of dampness cause paper to expand and encourage the cultivation of mold and infestation by insects. Extremes of dryness cause brittleness and other symptoms of aging to both paper and adhesives. The control of temperature, humidity, and light helps preserve collages. Humidity is a particular problem, since collages are made of composite materials that expand and contract at different rates. These stress cycles are exaggerated by fluctuating humidity.

Acid, both internal to papers and from external pollutants, is a further and most severe threat to paper permanence. Acidic conditions in paper are known to break down the cellulose fibers, causing deterioration and brittleness. For this reason the ideal collage papers, from the perspective of endurance, are acid-free.

Acid in paper can be measured in terms of pH units, which indicate hydrogen ion concentration. The pH scale is numbered from 0.0 to 14.0 with 7.0 as the neutral point. Values 0.0 to 7.0 are acidic; values between 7.0 and 14.0 are alkaline. For a paper to be relatively safe from acidic destruction it must register at least 6.0, which is nearly neutral. A higher numerical value in the alkaline range is even more desirable, since papers can pick up acidity from handling, contact with chemicals in the air, and oxidation which is accelerated by light exposure.

It is easiest to find new papers that are acid-free. Manufacturers concerned with the archival quality of their products generally strive to produce papers with a pH value between 8.0 and 10.5, and they advertise this information along with fiber content. Machine-made acid-free papers are often treated with alkaline agents, like calcium carbonate, that resist the paper's tendency to accumulate acid from handling and atmospheric pollutants. These are now widely available in all weights and textures from the lightest tissue to multi-ply mounting boards.

To the collagist, paper is more than a material. It is often a subject as well as a medium. For this reason, handmade paper is held by some in the very highest regard. The new reverence for "works on paper" in the 1980s emphasizes this aesthetic and places a greater demand on the collagist to meet the high standards of "permanent" paper art called for by conservators and curators. The availability of materials has made it easier for artists to make their own paper at home, even with simple kitchen equipment, if they choose. Some collagists, such as Robert Courtright and Robert Rauschenberg, have worked directly at mills with master papermakers, Rauschenberg traveling as far as Ahmedabad, India, to the famous, papermaking Sarabai family and to the People's Republic of China. But even without such extravagant means, the collagist can find an exciting selection of acid-free mold-made and handmade papers from around the world.

Japan is known for its variety of extremely tear-resistant papers, collectively known as *washi* and often mistakenly called rice papers in the West. Among them are the *kōzo* (*Brouissonetia kazinoki*) mulberry bark papers, the finest of which have been made by hand since the sixth century. Thin, pliable ones like Uda, Udagami, and Sekishu are especially useful in mending and backing collage elements. Buff Kitakata, another strong paper recommended for hinging collages, is made from a different combination of *mitsumata* (*Edgeworthia papyrifera* or *Edgeworthia chrysantha*) and purified wood pulp, which is a fine grade of wood-derived pulp that has been rendered acid-free. *Gampi* (*Diplomorpha canescens* or *Diplomorpha sikokiana*) is another native plant of wild growth that has been used in making a thin, tough non-absorbent smooth paper since the ninth century. Gampi Torinoko is an elegant contemporary example.

Japan also produces acid-free papers by machine, like Silk Tissue and Okawara, a very strong 100 percent *kōzo* paper which is more highly prized in its handmade version. Many of these papers, useful for mending and backing, also appeal to the collagist for surface textures and designs.

Among the best suited for applied design are the lace papers, made in several different patterns, that are created by jet streams blown through the newly formed sheets. Other papers, such as Natsume, Ogura, Kinwashi, and Unryu, derive their patterns from embedded fibers, which give them a soft, fabric-like appearance.

The particular fiber qualities of *kōzo*, *mitsumata*, and *gampi* are not found in European and American papers. On the other hand, there are very fine, acid-free Western mold-made and handmade papers that serve different elements of the collagist's aesthetic. Those made from fibers of nonwood origin, such as rags, manila, cotton, or linen pulp, are generally called "rag papers." Others are made from purified wood pulp.

Some of the European mills have been producing fiber papers for centuries. Names such as Barcham Green & Co. Ltd., J. Whatman (England); Moulin du Val de Laga à Richard de Bas, Moulin du Verger de Puymoyen, Moulin de Larroque (France); Cartiere Miliani Fabriano (Italy); Lessebo Handpappersbruk (Sweden); and De Zaansche Molen (Holland) are synonymous with the history of papermaking, which they reflect in their current productions. A sense of history and quality is shared by some manufacturers of mold-made papers like Arjomari Prioux, S.A. (France), the Van Gelder Papier Company (Holland), and the Inveresk Paper Company Ltd. (England), which are large-scale producers of distinctive fiber papers. But the increasing interest in papermaking as a richly original applied art has also led to the growth of many small handmade paper mills whose output is available for the collagist: Plant Paper Mill, St. Albans Paper Company, Sheepstor Handmade Paper Ltd. (England); CHO Mill and Press, Papersmith Mill, Papeterie St-Gilles and La Papeterie St-Armand (Canada); Paperart (Switzerland); Lawrence Barker (Spain); Jinn Hand-made Paper (Germany); Carriage House Handmade Paper Works, Twinrocker Inc., Imago Hand Paper Mill, Dieu Donné Press and Paper Inc., San Seriffe Paper Ltd., HMP Papers (USA) – to name only a few. Some papermakers and mills specialize in direct collaboration with artists. Silvie Turner and the late Brigit Skïold in their recent book, *Handmade Paper Today* (London: Lund Humphries, 1983), offer a worldwide survey of mills and papers. Their comprehensive book, which describes and illustrates available papers in useful detail, contains a list of manufacturers and agents that is an invaluable resource for the collagist.

Although acid-free rag papers are most plentiful in white, antique, and buff, many of the mills have a wide selection of colored papers. Fine mill papers have a tactile quality well suited to collage. And among the repertoire of colors are not only solids but speckled sheets and papers embedded with contrasting fibers. Artists working with handmade papers colored in small dye or pigment lots should realize that it may not be possible to match colors perfectly or purchase the same color at a later date. Nonetheless, the subtle tones and textures of handmade colored papers make them extremely desirable.

Among the most exotic of these are the marbled papers. This is a technique introduced in the Near East during the fifteenth century and later carried to Europe where it was used mainly for book endpapers. The technique involves floating colors on a size of gum tragacanth or caragheen moss. The discrete areas of color are then manipulated, "combed" into patterns, and transferred onto papers. Sydney Cockerell's handmarbled papers produced in England are well-known, as are the French papers of Michel Duval. Marbling is a process that the collagist can learn and apply to the collage medium itself.

There are other ways to transfer colored patterns to paper. The Japanese Mingei papers are *kōzo* sheets stencil-dyed by a fifteenth-century process known as *Katazome*. More than thirty different patterns of Mingei are commercially available. Miriam Schapiro, who uses them, also makes her own stencil patterns to apply color design. Batik is another dye process that can be applied to making colored paper patterns and has been used by Faith-dorian Wright in her collages. Nancy Grossman creates chance patterning with aniline dyes, which help preserve the papers by providing an alkaline saturation.

Collage artists working in color may want to experiment with patterned papers or patterning of their own. They will also find a good selection of existing solid colors among the Japanese papers: Moriki, Tarei, Unryu. Ande Lau Chen and Evelyn Eller, for example, make use of Unryu with its long decorative filaments to suggest the texture of vast landscapes.

Working in color has not meant for all collagists beginning with colored papers. Robert Courtright, for example, who is concerned with creating a sunbleached effect in color, has both painted used papers and made some of his own colored papers. Other collagists like Ruth Eckstein derive their colored papers from their recycled monoprints. Fritz Bultman in tempera, Elena Presser in pastels, John Evans and William Dole in watercolors, and a host of collagists using acrylics have all hand-colored papers to achieve special effects. Pencil, pastel, watercolor, gouache, and acrylics are all suitable media for coloring paper. Oil paint, on the other hand, may be seriously damaging to paper and should not be used in direct application. Many felt-tip marking pens fade rapidly, migrate in paper and are difficult to control. Inks should be selected with care since they vary greatly with respect to their color stability.

For many collagists the use of color may affect paper choice. Papers intended for drawing, etching, printmaking, calligraphy, or watercolor often come to be used in collage. Most important to the collagist is that these papers be of archival quality and acid-free. Swatchbooks and paper catalogs are immensely useful as guides. Many of the fine paper mills make these available at a nominal fee, and large paper suppliers often have their own books, listing fiber content, weight, texture, pH value, and suggested application of papers from many sources. Suppliers with paper catalogs and/or swatchbooks are listed in an appendix.

Collagists in search of papers for special effects are sometimes drawn to Japanese wood veneers or bark papers (*tapa*) from Mexico (Otomi Indian) and Hawaii. In using these they risk the introduction of elements with acidic content and should consider deacidifying them or treating them with a protective coating of acrylic to prevent their deterioration. These methods are also suitable for the preservation of used colored papers derived from magazine and various scrap sources (see p. 53).

Indeed, the introduction of nonarchival elements brings us to a broader consideration of collages made from recycled paper. The most familiar collages, in fact, such as the work of Kurt Schwitters or, even earlier, the typographically rich futurists and dadaists, made use of book illustration, newsprint, ticket stubs, wrappers – in short, papers with a history. Unfortunately the history of papermaking is not entirely a happy one, and these found remnants, though they symbolize industrial progress, are likely to be filled with destructive chemicals.

Early papers – papers produced up to the end of the eighteenth century – are relatively stable. Although the alum used in sizing rag rendered the paper acidic, this was stabilized by the alkaline compounds in the wood ash lye used to bleach the cloth and the chalk used to whiten it. Leo Manso makes elegant use of many of these very old European papers. In most cases, however, the collagist will not have access to papers of so early a date. Realistically, it is easier to find "breakers" – that is, damaged, torn, and incomplete volumes of books produced during the nineteenth century. And most of these books are made from woodpulp paper. From the 1860s onward, inexpensive books and papers were produced of unpurified woodpulp containing lignin and alum-rosin sizing, both of which render paper acidic, brittle, and subject to progressive deterioration, especially when exposed to light. The works of collagists who have used such materials may be in jeopardy.

This does not have to be the case. The collagist working with photocopies, for example, could have Xerographic plain paper process copies made on acid-free paper, or transfer the image, as Charlotte Brown does, to any number of archival materials. New archival chemistries exist for making photographs, and several different processes can be used to deacidify old or acidic papers.

The modern collagist, as a recycler of used paper, should be guided by a current knowledge of chemistry and conservation. It is easy enough to adapt practices of deacidifying or stabilizing papers before they are used in making collages. Indeed, it is much more sensible to take these precautions than to rely on repairs or reclamation later on. Since most galleries and museums have become extremely sensitive to the use of archival materials, collage can well profit from an updating of materials and techniques.

As paper composition cannot be determined by sight and touch, it is important to use a simple surface test to measure the pH factor of used papers of unknown origin. A test will make clear whether the paper has to be deacidified or otherwise treated.

Available from conservation material suppliers are commercial indicator pens and pencils that can be used for the surface testing of paper (The Archivists Pen; Micro Essential pHydrion Insta-Chek pH Pencil). In addition to these tools there are two other easy indicator tests that can be used. Both are wet methods.

Indicator test papers

These are available both in narrow (6.5–10.0) and wide (0.0–14.0) range. They are strips of paper with a color indicator at one end. When they come into contact with wet paper they change color to give an accurate reading of the paper's pH value according to a printed chart on the packet. The test, unlike the indicator pen or pencil, does not stain the paper.

For this technique you will need two pieces of clear plastic and distilled water, as well as the indicator paper.

1   Place a small piece of the paper to be tested on a sheet of clean plastic.

2   Using a clean eyedropper, put a few drops of distilled water on the paper.

3   Float a strip of the indicator paper colored side down on the water drops, agitating to make certain that its sensitive portion is thoroughly soaked.

4   Cover the wet papers with a second plastic sheet and press with weights for five minutes.

5   Check the color against the chart provided by the maker.

Papers that register between 7.0 and 10.0 pH are safe for immediate use in collage for they have a defensive reserve of alkaline. Those much below 7.0 are acidic. Certainly a paper that registers 6.0 or below might require preservation attention.

Chlorphenol Red

Another simple pH test uses the indicator Chlorphenol Red which has a narrow range of 4.8–6.4 or 5.0–6.6 (authorities differ). This is available in ready-made indicator solutions from chemical supply houses. With an eyedropper the indicator solution can be placed directly on a fragment of the paper in question. Since this is a stain test it should not be carried out near the whole sheet intended for use. If the spot turns yellow, the paper is acidic (pH below 6.0); yellow shaded with gray or green indicates mild acidity (pH 6.0–6.7), and if the spot turns purple, the paper is close to neutral or alkaline (pH 6.7 and above) – that is, safe for use in collage.

Paper conservators agree that acidic papers are in danger. They do not all agree on what is the best treatment for such papers. Three useful techniques used by library and fine art conservators that can be adapted to home or studio conditions are:

1   Nonaqueous magnesium treatments with *Wei T'o* or *pHizz*.
2   Immersion bath in magnesium solutions.
3   Immersion bath in calcium solutions (the Barrow two-step method).

With all forms of deacidification, a sample of the paper to be treated should be tested in advance to verify that the paper's ink, color, and surface are not affected by the process. The solubility of inks and dyes and the sensitivity of some dyes to a change in pH may influence the choice of a particular treatment. Furthermore, after immersion in water solutions, paper tends to dry with some cockling, and this too should be considered.

1. Nonaqueous Methods

A. *Wei T'o* (Dr. R. D. Smith method)
The treatment is water-free and therefore does not cockle paper. It basically works by impregnating the paper with magnesium carbonate and magnesium hydroxide, which further react with the carbon dioxide and water vapor from the air to form magnesium carbonate.

There are several variant formulations of solutions and sprays that are designed to meet different paper requirements. According to the manufacturer they all (1) neutralize the accessible acid present, (2) prevent the development of acids in the future, (3) reduce the rate of oxidative attack, and (4) ward off foxing – brown stains caused by molds. They can be used on woodpulp papers with little significant yellowing. The solutions exist in a product line modified to adjust to soluble inks and papers of differing thickness; there is a parallel line of spray products.

Pigment colored papers should not be affected, change color, or bleed in *Wei T'o*. Some inks and dyes, however, are soluble in alcohol and may therefore run. And some dyes are pH sensitive, which means that they may actually turn color if the deacidified sheet comes in contact with water. Thus collagists working with colored magazine photos, art reproductions, or other colored papers will need to experiment. Many colored and coated papers can be successfully deacidified using *Wei T'o* solutions and sprays without affecting hue or surface texture. Specific questions or problems should be referred directly to the manufacturer. The company will also supply complete technical descriptions of the whole product line and its

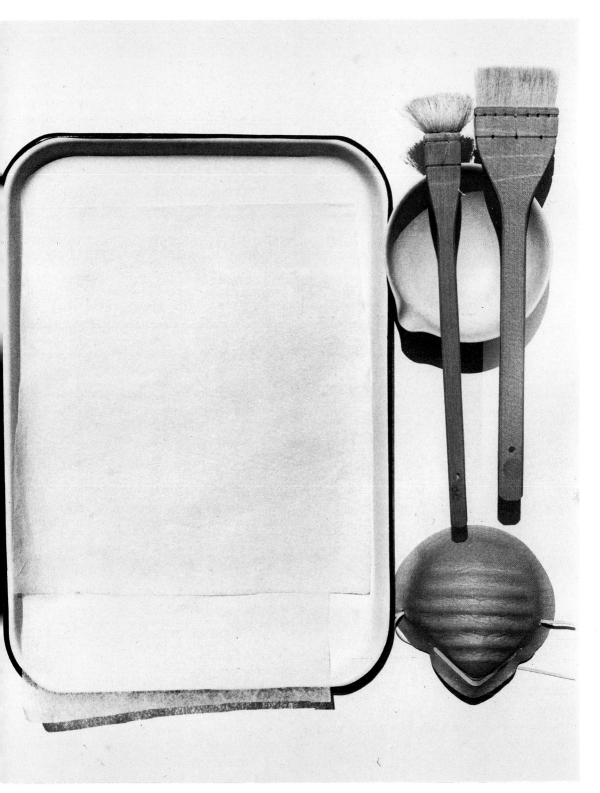

15 Tools for the use of Wei T'o solution (*left to right*): porcelain tray, random spun wove fabric, porcelain evaporating dish, *hake* brushes, surgical mask.

applications, along with suggested methods, equipment for use, and safety procedures.

While *Wei T'o* vapors are of relatively low toxicity, working with these products requires safety precautions. A vapor hood or adequate ventilation, and a surgical mask or respirator and goggles are recommended. The vapors should not be inhaled. For the collagist, *Wei T'o*'s great advantage lies in its being nonaqueous and fast drying. Paper can be treated and used within a matter of moments so that spontaneity is not lost. Papers treated do not buckle or curl. Even precut collage fragments can be treated in this way and made immediately ready for a paste-up.

B. *pHizz* (Archival Aids)

This new British product is a nonaqueous, nontoxic spray that contains methyl magnesium carbonate in a chlorofluorocarbon. A variable sprayhead permits flexibility and control of its application, and it dries instantly.

2. Neutralizing Paper with a Magnesium Bicarbonate Spray Technique*

A. To make the magnesium bicarbonate solution

EQUIPMENT

Household soda syphon, from whose long central tube $\frac{3}{4}$ inch has been snipped off so that its end will be clear of the sediment of undissolved magnesium carbonate

Carbon dioxide charged cartridges

$\frac{3}{4}$ teaspoon or 20 grams powdered magnesium carbonate

12 ounces or 400 milliliters distilled or deionized water

Large Pyrex or plastic funnel

Denatured ethyl alcohol (available from a chemical supplier)

A bottle with a tight cap, like the so-called French bottle (a glass bottle with a rubber gasketted glass stopper held with a metal spring clasp)

PROCEDURE

1 Measure the magnesium carbonate and put it in a clean dry container; put the water in the syphon bottle. Because more magnesium carbonate dissolves in water if the ingredients are cold, place both the container and the bottle in the refrigerator for several hours or overnight.

2 Remove both items from the refrigerator and, by means of the funnel, pour the dry magnesium carbonate into the syphon bottle. Cap the bottle and shake to be sure the powder is immersed in the water.

3 Place the tubes into the bottle and screw on the capping device tightly.

4 Following directions for making soda water, release the carbon dioxide cartridge into the bottle. Shake for about half a minute.

*Formulated by Anne F. Clapp.

5 Remove the cartridge holder from the bottle, cap it and shake again.

6 Place in the refrigerator and over the next hour shake 3 or 4 more times.

7 Allow to settle overnight.

8 Holding the bottle carefully upright, in order not to disturb the sediment at the bottom, syphon off the clear liquid into a bottle and cap tightly to hold in the carbon dioxide gas.

B. To use the solution

EQUIPMENT

Spray bottle

2 sheets of flexible, transparent plastic, like polyethylene, large enough to cover the object and extend generously on all sides

2 pieces of tissue paper to interleave between the object and the plastic sheeting

Denatured ethyl alcohol

PROCEDURE

Test the paper to be treated to make certain that the treatment will not be harmful. To test, place a drop of the neutralizing solution on an inconspicuous place on the paper and verify that the color of the paper is not altered by the solution.

1 Put into a spray bottle a measured amount of magnesium bicarbonate solution, plus 10 percent denatured ethyl alcohol (volume/volume).

2 Place the object face down on a plastic sheet with a tissue paper interleaf. Make sure that they lie smoothly.

3 Spray or mist the object by making passes first in one direction and then in the other until the paper is quite damp. Gently brush the paper with sweeping strokes of a broad, soft brush to distribute the solution more evenly.

4 Remove the excess water from around the object with paper towelling.

5 Cover with the second tissue paper and the second plastic sheeting. Seal the edges of the envelope with weights or some other means.

6 Allow the object to "marinate" for several hours, permitting the magnesium bicarbonate to spread into the fiber of the paper.

7 Open the envelope, let the object regain strength by becoming drier. Remove to a blotter and allow to air-dry completely. The carbon dioxide in the air will change the magnesium bicarbonate to the more stable, neutralizing magnesium carbonate.

8 If the paper needs to be flattened, it can be sprayed with water, "marinated" again for a short time, and dried in a blotter sandwich under flat pressure.

3. The Barrow Two-Bath Immersion Method

This method was formulated by W. J. Barrow.* In the first bath, the calcium hydroxide neutralizes much of the acid in the paper. The second bath carbonates whatever residue of calcium hydroxide is left in the paper from the first immersion and precipitates calcium carbonate in the fibers of the paper.

* Adapted by Dr. Joan Shields, C. W. Post College, Long Island University, New York.

Bath A

1 liter or quart bottle of water, chilled
2 teaspoons powdered calcium hydroxide (available
   from a chemical supplier)
2 wide-mouth half-gallon glass jars
Porcelain tray

1 Chill the water thoroughly, since calcium hydroxide is more soluble in cold water.

2 Pour the measured calcium hydroxide into one of the wide-mouth glass jars. Add a little cold water and begin to stir into a paste. The water must be added *carefully* and *very slowly* since the mixture builds up heat. Avoid any splattering.

3 Continue to add water until the full liter or quart is poured into the jar. Cap and shake the contents well.

4 Allow the suspension to settle. You will see the sediment come to the bottom.

5 Now pour off the top liquid into the second glass jar. Add another liter or quart of cold water. Stir.

6 Although there may still be some sediment, the clear upper liquid can now be poured into the porcelain tray for soaking the collage paper. Cap the jar until you are ready to proceed.

Bath B

2 liters or quarts of water
$3\frac{1}{2}$ teaspoons calcium carbonate powder (available
   from chemical supplier)
Carbon dioxide tank with regulator and tubing long
   enough to reach to the bottom of a 2-liter or
   half-gallon jar
2-liter or half-gallon glass jar
Universal indicator paper

1 Pour the measured calcium carbonate into the bottom of the 2-liter or half-gallon jar.

2 Add the water and stir.

3 Bubble carbon dioxide gas through the solution for at least 15 minutes. Be sure to bubble the gas close to the bottom of the jar. The gas enables the calcium carbonate to dissolve.

METHOD:

1 Pour Bath A into a porcelain tray. Immerse collage paper 20 minutes.

2 Pour Bath B into a porcelain tray. Remove the collage paper from Bath A and place it in Bath B for 20 minutes.

3 Dry deacidified paper between two sheets of acid-free blotting paper.
   Test pH with universal indicator paper.
   Press with weights to dry evenly.

Protective coating in acrylic

This is not a technique used by paper conservators but it might prove useful. Collagists who need to deacidify recycled colored papers have another alternative in protective acrylic coatings. Before using this method, the artist should be aware that a surface coating creates a certain aesthetic effect that is different from paper in its natural state; moreover, a surface coating undoubtedly makes more difficult any conservation treatment that the work might need at a later date. Bearing these two factors in mind, the protective effects of acrylic often weigh in its favor. Acrylic gives supportive strength to cheap and fragile paper, although there is some question about whether it can significantly reduce damage by light, especially to newsprint. But since acrylic medium is alkaline in its liquid form, immersion will have a deacidifying effect if the paper is porous. Claude Bentley, for example, uses this immersion technique, saturating his papers in acrylic medium. Miriam Shapiro uses four layers of matte medium or varnish as an overcoat. A glossy acrylic varnish is used by Georges Pinel to achieve an enameled effect and by Ande Lau Chen to emphasize gilding. Robert Courtright uses a painted layer of acrylic white to seal old papers and prepare a ground for his colors. Acrylic medium, varnish, and paint can all be used to protective ends by immersion, brush and spray methods.

There is, of course, great variety in the commercial formulations of acrylic artists' materials. Some contain ultraviolet light filters, others do not. Some yellow more than others or grow more brittle with age. Companies are frequently willing to supply technical information, but this will not always help the collagist know how particular acrylics will react in combination with particular paper and adhesives. For this reason the collagist may want to make simple experiments to simulate roughly the effects of aging. Three artificial aging experiments are useful. One subjects materials to heat; the other two are based on light exposure.

Heat. A broad indication of how materials will age can be determined by baking them at 100°C (212°F). Seventy-two hours at this temperature can be roughly equated to twenty-five years of aging – with certain qualifications. Since dry and moist aging are not comparable, oven baking gives no indication of aging under humid conditions. Still, the collagist might find it useful to make comparative heat tests, trying several papers, adhesives, acrylics, or combinations under the same general conditions to determine yellowing, strength, and brittleness.

Window Light Exposure. The simplest light test for aging materials uses natural window light. Experiments have demonstrated that direct sunlight is not necessary for good results and that the light transmitted during cloudy and even rainy periods will prove adequately conclusive in the testing of materials. By exposing paper, adhesives, tapes, and pigments to window light, you will be able to determine fading, yellowing, and other discoloration. Since the most dramatic aging of these materials occurs during the first few months of exposure, this test will allow one to know quite rapidly whether to use a particular material or particular materials in combination for collages.

In testing materials by window light you should put two sample swatches side by side on an acid-free board. Cover the one side (and swatch) with a piece of reflecting aluminum foil, leaving the other side (and swatch) exposed. Now tape the sample face out to the inside of a window. Within a few weeks, possibly days, you will begin to see a change in color, cracking, or brittleness if they are characteristic of the material's aging tendency.

Artificial light box. A light box testing device can also simulate aging artificially without giving up the use of the kitchen! This can be built with a wooden crate, a slatted vane covering, and a 50 watt ultraviolet light (in a housing) or a fluorescent light used for raising indoor plants (plant grow light). You will also need black paint, hinges or latches, aluminum foil, and a small fan.

1   Paint the inside of the wooden crate with black paint.
2   Turn the box on its side, leaving the front side temporarily open. Cover the back and sides with squares of aluminum foil, shiny surface facing out.
3   Saw an opening in the top large enough to install an ultraviolet light or fluorescent plant grow light set in a metal housing. Cover over the top with aluminum foil.
4   Drill air holes in the back of the box.
5   Build a front open vane vent that can be fixed with hinges or latches.
6   Place collage in the bottom of the box.
7   Cover the front so that your eyes are not exposed to light.
8   Place a small fan in front of the vanes, so that air can circulate gently through the box.
9   Turn on the light and expose the collage for a few days. This exposure will be the equivalent of several years under ordinary conditions of exposure.

CAUTION: be careful not to expose your eyes to ultraviolet light. This experiment is best conducted in an infrequently used room. Never remove the front vane panel with the light on.

Backing papers and support fabrics

In working with old papers, thin papers, or long pieces of fragile paper, it is sometimes useful to paste up in layers, fixing the image first onto a backing paper, then the double or multiple layer onto a mounting board. Any number of acid-free papers are suitable for this purpose, from a light Silk Tissue to the heavy support of Powell Repairing Paper (Barcham Green). Choice will depend on the final stiffness or pliability that the artist wishes to achieve in bonding the two papers.

The perfect combination of image paper and backing paper is a matter of trial and error. It is related to the choice of cutting tool and adhesive as well as to the hand skills of the artist and the desired effect. A white backing paper or a deep tan might, for example, drastically change the tonal quality of the surface paper. Changes in humidity, too, might play a role since each paper expands and contracts at its own rate in response to humidity. Some papers work well together in the context of atmospheric change; others buckle. The collagist who wishes to experiment with backing papers should therefore attempt to paste the papers together in an airtight bond and press the papers with weights to dry. They can then be exposed to normal conditions for some period to allow any changes to be observed.

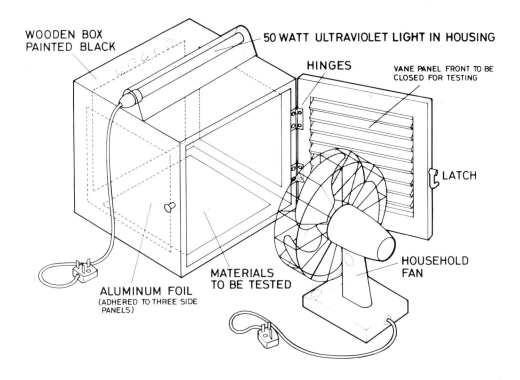

WOODEN BOX
PAINTED BLACK

50 WATT ULTRAVIOLET LIGHT IN HOUSING

HINGES

VANE PANEL FRONT TO BE
CLOSED FOR TESTING

LATCH

HOUSEHOLD
FAN

MATERIALS
TO BE TESTED

ALUMINUM FOIL
(ADHERED TO THREE SIDE
PANELS)

16 Artificial light box.

Generally collagists aim for flat surfaces, and for this reason long-fibered Japanese papers like Kitakata and Okawara are often good choices for a durable backing. These porous papers encourage adhesion. Although they wrinkle when moist and require handling with care, once they have dried together under the pressure of a heavy glass, the bond is firm.

Many fine Western papers are also suitable for backing materials and easier to work because they are generally smoother and more even in surface tension. These include Bodleian and the heavier Dover from Barcham Green, Firenze, and lightweight Rives. Even acid-free bond or interleaving paper may serve this purpose.

In some cases, the collagist may not wish to back an entire image, but may need to reinforce delicate or torn pieces of paper. For this purpose a number of products are available, all of archival quality and neutral pH. These include paper tapes, thin Japanese 100 percent *kōzo* papers such as Udagami, Uda, Sekishu, or *gampi* Silk Tissue. English manila L Tissue can be adhesive-coated and heat-set. Many new synthetic fabric tissues designed for conservation work are also applicable as collage paper supports. Promatco Heat Set Tissue (Process Materials) is an acid-free polyamide resin adhesive that resembles Japanese tissue and can be bonded to paper and fabrics with a dry-mount tacking iron or household iron. Other spun nylon fabrics are manufactured for similar purposes and designed for use with a variety of adhesives. Lamatec (Ademco Archival Aids) is an adhesive developed for use with many different support materials, from Crompton Tissue to heavyweight cotton cloth. Unglazed Lamatec Coated Repair Tissue was specifically developed for laminating lignin-based papers and may therefore be of special use to the collagist in repairing or backing ground wood papers.

Double-sided Lamatec Repair Tissue, intended for the archival mounting of photographs, has a modified application in its use by the collage artist working from original prints in photomontage. (See also Fusion 4000 under *Adhesives* below.) In backing photographs paper conservators point out that 100 percent rag boards (pH 6.5–7.5) without a reserve of alkaline may be safer for dye-transfer and albumin prints than boards with an alkaline reserve.

In all combinations of backing papers and adhesives the goal is more durable papers that contribute to the permanence and solidity of the final collage.

Mounting materials

Once the collage or elements of the collage are backed for support as necessary or desired, the piece should be mounted for framing. Many collagists mount their work on 2-ply, 4-ply, or even 8-ply mat board, which, of course, should be acid-free. If you choose acid-free colored mat board, it is wise to take the special precaution of separating the work from the back board by a barrier paper. This is necessary because in most cases the colored paper itself is not acid-free.

Collagists who prefer a textured mounting surface often choose heavy acid-free papers like Arches Cover, Rives or Dutch Etching Paper, but many other materials exist that meet specific needs. Because of their size and complex structure, Fritz Bultman backs his large, abstract shapes onto a thin, muslin-weight canvas which he sometimes adheres to a second support canvas. This French technique, called *marouflage*, has its origin in backing large paper posters. Conventional, sized canvas is used by Robert Goodnough, who staples his treated canvas collage elements directly to the prepared ground. Claude Bentley also uses acrylic sized canvas for large collage paintings. For artists who combine paper, cloth, and paint, canvas is extremely suitable.

A less conventional mounting material is used by Sari Dienes, who irons her collage elements directly onto a map-backing fabric coated with a heat/pressure adhesive. In his resin-colored fiberglass collages, Jim Zver has been able to eliminate altogether any mounting material. Using Velcro, he can mount the large free-form shapes directly to the surface of a wall, unframed.

Even collages intended for framing may require very solid mounts. Robert Courtright's modular components are composed and mounted within gesso-surfaced, deep wooden box frames. John Urbain uses masonite, Ray Johnson chipboard, and Kathleen Zimmerman canvasboard. Romare Bearden, whose collages are sometimes worked to the size of murals, has developed a masonite and wooden support frame structure, covered on the back with heavy brown paper to balance tension.

In working with these rigid mounting materials it is recommended that a protective layer of gesso, acrylic, Mylar, or other acid-free barrier be used between the mount and any paper elements employed. Once you have taken the care to make a collage that is acid-free in its essential materials, you should not permit it to come into contact with wooden or other surfaces having acid content. New materials are being developed all the time that can assist in these precautions, such as polystyrene archival mounting board and acid-free corrugated boards.

A collage mounted on board should be hinge-mounted at the top corners. This can be done with archival white gummed cloth tape. A flatter, less textured hinge can be made for small, light collages simply from a long-fibered Japanese paper like Kitakata. Adhered with a water-soluble paste, these hinges can provide vertical or horizontal support for the hanging work.

Adhesives

Collage gets its name from the French verb, *coller*, to paste, and indeed paste is central to the whole art. The texture, fluidity, and application method of every adhesive must be considered with respect to paper texture first, then the handling procedures in collage construction. A thin, porous paper, for example, would look opaque and wrinkled if an unsuitable paste were applied to it. Heavy papers worked in layers require strong adhesives with lay-flat properties. And since the magic of collage is in its unity, no collage should show the marks of dried paste revealing the seams of its composite parts. For aesthetic reasons, then, as well as practical ones, it is essential to have a variety of adhesives available for different uses. In working with archival papers, moreover, it is equally important to choose conservation quality pastes or synthetic adhesives that are resistant to aging.

As in paper, neutrality or alkalinity is a positive value in adhesives. But acid should not be considered the only factor determining adhesive choice. Some adhesives, even pH neutral ones such as dextrine pastes, may turn yellow or brown as a result of aging. Some grow brittle and flake. Others, like rubber cement, oxidize, lose their bonding force, and stain. All such adhesives are unsuitable to collage.

For hundreds of years *starches* have been used as adhesives, and today rice- and especially wheat-starch are still widely preferred by paper conservators. They are water-soluble and reversible. The natural starches, available in powdered form, must be cooked with water to a gelatinous consistency and treated with a bacterial and fungal retarding agent, such as thymol, eugenol, or formalin. Here is a working recipe for wheat-starch paste:

Wheat-starch paste
$12\frac{1}{2}$ teaspoons wheat-starch
5 ounces distilled water
10 drops thymol*

In the top of a double boiler, soak the starch in the distilled water, stirring occasionally for half an hour. Cook over boiling water, stirring constantly for 15–20 minutes. Remove from heat and stir in the thymol. Bottle in a tightly sealed jar that has been swabbed with thymol. Store in a cool, dark cupboard.

*A solution can be made by dissolving $\frac{1}{2}$ teaspoon thymol in one ounce of methyl alcohol. Store safely in a medicine bottle marked with a *TOXIC* label. Use a measuring dropper to add the solution to the paste.

Before using this paste, you will need to strain and dilute the stock with distilled water to a working consistency. This will depend on the brushes and papers you are using. The advantage of organic starch pastes is that they can be prepared freshly at home and modified to desired consistencies relative to different materials.

Rice-starch paste
2 tablespoons rice-starch
$\frac{2}{3}$ cup distilled water
10 drops thymol

Put the rice-starch in a small bowl and add enough cold water to make a smooth paste. Finish adding the cold water, stirring to ensure that there are no lumps. Transfer to a double boiler and cook over boiling water, stirring until thickened. Remove from heat and stir in the thymol. Store in a cool, dark place, as in the case of wheat-starch paste.

Both wheat- and rice-starch pastes require considerable skill in manipulation since they cause wrinkling and need a long drying time and weights to return the papers to perfect flatness. These pastes, too, must be applied with a delicate brush so that they do not touch any visible surface of the collage, since they dry to a shine. Ande Lau Chen has commented that rice-starch paste can be used to make thin Japanese papers look even more transparent.

A note on wallpaper paste
The various preparations of wallpaper paste made from starch or cellulose vary considerably and may contain impurities. It is preferable therefore to use pure organic materials of known archival quality.

Methyl cellulose is an adhesive recommended by conservators. Mixed with distilled water at room temperature to any desired consistency, it is an uncooked material that is similar in working properties to the starches, though it reacts more easily to atmospheric moisture and is not as firmly adhesive as the pastes.

Combined with natural starch, methyl cellulose is more effective. It is best to work with the two stocks, roughly 55 percent wheat-starch paste to 45 percent methyl cellulose mixture.* These should be combined just before use, since the mixture loses its adhesive properties after about twelve hours. Magnesium carbonate powder (one teaspoon to a pint of the mixture) can be added as a protective alkaline reserve.

Methyl cellulose in its mixed form can also be combined with Polyvinyl Acetate (PVA) to form an adhesive that is strong, plastic, maneuverable, and *slow*-drying. This strong adhesive can be achieved with proportions of 10 parts mixed methyl cellulose to 1 part PVA.

Sodium carboxymethyl cellulose is a water-soluble cellulose powder that can be used as an adhesive for both paper and fabric. It is frequently employed in bonding these materials to nylon or polyester, but can also serve in collage construction, backing, or mounting.

*Proportions suggested by Anne F. Clapp.

Casein

Casein pastes, manufactured from milk, are among the strongest organic adhesives. They have been used for centuries but because of their acidity should not be used directly on collage papers. They may be useful to bond other materials where a barrier separates them from direct contact with paper. In mixing casein from powdered form a preservative should be added. Premixed casein paste may already contain a bacterial and fungal retardant. Check with manufacturer.

Polyvinyl Acetate (PVA)

Many versions of these emulsions have been developed as adhesives for bookbinding, art, crafts construction, and conservation. These are basically of two generic types. The *homopolymer*, a brittle film that requires an added plasticizer to become flexible, is not suitable for collage work. The *copolymer*, designed for permanence, is internally plasticized and has its flexibility built into the molecule itself. It is this kind of PVA that the collagist should use. Each manufacturer of copolymers has a number of modified formulations. Although they vary considerably in pH factor, viscosity, molecular weight, and light stability, the copolymer PVAs are generally flexible and resistant to aging when they are not exposed to direct light. Technical specifications, heat and light box tests will be helpful in checking a particular product for yellowing or brittleness. The most appropriate to collage are close to neutral in pH, flow easily, dry quickly, and have excellent lay-flat properties. Elvace 1874 and Jade 403 are two current formulations that have been tested for archival work by paper conservators.* Because manufacturers may change their formulas from time to time, it is essential to get current information on any product intended for use.

Since PVA can be thinned with water, it is adaptable to various paper requirements for collage. Many formulations can also be reversed in alcohol, which allows the collagist to correct errors or alter an original design. A certain care must be exercised in working with this type of adhesive since it dries to a shine and exposed areas tend to yellow most readily. It is therefore important to apply the emulsion sparingly with a brush to prevent any flow from reaching an exposed surface. Though fast-drying, PVA allows enough time to manipulate collage elements into exact position. While it does not buckle wet paper as radically as the organic pastes, the use of a roller or a bone folding tool, followed by a glass weight or a press, will insure a perfectly unwrinkled bond. Some formulations such as Elvace 1874 heat-set, so that collage fragments can be bonded with a moderately hot iron.

Acrylic medium and gel

Other synthetic adhesives that have come into favor with collagists are acrylic matte medium and acrylic gel medium. These translucent polymer resins dry clear but can also be mixed with pigment for special effect. As adhesives, they are used both by pure paper collagists and by those who combine paper collage with paint and other

*N. S. Baer, N. Indictor, T. I. Schwartzman, and I. L. Rosenberg, "Chemical and Physical Properties of Poly (vinyl acetate) Copolymer Emulsions," ICOM Committee for Conservation, 4th Triennial Meeting, Venice 1975.

materials. Since acrylic medium has a pH value in the alkaline range (generally between 9.0 and 10.0), it can be used, as described earlier, not only to adhere but also to coat acidic papers in order to prevent their further deterioration. Most of these products are manufactured with retardants to prevent bacterial and fungal growth, but like PVA adhesives some tend to yellow with age and the collagist is advised to test intended products or consult the most recent experimental literature.

Solid polymer resin
For broad piece work, touch-up work and repairs, solid polymer resin gluesticks are convenient. Look for those which are alkaline and water-soluble, therefore reversible (at least when first applied), like the Pritt Glue Stick. The solid polymer resin adhesive bonds both paper and textiles.

Spray mounting adhesives
These synthetic polymers, developed for design layout work and photography, are formulated to replace rubber cement. They are intended to retain their tacky quality for long periods of time.

  Heat and light tests can be helpful in determining more exactly the active lifespan and aging characteristics of particular formulations, which vary considerably. They are not recommended by paper conservators for archival work. Many of them, furthermore, are highly toxic and should be used with great caution.

Dry-mount adhesives
From photography, collagists can also borrow sheet adhesives. These are convenient to work with since they are thin and easy to cut with scissors or blades. The dry-mount tissue can be tacked to the collage paper and cut, then bonded to the surface paper exactly as desired in a dry-mount press or with an iron. The double layer can then be mounted directly in place on the collage. Along with the development of archival photographic chemistry there are new dry-mount tissues. *Fusion 4000* (Seal) and *Double-Sided Lamatec* (Ademco) are dry-mount products that manufacturers claim as suitable for archival work.

Adhesive fabric
Adhesive-coated textiles generally used for map or document backing can also be applied to collage, especially large pieces or works intended as hangings. *Lamatec Coated Archival Cloth* (Ademco) is designed for heat/pressure application. It is treated with a fungicide and a bactericide, and is also mothproofed. The manufacturer's promotional information claims that it is of archival quality and reversible in ethyl alcohol. *Chartex Dry Backing Cloth* (Seal) is intended for use with Seal laminating tissue.

  For adhesive tissues see Backing Papers and Support Fabrics, pp. 54–56.

Adhesive tapes
For repair work, mounting, hingeing, framing, and in some cases even in surface design, various adhesive tapes are essential. These also should be acid-free.

Archival Document Repair Tape (Ademco) as described by the manufacturer is non-yellowing, reversible in alcohol, and neutral pH. This is a pressure-sensitive, acid-free wood tissue material that is easy to use on fragile papers that require mending. Paper surgical tape is also useful and acid-free.

Although collagists may prefer the conservator's technique of hingeing their works with Japanese long-fibered paper and water-soluble paste, acid-free gummed linen tape is another alternative. It is lay-flat and can be reversed in water.

Archival Framing Tape (Ademco) can also be used for hingeing and mounting. This is made from base paper, pH 6.2 buffered with 0.3 percent calcium carbonate. The tape is coated with a PVA of pH 7.0 and is moistened with water.

Acetate film tape (like *Scotch Magic Mending Tape* #810 or doublecoated #415) can be used to seal glass or plexiglass to the frame and secure a dust-free condition for the collage.

In the choice of adhesives, chemical properties and practical working properties must both be considered. How do particular adhesives work with particular papers? Can papers bonded with this or that adhesive be cut easily? Will marks of the adhesive be visible through the paper? Indeed, though traditional collage is *papier collé*, pasted paper, not all collagists work exclusively with paper. Cloth, leather, feathers, wire, wood, shell, metal, and plastics may all enter into collage designs along with even more exotic materials. For this reason the collagist must be prepared to face special problems in bonding these materials to each other or to paper surfaces. Many polyvinyl acetate resins, for example, exist specifically for use in bonding textiles, leather, foil, wood. Other strong adhesives made from animal hides and fish, as well as epoxy resins, are also readily available. Each has specific applications that should be considered before using, especially since many adhesives are acidic and therefore unsuitable for contact with paper elements of collage. Most manufacturers will send technical specifications on request. Many, conscious of archival concerns, are endeavoring to produce new adhesives that are permanent.

Although collage often gives the illusion of delicacy, even fragility, the actual architecture and construction must be solid in both design and technical composition. A collage may "look" antique, even aged, but the art work itself should be enduring and free from materials with rapidly aging properties. Thus archival papers and adhesives are much to be preferred.

Despite all precautions, every collagist is likely to face problems. These might arise from particular materials or materials in specific combinations. Even more distressing is damage to completed work. Accidental stains or tears, airborne pollutants, light, a flood in a storage area, mold or fungus growth are all aggressively destructive to collage. Whether the problem is one of construction or conservation, it is best not to attempt a home remedy, which can often cause further damage. The nearest major art museum or library should be able to supply a list of certified paper conservators who are trained in the chemistry and practical handling of works on paper. Their expertise is the collagist's most essential resource in problems pertaining to construction materials and the repair of damaged work.

TOOLS

Cutting instruments

The ways in which paper and adhesives are brought together leads to the subject of cutting instruments. The collagist literally imagines and draws with a cutting edge, so that the tool itself defines the line. It is possible to work so directly with the materials that no tool intervenes. The torn edge is itself a statement and a texture subject to great variety. Freehand tearing can impose curves or make gashes, can be clean or leave a ragged edge. With great finesse paper can be crisply torn against a ruler's edge. A subtle shape can be torn using a wet brush technique. By this method the brush dipped in water marks the desired tear line. When the paper is pulled apart at the water line, the tear leaves a gently feathered edge that can be exaggerated if the technique is applied to long-fibered paper.

For most collagists concerned with the finesse and polish of the line, a blade is important. Many instruments are good for cutting paper. Scissors of all shapes and lengths can provide variety, from long straight shears to the definitive markings left by pinking shears. Delicate work can be done with short, curved nail scissors or even micro-surgical scissors. Surgical scissors are generally recommended for their quality and precision.

Another kind of surgeon's instrument, the scalpel, is also useful. Since the handle can be fitted with many different shaped cutting blades, the scalpel is a versatile tool that can be manipulated as precisely as the thinnest drawing pen. With its long, balanced handle, the scalpel is easier to use and more flexible than the razor blade. Stanley and X-acto knives, like the scalpel, have a great number and variety of interchangeable blades. All have a place in the collagist's cabinet of cutting instruments.

The tools that any collagist uses are, of course, a matter of personal choice. They depend in part on comfort but also on the textures of the papers themselves and on the aesthetic impact intended. Before you choose one particular instrument or even a combination, it is advisable to try them all. Expertise and refinement develop with continued practice.

Visual aids

Careful cutting depends in part on good illumination and eyesight. Both can be assisted to some degree. It is important to work with a strong and flexible light source that can be manipulated in every direction to eliminate shadows as you work. If you normally wear eye-glasses for close work, you may want to consider working under more intense magnification. There are many tools available for magnification, from table-top lenses on a pedestal to ocular loupes attached to headbands or eyeglasses. Increasing comfort and visibility should decrease strain.

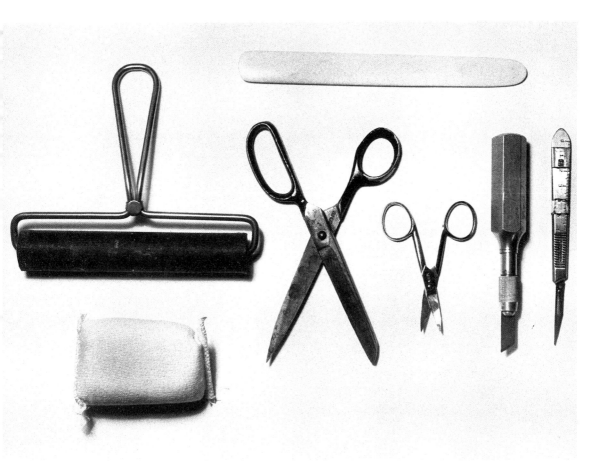

17 Tools (*left to right*): archival roller, Draft Clean Pad, scissors, bone folding tool, X-acto knife, scalpel.

18 Brushes of different widths and shapes for cleaning and pasting.

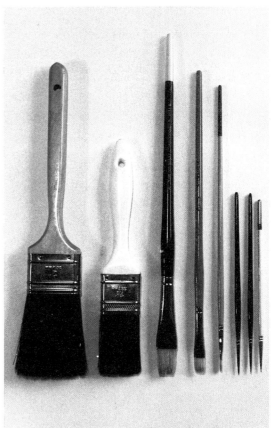

Brushes

For most collage work you will need an assortment of brushes in varying shapes and sizes. Flat brushes of differing widths are most useful for even paste-ups. Thin, round brushes of oo widths are easiest manipulated for repair work on narrow edges. In working with delicate papers it is advisable to use soft-bristled brushes, and these should be thoroughly washed with soap and water or cleaned with an appropriate solvent after each paste-up. Brushes should be wiped clean and stored upright.

Additional tools

Plate glass of $\frac{3}{4}''$ or $1''$ thickness can be cut to size according to your demands. These glass sheets are useful as weights in drying and can be used as surfaces for repair and paste work.

Mylar or *polyethylene sheets* can also be used as a protective work surface, especially for pasting. The sheets prevent contact of materials with acidic surfaces.

Self healing cutting mat is an excellent surface for work done with blades. It is possible to obtain these in archival quality materials.

Tweezers and *forceps* may be helpful in manipulating small fragments.

Cleaning pads containing a grit-free powder can be used to remove dirt from old papers. Conventional *erasers* may be helpful.

Rulers, *curves*, *T-squares* and *templates* may assist in cutting patterns.

Archival rollers can be used to apply pressure for an even application of adhesive.

Bone folding tools. These polished instruments used in bookbinding come in several different shapes. They are helpful in rubbing surfaces to insure adhesive bonds.

Tacking iron and/or dry-mount press is used for lamination bonding.

FRAMING

Standard framing should conserve a collage by providing a closed housing that is both dust- and acid-free. Most recent procedures suggest that the best protection against ultraviolet ray light damage is plexiglass (polymethyl methacrylate sheeting). Whether this material or glass is used, the sheet should be properly cleaned and sealed to the inside of the frame with a transparent, acetate tape that acts as a dust seal. The collage hinge-mounted onto a backing board can be matted and mounted in a 4-ply, acid-free window mat or floated on an acid-free mount alone, provided that the piece can be kept from touching the glass. In either case it is important that the collage does not come in contact with the glass or plexiglass surface. Once the piece is lowered into the frame, a sheet of buffered paper is placed over the back mat. If a stiffer backing is still required because of the depth of the frame, acid-free corrugated board or Fome-Cor can be used. Finally the frame is closed with retaining devices. Acid-free wrapping paper, cut to the dimensions of the frame's outer edge, is sealed to the back of the frame with PVA or framing tape.

STORING COLLAGES WITHOUT FRAMING

Unmatted or matted but unframed collages should be stored in protective cases that prevent light and atmospheric pollution from reaching them. If they are stored one on top of the other, they can be separated by sheets of acid-free glassine. It is a good idea to store collages away from dampness, so that bacteria, fungus, and mold are not encouraged. It is also wise to keep them away from extreme heat, which ages paper and adhesives.

Finally, in displaying and storing collages, it is essential to remember that all light, not only ultraviolet light, can have bleaching and yellowing effects on papers, adhesives, and colors. Avoid light damage by keeping collages away from exposure to direct sunlight.

Collages can be easily stored in transparent Mylar folders (Type S and Type D) which are inert and also protect the works from handling. Acid-free paper sleeves are also available, as well as acid-free storage boxes, which keep them dust-free and well-protected.

See the list of suppliers for all the materials mentioned in this chapter.

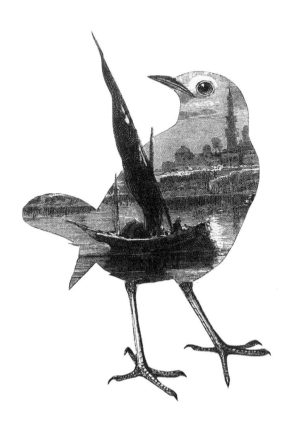

19   John Digby: *Bird* (1982–83). Paper collage, 12 × 16 in. (framed). Courtesy of the artist.

20   John Digby: *Dog* (1982–83). Paper collage, 12 × 16 in. (framed). Courtesy of the artist.

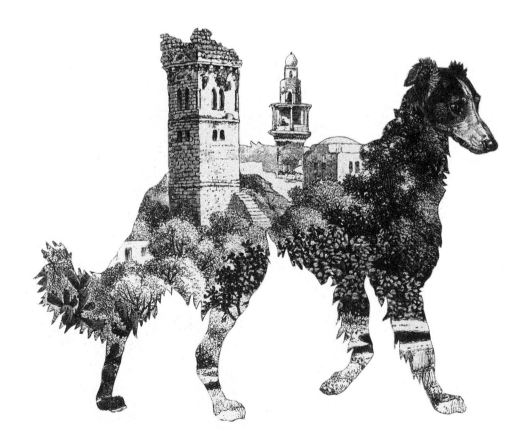

CHAPTER FOUR

Archival Technique: A Personal Example

John Digby

In my own collage work, studies of birds and animals are fundamental to the lyrical expression I seek in the medium. As a subject, animate nature goes back to my childhood when I developed a passionate interest in birds. For six years I worked as a keeper at the London Zoological Gardens and much later, when I came to poetry, the movement and grace of animals remembered still exerted a strong metaphorical influence on my work. In collage I can isolate the metaphor and bring it to a visual immediacy that is mysterious yet whole.

As a lyrical form, these collages seem to me very much like two-part inventions. The one hand attempts to capture the purity of animate form, the lines and curves defining the essence of organic shape. The other hand interprets the animal, its place in nature, the hills, forests, treetops – the topography of its habitat that becomes so much a part of its consciousness as to shape its living expression. In unifying these two elements, it is important that the collage itself remain invisible; that is, the manufacture, the piecing-together, must remain invisible in order to achieve a mystery of unity. The complete image, the metaphor, as I see it, should strike at once as a convincing original. The collage should not reveal or emphasize its natural history, but rather the deceit necessary to arrest disbelief. When the lyrical invention is harmonious it transcends reason and opens a new depth of perception.

When we *think* of birds and animals as being *in nature*, we still imagine them as separated from nature by the outward circumference of their opaque skins. We are really thinking, in this case, of nature as a background outside of its inhabitants. But in my collages I have deliberately internalized natural habitat so that we can *sense* nature, not as an external place, but as the inner reality, the muscles and fibers of the animal's intuitive self.

Even this relationship, this unity, is a formal idea, and for me it is one best expressed in black and white. Between these clear delineations there exists such a subtle vocabulary of grays as to evoke everything I perceive about line, shape, volume, and movement in nature.

The transcendent idea contained in my collages also led me to consider their permanence. I was painfully aware that species in nature were vanishing and nature itself was disappearing. Even the paper images that recorded their presence were organic and fragile. This realization pushed me to new methods and materials. The use of engravings drew me quite naturally to paper conservation, which has become an integral part of the art and its precision. In fact, collage is for me a process of restoration and retrieval, of rescuing images from the past and giving them new life and meaning. Thus archival considerations have, in turn, become a part of the lyrical statement about permanence implicit in the forms themselves.

Fortunately, archival technique is largely a matter of habit and adaptation. It can, so to speak, become "natural" and in this way preserve collage as a species of permanent art. My own working practice may serve to illustrate many of the basic materials and methods suggested in the previous chapter. We begin here with black and white. Other collagists, whose works are described in later sections, provide diverse techniques for working in color.

In making a bird or animal collage, I am always working with two kinds of images (both wood engravings): the primary figure and complementary or contrasting elements of landscape. As I never precut and file images, my initial process involves long hours of turning pages in picture books. These are usually "breakers," that is, broken volumes of old books that are unmarketable as complete editions. Almost invariably I fasten onto an animal image first and allow my association with either its shape or movement to suggest a juxtaposition of imagery. In this way I start to conceive the collage.

The zebra, for example, with the mystery of its stripes, brought to mind the shifting play of light and darkness in the African landscape. This association of rhythms led me to compose the particular collage shown here in the making, of the zebra peering from among the acacia trees that shade the village house.

My first concern is with the papers themselves. As the zebra and landscape plates both come from "breakers," I need to remove the fingermarks and soils in order to bring them up to their true value. For this I use a print eraser, rubbing the flexible bag of white powder gently across the surface. The soiled dust can then be brushed away with ease. I always keep a clean household paint brush solely for this purpose.

Once I have given them a superficial cleaning, I begin deacidifying the collage papers. This is important in my work because all the images are from paper sources that contain lignin. Although these papers are brittle and somewhat yellowed with age, the process will neutralize them chemically and render them permanent. Thus

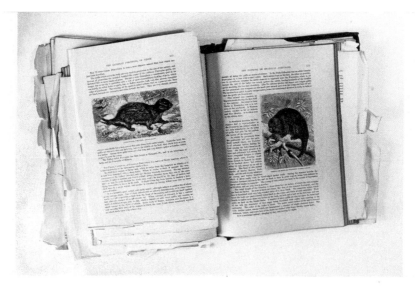

21 A "breaker".

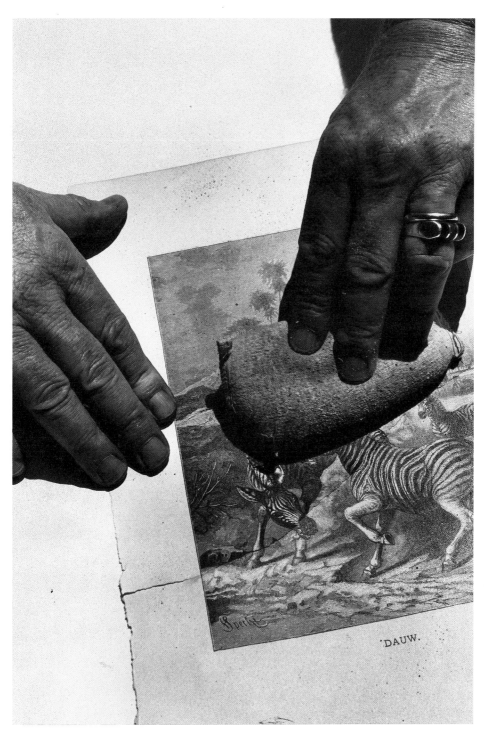

22 To clean an old page with a Draft Clean Pad, rub the paper gently, then dust away particles with a clean paint brush.

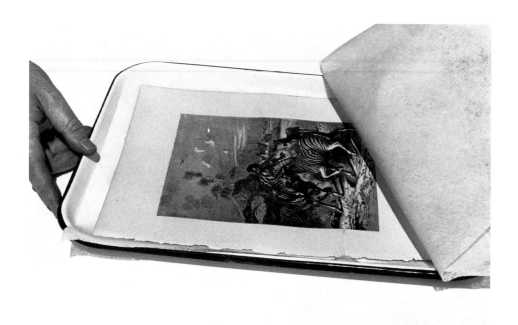

23 Sandwich the paper to be de-acidified between two sheets of random spun wove fabric in the porcelain tray.

the warm tones they have achieved in aging can contribute to the collage without any destructive effect on the piece itself.

I deacidify, using nonaqueous *Wei T'o* solution #2. As the fumes of this volatile liquid are quite potent, I work near an open window and wear a surgical mask. The image itself is sandwiched between two sheets of acid-free spunbonded polyester fabric. This enables me to lift and turn the image on a flexible support without any danger of tearing the paper. The permeable, random weave also helps disperse the solution evenly into the paper. First I place one layer of the cloth in an enamel tray. Then I put the image over it and place the second layer of cloth on top.

I pour a small amount of *Wei T'o* into a porcelain evaporating dish. Using a Japanese water brush (*hake*), I apply the *Wei T'o* evenly across the top of the sandwiched layer. Immediately, I can turn the paper by grasping the edges of the fabric. Then I brush the *Wei T'o* over the reverse side of the sandwiched sheets. The liquid quickly penetrates the paper, and within minutes it is dry and ready for cutting. I repeat this process for each of the pages I will use, or even fragments of paper that can easily be handled the same way using the support fabrics. Once the papers are dry, I clean them with a flexible household paint brush, dusting to remove any crystals that have formed on the paper. Since the solution crystallizes rapidly in open air, I wash the porcelain dish, tray, and *hake* brush thoroughly with soapy water for clean storage. In time, however, a residue of the crystallized solution will form on the brush, bowl, and tray. In order to dissolve and neutralize these alkaline deposits, I clean the instruments in ordinary household vinegar, after which I wash them thoroughly in hot water.

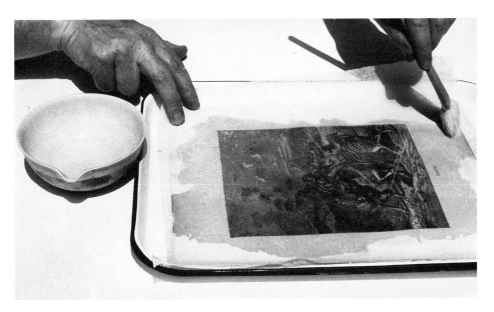

24 Pour a small amount of Wei T'o solution into the evaporating dish, then brush it evenly over the surface of the sandwich. Repeat procedure on reverse side.

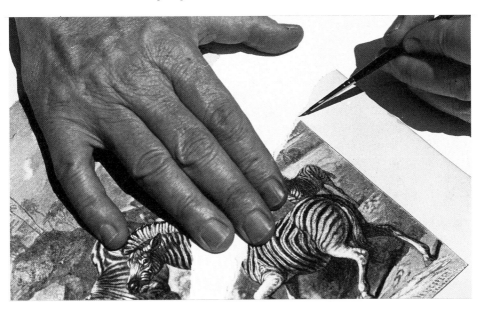

25 Repairing torn paper with a fine circular brush and PVA.

Although it is now free of acid, the engraving of the zebra is still severely torn. Before I can begin to work with the page, it has to be repaired. I do this by carefully aligning the tear marks to match the zebra's stripes. Then I paste the two sheets together using a very fine brush dipped in Jade 403 or Elvace 1874, the polyvinyl acetate adhesives that I typically use in making collages. Now, laying the bonded tear image upside down, I apply acid-free Archival Document Tape, pressing it firmly in place.

As the image papers are old, they can use the additional support of a backing. My choice for the zebra image is Japanese Okawara, a long-fibered paper often used by conservators for reinforcement. Sturdy and thick, it will give me an excellent edge to assist in cutting the zebra's round contours. Its rough side takes adhesive especially well, insuring a perfect bond. In pasting down a backing paper, I begin at the bottom edge. With my image paper (zebra) face down on the work table, I begin by brushing a thin layer of adhesive across a one-inch strip at the lower edge of the Okawara sheet. Then I lay it down on the reverse side of the zebra and press the paper firmly into place. Inch by inch I brush the backing paper with adhesive and roll it into place, smoothing the pasted sheets together with my fingers to prevent wrinkles. I always hold the backing paper up as I paste, being careful never to bend or crease it. Finally, when the whole backing sheet is laid in place, I use an archival roller to secure a wrinkle-free bond. Then I press the two sheets between heavy plate glass and allow them to dry.

Like the zebra image, the landscape sheet that I intend to use is also backed. But because I must cut out the delicate branches of trees, I choose a thin, transparent Sekishu paper which allows me greater flexibility with the cutting blade.

All my images are cut with surgical scalpels, using a number 11 blade. I cut on a drafting table against an acid-free self-healing mat. Because the surface mends, I am never in danger of an old cut mark running my blade out of its intended course. This is crucial since I am essentially drawing with the scalpel.

In the first stage of cutting I hollow out the zebra's shape. Since this also removes the tail (hanging between its legs in the original plate), the form loses some of the dramatic movement that I want to retain in the final collage. Luckily, the plate portrays a second zebra with tail erect, and I can use this tail's shape as a pattern, transposing it onto the image I have chosen.

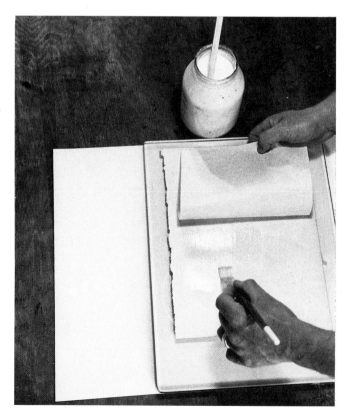

26 Paste is applied evenly and the backing sheet is rolled carefully into place.

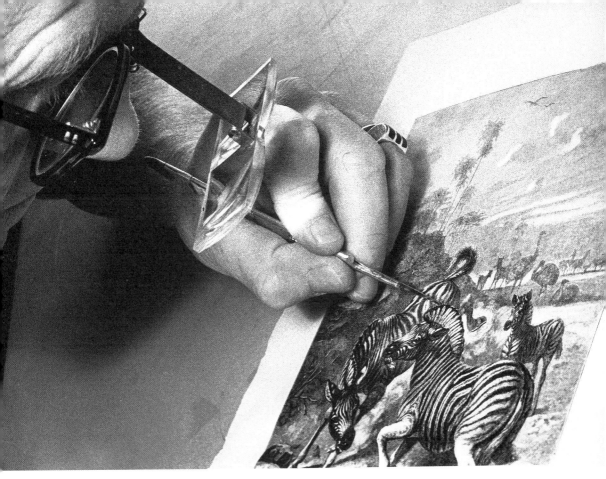

27 Cutting out the zebra with a scalpel (#11 blade).

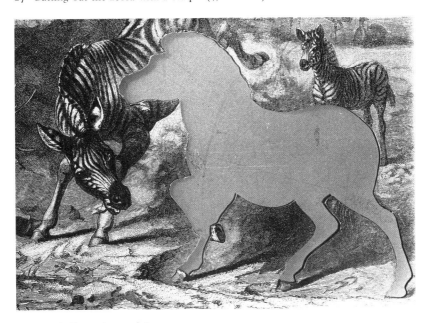

28 The hollow zebra template.

Now, in the hollow form I can see exactly how to arrange the landscape with respect to the zebra's shape. Since the treetops and round hut will rise above the zebra's contour in the finished collage, I cut along the edges of these images so that I can study their shapes overlaid against the animal's form.

Cutting the trees is a most difficult process, for the final image must not show elements of sky between the branches and the whole outline must not appear as if it were extracted from another place. It must convincingly belong to this image only. For the delicate carving of such minute contours the extreme tip of the scalpel blade is my only cutting tool. The instrument, though firmly grasped, is moved with a loose wrist motion, like a drawing pen, so that the trees are rendered with natural curves. As I am cutting, I frequently stop to match the two plates. Until the final pasting, there is much flexibility in positioning and changing the related images. Moving the trees to the right or left, slightly higher or lower, can alter the collage drastically. Proportions are essential. In this case the trees, once in place, need a pruning to prevent them from overpowering the animal shape.

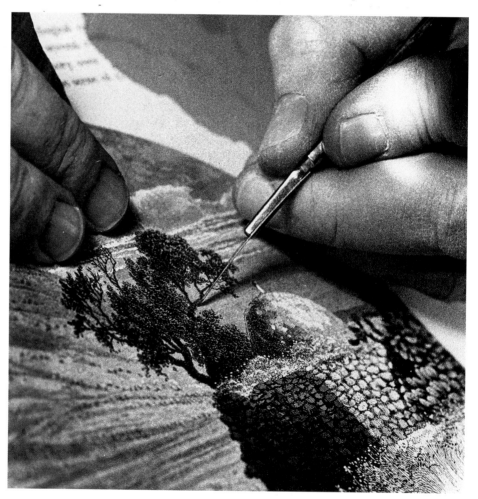

29 In the delicate cutting of landscape, each separate branch must be shaped.

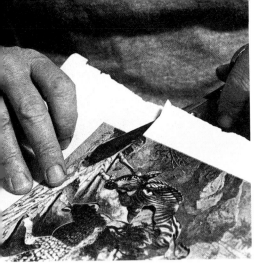
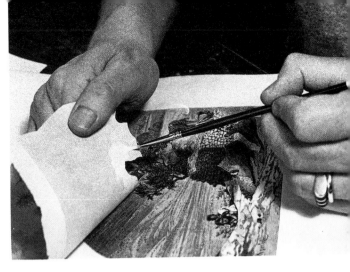

30 A scissor-cut from the paper's edge slits the zebra into two connected flaps that are easy to manipulate.

31 Pasting the hollow zebra template to the landscape.

Once the two papers are perfectly adjusted, I paste the trees and dome in place on the zebra plate. Then, turning the image as I work, I continue to paste the zebra plate onto the landscape. With a brush, I apply an even coat of adhesive following the animal's form. Every inch or two I pause to press the pasted paper down firmly, using an archival blotting paper to pick up any excess paste that might have seeped through an edge. In order to liberate the zebra's shape, I first make a single cut with a pair of scissors from the paper's edge to the animal form. This slits my pattern into two connected flaps that can be freely manipulated without breaking the template itself. Once I paste them both down, the zebra image will be whole and the two layers of imagery bonded perfectly in place.

Again I will cut out the zebra's shape, this time using the edge of the hollow form as a cutting guide. Since the zebra plate has been backed with Okawara, its thickness provides a firm support for the scalpel blade. By degrees I free the internal landscape, which gradually becomes the zebra of my final collage. As I cut, I slice away the shell that has served as a pattern.

Now, from the original zebra I cut the hooves and head, pasting them carefully in place. In order to bond them securely I use the tip of a bone bookbinder's folding tool. With this smooth instrument I am able to apply firm pressure to small surface areas, rubbing gently.

This brings me to my most fragile cutting. The whole form must be refined to a unity of shape and proportion. The separate branches of the treetops must be shaded, drawn with a scalpel, to their final form. At this point I am frequently cutting between lines only a few millimeters thick, and it is probably for that reason a surgeon once described the work as "bloodless surgery." My concentration requires that I forget the overall image and think only of unnecessary detail that can be eliminated. Minute spaces give depth to the trees, and further definition is possible with ink drawing over the image.

For this I use waterproof India ink and a pen with fine nibs. Since I work at an angle, I prefer this to an architect's pen that must be held in a vertical position. With the ink I emphasize the black branches of the trees and other contour lines in the

75

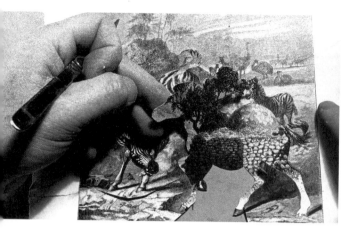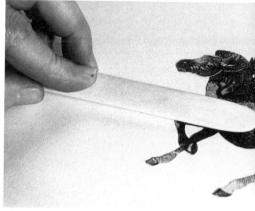

32 Freeing the zebra form.

33 Securing the bond with a bone folding tool.

shape of the collage. With stipple drawing I add texture to the stones. By outlining the zebra's form I can eliminate the white paper edge and discover any imperfect cut that might require touching up with the scalpel. Using another pen dipped in white ink, I add contrast to the eye and facial stripes as well as dense areas of leaves that need visual separation. Finally, I check the complete collage against a white surface, the 4-ply acid-free board on which it will be mounted.

Since my aim is to isolate the complex image, I want to give it space on the mat board. With a soft pencil I rule a 4″ bottom edge and at right angles a 4″ side margin. This will give me a pasting guide for the collage to be mounted perfectly square within wide borders. I complete ruling these, then cut the mounting board to size. This makes it easy to manipulate, which is important to me since I rotate the collage as I paste it.

The finished piece is pasted with the same PVA used in its making. I begin on the reverse side of the zebra's face, applying the adhesive evenly with a thin round sable brush (#1 or #2), making certain that there will be no excess at the edge. Turning the collage over, I set it down in place on the mounting board. The hooves are about $\frac{1}{4}″$ above the ruled guideline, to make erasure easy. I press the pasted head section firmly down with archival blotting paper. If it lifts off without resistance I know that the adhesive has not leaked through an edge onto the mount. Now I smoothe the face gently with the bone tool.

Once this crucial tacking is achieved, I paste the animal's body, working in zones. Holding the body up, I am careful not to bend back the paper image, but roll it against supporting fingers. With a fine brush, I apply the adhesive liberally to a zoned section of the back of the image and roll it into place on the board, first blotting then rubbing with the bone. Since I work in zones I can be sure that each area is pasted properly. The zone system permits me also to rotate the piece so that I can work consistently in one position.

With the legs fixed in place, the collage is finally secure on its mount. Now I cover it with archival blotting paper and, using the archival roller, apply even pressure passing over it from every direction. Finally, with a clean soft gum eraser, I remove

76

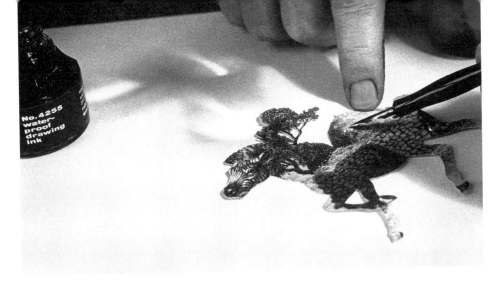

34 Over-drawing with India ink.

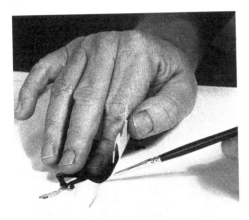

35 Pasting the collage by zones. The image is held firmly and rolled into place.

36 After each pasting the image is touched gently with archival blotting paper to pick up any excess.

the guide lines and, using an ordinary household paint brush, clear the surface of any remaining particles. The finished collage, pressed under a piece of heavy plate glass, will dry perfectly flat.

If the zebra is to be stored in a print cabinet or acid-free paper box, I cut a protective layer of acid-free glassine to serve as an overlay. For framing, I hinge the mounted collage with linen tape on a 4-ply acid-free mat board and cut a double window mat. This enhances the animal's depth and freedom in the visual field.

The working technique that I have described has, of course, many variables in the number and source of composite images, in the choice of backing paper, adhesives, and finally in the subject of the collage itself. While animate nature persists for me as a recurring theme, I also work in abstract geometrical compositions on a large scale. For these I adapt my method, placing the backing sheet of Okawara directly on the work table, applying the adhesive to the backing paper and laying the image fragments down in place. Despite the differences in conception and execution, I still deacidify the image papers and work with acid-free adhesives. Whether the piece has

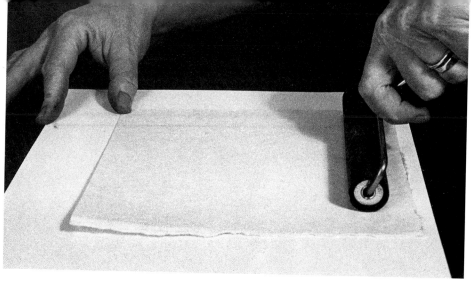

37 After the pasting is complete, the collage face up is covered with archival blotting paper and pressed with an archival roller.

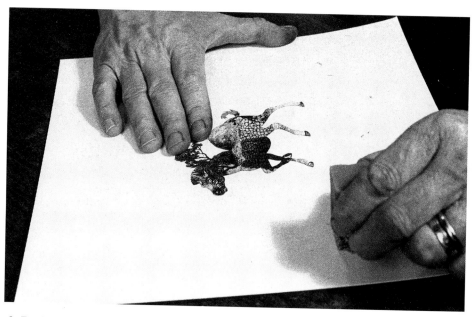

38 Erasing ruled guidelines used for pasting.

dimensions of 4 inches or 4 feet it can be constructed with techniques and materials that insure its solidity and permanence.

In the handling of papers, materials, and pastes there are many methods quite as elaborate and individual, requiring perhaps a new vocabulary to describe them fully. At present collage is widespread and so diverse that my illustration of personal style can serve only as an introduction to archival considerations that have lately influenced the medium.

The next chapter will be devoted to a cross-section of collage in contemporary practice. It it is not intended as a definitive survey but as a representative sampling. There is no one way to work, even in black and white, as a number of collagists will illustrate by their extreme diversity. Even more artists explore collage in color, working in everything from magazines and photocopies to handmade stock, dyed, pigmented, crayoned, and painted. Their profusion is full of suggestions that artists working in the medium might care to pursue. Many of the collagists whose work is described have shared their techniques and even technical information. Their generosity provides not only practical information but a means for understanding the state of the art and how its aesthetic is related to methods and materials.

39 John Digby: *Zebra* (1983). 12 × 16 in. (framed).

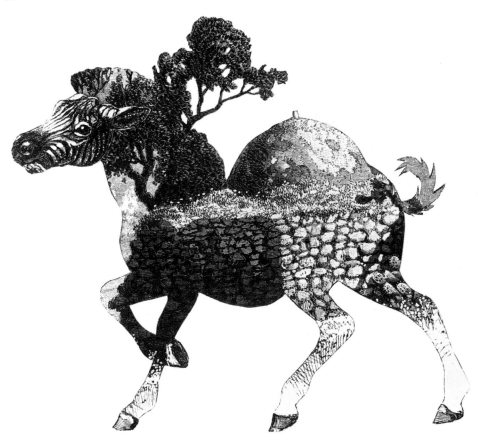

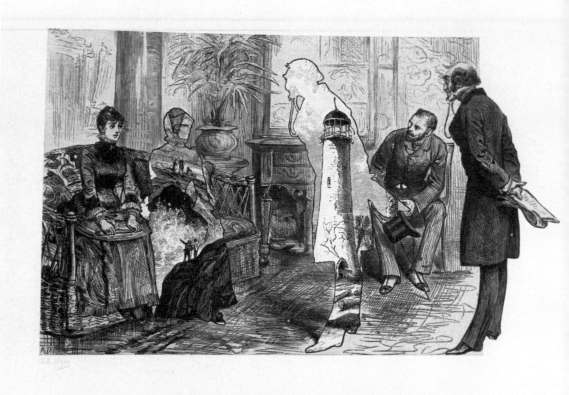

40 John Digby: *The Interview* (1984) from the series *Beside Themselves*. Paper collage with pen and ink, $10\frac{1}{2} \times 6\frac{1}{2}$ in.

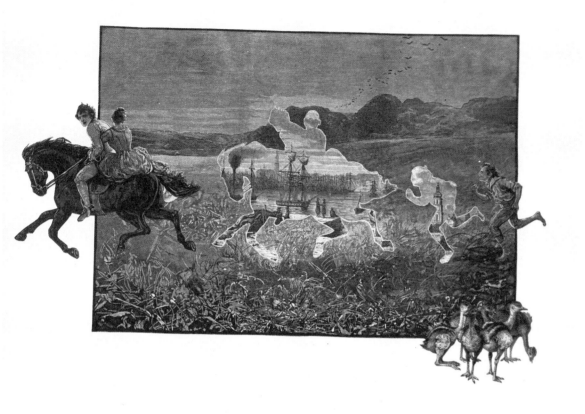

41 John Digby: *The Elopement* (1984) from the series *Beside Themselves*. Paper collage with pen and ink, $11\frac{1}{2} \times 7\frac{1}{2}$ in.

CHAPTER FIVE

Collage in Current Practice

HANNELORE BARON

In the collages of Hannelore Baron it is possible to pass through the innocence of a child into the experience of a dangerous and fragile world. Above all, her collages are political statements about the human condition, reflecting the facts of war and violence. At the core of her work is a poetry of protest.

"I need to work for my own well-being," she admits. The need is also mirrored in her desire for order and neatness. She describes the tidy, geometric elements of her collages as "war memorials" set against the destructive impulses that surround us.

She is utterly opposed to war, not only that which she experienced as a Jewish child in Germany, but also the Viet Nam War and every clash that has endangered us since. Her work expresses the resignation of an artist who has turned fear and protest to creativity.

The human figure has a double potency in her collages. It is a childlike figure, man imagined in innocence. But it is also "the shapes of people, which were dug up somewhere at an archaeological dig." These she composes by cutting figures from thin copper sheets, then wrapping them in string and cloth "like Egyptian mummies, American Indian burial costumes . . . the body-bags in Viet Nam. The string has to do with imprisonment, but much of that is on a subconscious level and I can't really tell which of these things I do just for visual effect, or for conscious or subconscious reasons."

The visual effects are strong. She inks her simple cut-out elements, printing the patterns in uneven, muted tones that sometimes look like faded frescoes or worn Oriental carpets. They are disturbing, but the allusions to childhood, to crayons, to direct and simple evocations are also protective. Her collages are soft graffiti of a hard world.

Typically, she works in series, preparing five pieces of Kitakata background paper, then composing the collages one after the other. Her imagery is set down with various techniques. Sometimes she paints with oils on glass, then impresses reverse images on bits of paper which she applies to the background or pastes directly. She also prints monotypes from her copper figures using a printing press. She may introduce pieces of fabric or small pen-and-ink drawings on *washi* paper, applying the overlays with acrylic medium gel.

A prolific artist, Hannelore Baron works collages in cloth as well as paper and in three-dimensional box constructions as well as flat work that she irons to a smooth finish. Her images are a kind of pictorial conservation that seems to trace the history of human impulse from cave walls to city squares. Even her newest collage looks old, like a palimpsest scratched deeply with layers of meaning. And paradoxically, though she repeats her imagery, each piece looks new.

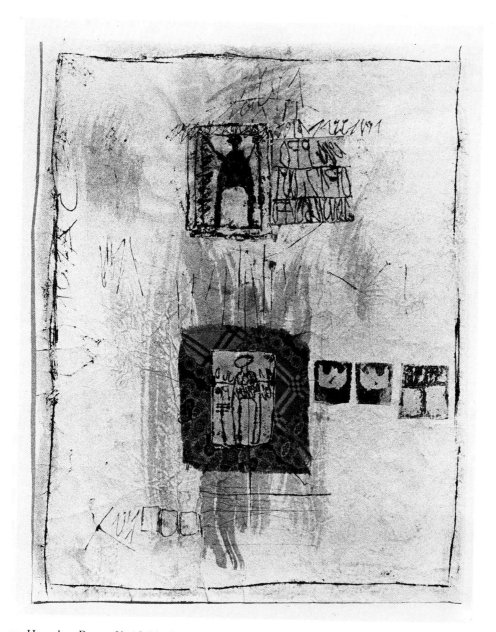

42 Hannelore Baron: *Untitled* (1982). Japanese paper and mixed media, $19\frac{1}{2} \times 14$ in. Collection of the artist.

SUSAN BARRON

In 1979 Susan Barron was printing 3,200 photographs for her limited edition book, *Another Song* (text by John Cage, New York: Callaway Editions, 1981). During that time "I couldn't bring myself to make another print," but the need to work was there, and she began collaging. A palladium print of one of her earliest collages appears on the cover of *Another Song*, and from that beginning the photographs and collages have become inseparable. In fact, they share the same studio; on the tables and ledges of her darkroom are the files of minute fragments of maps, music, and intriguing old papers that she stores for her collages.

These, like her photographs, are worked on a small scale. "My ideas," she says, "represent an intimacy that I don't wish to throw open to the skies." Most of the collages, like the photographs, have dimensions of only a few inches, and yet her private spaces are dense with layers of mystery. On this scale, for example, she has composed a Book of Hours in the style of an illuminated manuscript. The feeling of each month is evoked by oblique allusions, tiny figures from old prints, a miniature heart buried in February, scraps of Hebrew, a shred from an old map of Paris and calligraphic markings of a "language" she has invented to preserve her secrets. The buried and the hidden also speak a secret language in her work. We are conscious of layers, a building up of surfaces like maps defining the hills and rivers of an imaginary world. Sometimes she colors the landscapes with a blush of pigment, gouache, and watercolor. Sometimes she leads us through the labyrinth by a single thread of hair. In all, the final gesture must be a total shape. "I'm not satisfied until it can't be broken down into its finite pieces."

In her Book of Hours there are thirteen months. The thirteenth, nestled between May and November, is "Remember," a clue to the essence of her work. An inveterate habitué of libraries, digging everywhere with pleasure for unknown information scattered in deep retreats, she makes her collages a sort of "library retrieval system" of remembered images.

Memory also plays a role in the musical quality of the pieces. Barron studied piano, playing more from memory than notation, and in the collages allusion to musical notation is yet another secret language. The influence of music is strong in her work – particularly medieval and French court music, and also the complexities of more modern composers like Erik Satie and Charles Ives.

Even the dissonance of modernity has a place in her collages. Though she rarely collages her own photographs, she uses borrowed photographic images in some of her more expanded pieces, the largest of which is 11″ × 14″. Interestingly, when she borrows images from the history of art, she chooses black-and-white reproductions – for example, her Mona Lisa placed in the context of a concentration camp. In these larger pieces disturbing anatomical figures also appear.

Anatomy may be part of her secret self-landscape, since she is by training and occupation a diagnostic chemist who, in another sense, probes for unknowns on a

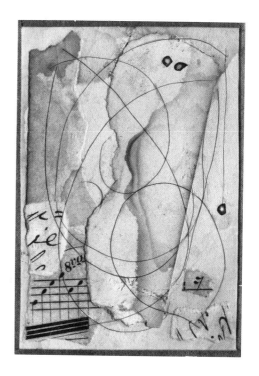

43 Susan Barron: Collage book cover for *Another Song* (1979). Pallodium print of a paper collage, $3\frac{1}{2} \times 2\frac{1}{2}$ in. Collection of the artist. (Actual size)

microscopic scale. Certainly her laboratory technique gives here a special facility as a collagist. In setting down fragile elements of paper, even paper from a wasp's nest, she applies adhesive (O'Glue) with a syringe. She buffers her PVA (Jade 403) with calcium carbonate and mounts the work with acid-free papers and boards. But, for the actual piece, she also chooses to work with old, discarded papers, which she treats carefully, sometimes with acrylic matte fixative and archival adhesives to stabilize them as well as she can. Her collages evoke the lyrical imagery of worlds retrieved from loss.

ROMARE BEARDEN

Citing Goethe, Romare Bearden meditates on the human condition: "We're all locked into our particular time by at least one or more of the major faults of that period." In the twentieth century we live under stress in a quickly changing world. The French poet Paul Valéry once commented that "the machine has robbed man of his patience"; therefore, Bearden adds, it would be impossible today to paint in the manner of, say, Van Eyck or Dürer. Collage is Bearden's response to this situation, a medium perfectly suited to the age and one that sets him artistically free.

His freedom unlocks the past, which floods him with childhood memories of Charlotte, North Carolina, where he was born in 1914. Mecklenburg County was then a rural world, of which he recalls the sensations of magnolias and cotton fields, his Cherokee grandmother cooking catfish, and Mrs. Maudelle Sleet, the lady with the green thumb. In his collages, the people and aromas return and by means of them he salvages the vitality of a particular kind of American life.

Bearden is an epic artist whose narratives depict the life, adventures, and sometimes tragedy inherent in his culture. Paradoxically, this great master of figurative collage is also profoundly abstract. "People in America have misused the word abstract," he contends. For Bearden, abstraction refers to compositional relationships that create an illusion of volume in flat space. Instead of shading by a light source, collage permits the various flat planes, in opposition, to suggest the volumes. Bearden derives his abstract geometries from proportionate ratios (3×5 or $1\frac{1}{2} \times 2\frac{1}{2}$) that define the spatial relationships of his compositions. Every collage begins for him by a laying down of areas that are proportional to the full canvas, or board, on which he is working – the ground against which his figures come to life.

His principles of composition are consciously indebted to the tradition of painters such as Rembrandt, Vermeer, Ter Borch, and De Hooch. Like them, he has a powerful sense of the interior room, its space, light, mood, and extreme sense of personal privacy. He translates this into expressions of cabin life in his own black South, or mealtime gatherings in Harlem apartments. Always the table, with its coffee pot, forks, and spoons, rests at the center of human relationships, presided over by mother and child, cat and dog. The measurements and figures are archetypes as well as individuals. They link his epic narratives also to the Homeric tradition, which he explored in an early series of paintings from *The Iliad* (1947), then in the "Odysseus" series of collages (1977). They are also strongly connected to icons of Christian art, which are a perpetual spiritual presence in his work. The freedom of every bird is a potential annunciation, the mother and child a potential madonna, and every girl dipped in the river of her battered tin tub recalls Susanna at her bath. These forms never change.

Their permanence is a mathematical as well as a figural reality, as Bearden understands. Having evaded his parents' intention that he become a doctor, he graduated from New York University in 1935 with a degree in mathematics. But his abstract sense of number and interval also comes from the applied mathematics of music – jazz and the blues. In these forms, as in his collages, rhythm and dissonance play on the sensibility. From the blues he gathers an essential patterning and balance of opposites, a call and response that sound like echoes of isolation.

His people are caught between conflicting images; the fields are open but the figures often appear confined by spatial arrangements and blocked in by fences. Birds appear everywhere as symbols of flight and freedom, the train by contrast as a recurring emblem of mystery, transience, and mechanism. His country guitarists with their absorbed faces seem to compose a sympathetic response to the lonely whistles of passing trains.

Like the jazz that inspires them, Bearden's collages work by intervals, the fine sequence between what is struck and not struck. Most of their political overtones are left unstated. The cut-up faces, composed from magazine photographs, are intercut with images from African masks. The historical allusions are unmistakable, yet they never dominate. The people do, with their energy and density of movement. Like Bruegel, whom Bearden greatly admires, he invests folk life with a transformational reality that elevates it to art.

The collages have the inner truth of the caricature. Significantly, during high school, Bearden met E. Simms Campbell, a black cartoonist for *The New Yorker*, *Life*, *Esquire*, and *Judge* magazines, and determined on following the cartoon tradition with the express purpose of creating art that would inspire social change. Later, in 1936–37, Bearden studied at the Art Students League in New York with George Grosz, who had already earned his reputation as a political satirist. Grosz introduced Bearden to Ingres, Cranach, and Dürer, the great draftsmen of the past, and taught him the necessity of looking and learning as a prelude to distortion.

It was the American painter, Stuart Davis, who taught Bearden how to listen to the music of Earl Hines and to see the relationship of its intervals to the laying down, separation, and distortion of colors and patterns. In those days Bearden was still working with paint. He went through many styles that included semiabstract watercolors based on literary texts (*The Bible*, *The Iliad*, the poems of Federico García Lorca), then formal studies of Old Masters. A stint in the army intervened. In 1950 he went to Paris to study philosophy at the Sorbonne, and at that time met Brancusi, Matisse, and Braque, whom he remembers vividly.

When he returned to New York, earning his living was a problem. He tried songwriting, and his one big hit, "Seabreeze," was recorded by Billy Eckstein, Dizzy Gillespie, Tito Puente, and many other musicians. But his real voice was still silent, and only under the influence of his wife, Nanette, whom he married in 1954, did he return to painting. Collage came later, in 1963, as a response to the civil rights movement. Working in a collaborative group of black artists, Bearden came up with the idea of rendering scenes drawn from black life in collages made from magazine imagery. The monumental photographic enlargements of these pieces were shown in 1964 under the title "Projections" and introduced the style for which he has gained his reputation. It is a style based on found images that derive much of their mystery from the fracturing and juxtaposition of objects from one spatial environment into another.

But that style, too, is subject to perpetual change. "Suddenly," as Bearden puts it, "you're doing something else." The found magazine papers have disappeared from his recent works, which are composed of papers he paints himself with a luminescent imagery that still transports him from his Long Island City studio to the gardens and fragrances of Mecklenburg County. He still constructs by putting colors down in ratios and building by layers as the figures and movements define themselves. He points out that it requires faith to work this way, keeping the collage open, not closing too quickly, knowing the point at which the picture is saved.

Bearden regulates his choices by working color, space, and form as one. He constructs one collage at a time, over successive days, often thinking in terms of a series, although each piece maintains its independence and integrity. In making collage he works with a resin emulsion adhesive (Gluefast 7256), pressing his work as he composes with a printmaker's brayer, or hand-roller. At the end of the working day the boards are weighted down with paving bricks to help prevent warping. The pieces are constructed on the firm supporting of a masonite backboard, and the latest work, of hand-painted papers and fabrics, is spray-coated with Blair acrylic matte varnish applied under 100 pounds pressure to form a perfect, even seal. Bearden's masonite boards are reinforced by a wooden stretcher fitted with a central beam. Over the back surface he pastes a heavy piece of brown paper to distribute the tension evenly. This engineering has successfully enabled Bearden to work even in mural-size collage. *Color illustration I.*

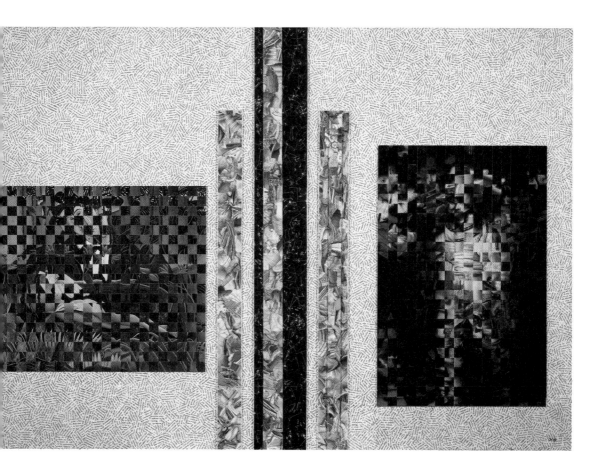

XI Jiři Kolář: *Homage to Bartok* (1980). $39\frac{3}{8} \times 27\frac{5}{8}$ in. Courtesy Maeght Galerie, New York.

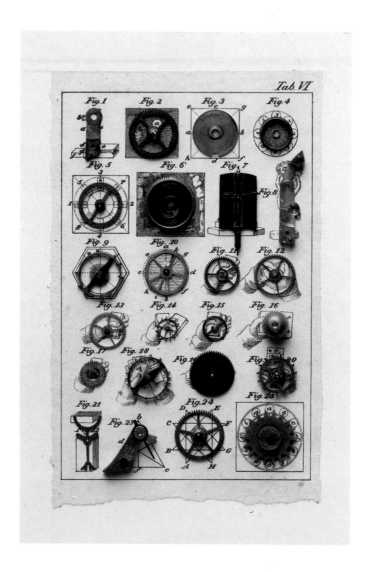

XII Friedrich Meckseper: *Sammelsurium* (1978). Paper collage with mixed media, $5\frac{1}{2} \times 3\frac{1}{2}$ in.

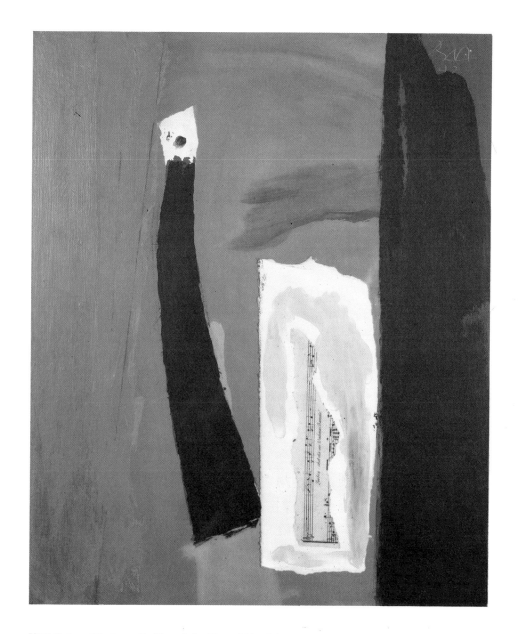

XIII Robert Motherwell: *Sign of the Mermaid* (1980). 24 × 20 in. Courtesy M. Knoedler and Co., Inc., New York.

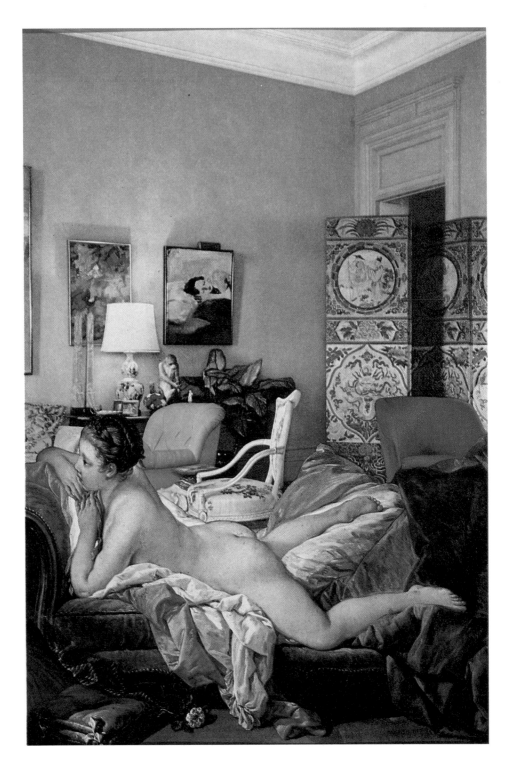

XIV John O'Reilly: *Untitled* (1981). Paper collage, $8\frac{7}{8} \times 13\frac{1}{4}$ in.

XV Alfonso Ossorio: *Money is Energy* (1967).
Collage and drawing, incorporating the
artist's earlier work, 22 × 6 in. Collection
Mr. and Mrs. Joseph V. Ossorio, Greenwich,
Connecticut.

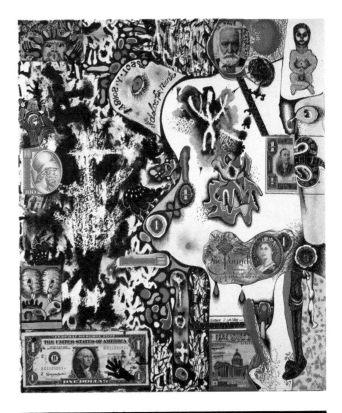

XVI Georges Pinel: *Madones Anatomique*
(1977). Paper collage with spray varnish, 20
× 16 in.

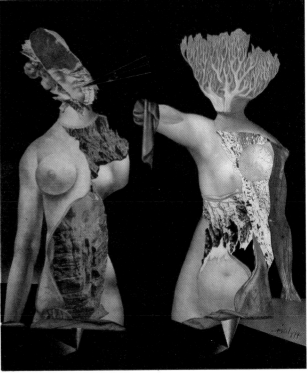

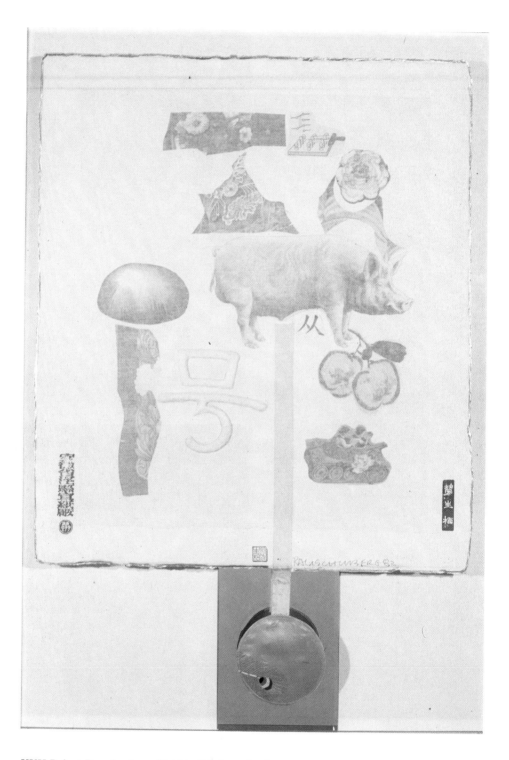

XVII Robert Rauschenberg: *Howl* (1982) from the *Seven Characters* series. Mixed media on paper, 43 × 31 × 2½ in. Courtesy Leo Castelli Gallery, New York.

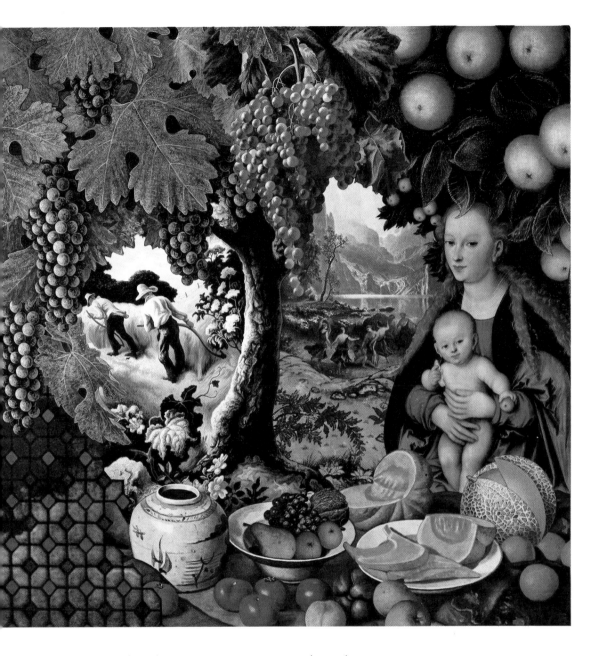

XVIII David Singer: *Harvest* (1981–82). Paper collage, $20\frac{1}{2} \times 20\frac{1}{2}$ in. Collection of the artist.

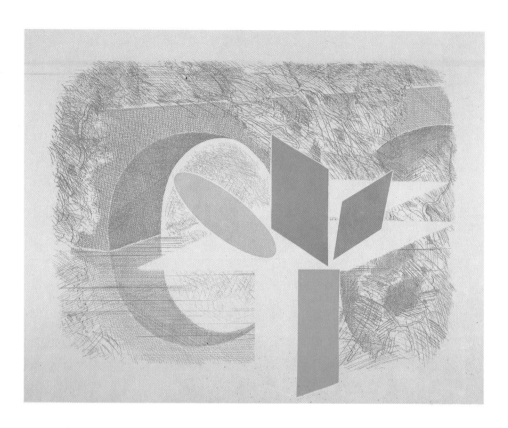

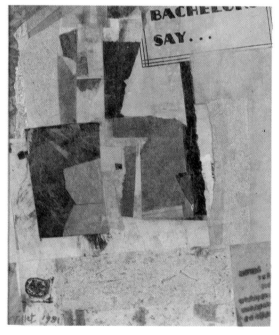

XIX William Tillyer: *Thorneywaite IX* (n.d.) from the *Esk Bridge* series. Courtesy Bernard Jacobson Gallery, London.

XX Cynthia Villet: *Bachelors Say* (1981). Paper and mixed media, 10 × 12 in. Courtesy Kouros Gallery, New York.

BARTON LIDICÉ BENEŠ

To shock is to connect. In Barton Lidice Beneš' world, ideas are barbed lures intended to hook the spectator. Although aesthetically pleasing and masterfully constructed, his collages are in essence totems jeering at taboos, turning serious and sacrosanct subjects to jest.

Beneš adds a further dimension to the outrage by insisting on using, in his own words, "real and original objects" – real books, mummies, money, box tops, beetles, pencils, plates, Picassos, ancient pot shards, sacred things, and even real ash from crematoria. His inventory has the passionate eccentricity of an obsessive collector preoccupied with the logic of rearranging his specimens.

Beneš is, in fact, an avid collector of African and ancient Egyptian artifacts, and all his work is directly inspired by the pieces of his collection. In 1978 he went to the Ivory Coast to complete a mural commission on a plantation at Grand Bassam. During his visit, he met people who made the art that he collects; they were ordinary

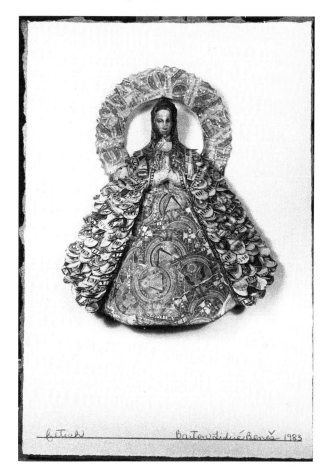

44 Barton Lidicé Beneš: *Fetish* (1983). Money and glitter on rag paper, $10\frac{1}{2} \times 15\frac{1}{2}$ in. Courtesy Kathryn Markel Gallery, New York.

people, craftsmen for whom art was not a conscious pursuit but simply the work they did. And their work appealed to Beneš, particularly the masks and fetish figures covered in loose straw, shells, beads, and exotic pouches.

These images are the conjuring objects of Beneš' collages. Not only does he make masks and fetishes of his own, but much of his collage work is about collecting, particularly the multiplicity of objects that become structurally a collection. He has made, for example, his own museum collage, a floor-to-ceiling specimen cabinet with perhaps a hundred visible collaged sections made from genuine antiquities. In a satiric spirit he has also done a series called "Snips," made from pieces sliced out of original art. "Nasty Stains" of every imaginable kind constitute another wing of his collage museum, and at present he is working on "Smorgasbord," an array of collaged objects typifying each nation of the world by its food reconstructed in currency.

Money is one of Beneš' favorite materials – also a comment on collections and, he says, ironically cheaper to use than art supplies. Beneš has the unusual distinction of having bartered with the U.S. Federal Reserve Bank for six million dollars in shredded bills, which he weaves and otherwise transforms into nest eggs, ice cream scoops, filled purses, and icons of great imaginative power. His completed collages, isolated against their clean white grounds, have the strength of the African masks which are his inspiration.

They also have a sense of display. Beneš, who was born in New Jersey in 1942, counts as more significant than his art training the six years he spent doing commercial displays, which taught him the transformative potential of materials; and even now much of his jesting derives from the game of making one thing look like another. He burns, cuts, crushes, tears, paints, models, and draws, working every day and rarely leaving his New York studio. Although the work itself has a pristine clarity when complete, he chooses to mount his collages on foam board and Arches paper with deliberately torn (simulated deckle) edges that play against the sharply defined images. Beneš makes and mounts his pieces with acrylic matte medium conscious of his craftsmanship simply as an element of the work he does by nature.

CLAUDE BENTLEY

In the autumn of 1944, when Besançon in eastern France had just been liberated, Claude Bentley, an American artist who had sketched throughout his war service, walked into the town and arranged for an exhibition of his work. "The experience of war gave me a sense of urgency," he says, an urgency which still drives him to work at his art daily.

Both in paper and on large collage canvases, his work derives impact from bold and stable forms that often gain their energy from diagonal patterning. The assertive, rectilinear geometries are keyed to a subtle range of earth tones, touched discreetly with reds. "In many instances I limit color. Black is a strong element. I cannot think of working without black." Even the black of lettering on a torn envelope, or charcoal, or an ink stroke slash through his compositions in black, are focal points of interest.

Bentley works collage on a large scale, concerned with the movement of his broad shapes from the upper edge down. He composes with a deliberate sense of gravity. His papers are 100 per cent rag, some handmade (Plum Tree) and densely pigmented.

His works are never descriptive in a traditional sense but depend on an organization of the elements of form and color to give them structure and unity. Bentley, who spent some time in North Africa during the Second World War and traveled extensively in Mexico, Spain, and Portugal, acquired a sense of color and mood that pervades his work. Now living in Hispanic northern New Mexico, he continues to be influenced by the natural forces of the rugged landscape. His fascination with primitive forms draws him, as well, to pre-Columbian and African art. In his earlier days, as he recalls, Antonio Tápies was also an influence.

Working on Arches as a background paper, Bentley brings his collages one at a time to completion. "I cannot leave a collage in an unresolved state," he remarks. Making the resolution work in paper involves a progressive accumulation of shapes which he rearranges to his satisfaction before pasting them down with casein adhesive.

The canvas compositions are technically more difficult. First he sizes the canvas with two coats of acrylic gesso. When he has decided on the approximate placement of papers, corrugated cardboard, burlap, and elements of painted canvas, he saturates them, painting on both sides with acrylic medium before setting them on the canvas to adhere. The front coating of adhesive insures protection against atmospheric pollution and aging.

The permanence of Bentley's collages is impressive not only in the material sense, but as formal compositions that have the solidity of boulders resting on bedrock. *Color illustration II.*

TONY BERLANT

The working of metals into art forms is almost as old as the history of man. Metal associated with collage in particular has historical implications linked to folk craftsmanship and icon-makers, as well as to the constructivist fascination with tactile relief patterning from machine-age refuse.

Tony Berlant brings to his ornate metal surface collages a synthesis of all three traditions. He works in the manner of a tinsmith from sheet metal biscuit boxes, steamer trunks, and serving trays, making use of their color and even pictorial designs. By cutting, patterning, hammering, and nailing his shaped tin fragments to found wooden surfaces, he builds his collages (a method that definitively solves problems of adhesion!). The foundations are often old frames, into which he may set a found painting that becomes an icon in the context of his hammered metal collage borders. Even the profusion of nails, clustered in patterns, becomes an element of the crafted surface with stylistic reference to folk art.

Berlant has, in this way, collaged whole doors in tin plate to look like avant garde bulkheads, and he has extended the method to three-dimensional sculpture, collaging cubes and house-shaped boxes that suggest personal reliquaries or roadside shrines.

For many years Berlant has collected and traded Southwest American Indian artifacts, and his collaged metalwork is frequently reminiscent of their patterns. But if the folk element is strong, Berlant also carries into his collages his training in painting and sculpture. His emphatic substitution of metal and nails for paper and paste is a sculptor's solution to problems of material fragility. Within the self-imposed limits of working with found materials, his compositions have classical components of structure and imagery that are easily understood in the context of traditional painting. As a collagist, moreover, he is somewhat unusual in having both a figurative and an abstract style.

Born in New York City in 1941, Berlant took his B.A. and M.A. in painting at the University of California at Los Angeles, and in 1963 took his M.F.A. in sculpture. In the same year he began to collage. He continues to live and work in Santa Monica, California. *Color illustration III.*

VARUJAN BOGHOSIAN

The collages of Varujan Boghosian are blueprints of spatial order. Trained at the Yale University School of Art and Architecture, he invests even the most personal memorabilia with formal dimensions. Like the still-life *trompe-l'oeil* paintings of the nineteenth century, his collages seem arranged to simulate the contrasts of ephemera. In the paintings artificial shadows trick the viewer into the perception of a third dimension. In Boghosian's collages loose and folded papers cast real shadows that play against the flatness of the page with suggestions of textural life akin to his three-dimensional assemblages.

In his collages the page itself is a basic architectural frame. From old bookplates he borrows decorative borders that define the spatial proportions of his work. But he

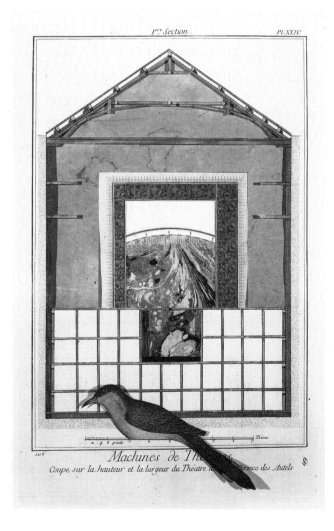

45 Varujan Boghosian: *Untitled* (1978). Paper collage, $14\frac{1}{2} \times 9\frac{1}{2}$ in. Courtesy Cordier and Ekstrom Gallery, New York.

tends to choose those with torn and folded sections which reveal to the viewer his artful deception. Within the frame he breaks his space into cubes, rectangles, thirds, triangles – the proportions of architectural regularity, which maintain stark order against irregular or broken figures.

The imagery he chooses is also anatomically proportionate. He appears fascinated with the eye as a structural organ and the doll as a spatial rendering of human contours. His human faces are idealized, like Vasari's Renaissance man. Animate life – birds and horses especially – figure strongly in his work, and their engraved images are taken from nineteenth-century illustrations that aim to catalog the species, showing correctness of movement and form.

Although he frequently uses line engravings and drawings with reference to their precise draftsmanship, the spatial organization of man and animal is equally important. For this reason he may present the image simply as a silhouette or, omitting the figure altogether, leave the yellowed page with its suggestion of where the man or horse had been. The negative image in this way becomes the shell, the house of organic form.

Buildings, too, occur as central figures, and though they are reminiscent of paper castles and model projects, their geometry is dominant. Even the triangle of an envelope flap, decorated with a classical head and set against graph paper, becomes the pediment of an imaginary structure. His architectural imagery has a strong New England sensibility. Born in 1926 in New Britain, Connecticut, Boghosian is Professor of Art at Dartmouth College, New Hampshire. The clean frames of clapboard houses, vacant mills, and Greek Revival banks come to mind obliquely as correlations of his space.

Against formal line and proportionate volumes, Boghosian establishes curves. These might come from a silhouette shaped like a weathervane horse or patterns of old wallpaper. By contrast with the straight edges he cuts with scissors or razor, the curves often come from torn edges or irregular stains in the papers themselves. Sometimes he cuts a fan of feathers from engraved birds. Marbled papers, valentines, playing cards, and printed stencils inject strong color against the yellowed pages of old books. Each of these elements defines a space as crucial to the visual stability of Boghosian's formal collage as a keystone in a house of cards.

CHARLOTTE BROWN

Even the chance rhythm of the earth's surface can yield a patterning for art. This was the discovery of New York artist Charlotte Brown, whose early paintings and paint-stained paper collages transformed earth shapes into formal structure. A graduate of the Pratt Institute, Brooklyn, she worked in both media for twenty-three years. In 1975 an accidental encounter with a copy machine inspired her to pioneer explorations that opened a future of machine-generated collages.

Since then collage has become her sole medium, and the center of her invention is the relationship between art and the machine. "The machine with its immediacy allows more time and energy for creativity. For me it is an instant image-making tool."

The imagery of her new work is exuberantly filled with the colors she has in her complete control. They are derived from 1,500 computer cards, each one keyed to a shade of her vast color memory. All are achieved by the relative balance of yellow, magenta, and cyan (blue). Using the 3M Color-in-Color copy machine as a palette, she reinterprets the flowering vines, geometries, and paisleys of Persian, Indian, and Far Eastern designs. From one image she reproduces a quantity of photocopies based on a dominant color of her conception. These then become the image sources for her abstract collages.

The collages are generally not made from paper copies. By the process of electrostatic printing, Brown has developed ways of transferring the patterns onto stable materials such as cloths, *washi* papers, and handmade stock. She does this by photocopying multiples of the original image onto coated transfer papers. Then, using a heat press or iron, she is able to shift the image onto an absorbent material that becomes permeated with the inks. The technique employs a front and back barrier that prevents the inks from migrating into the paper or fabric, so that the final achievement is a permanent color image. By this process Brown also transfers prints onto wood and clay, which she uses for mounts and embellishments. Thus, from the machine-made image she generates a vocabulary of textures complementary to her colors.

Indeed, despite her response to the immediacy of the machine, Brown's process is an elaborate manual fabrication, which perhaps explains her admiration for traditional craft and design. The most poetic paradox inherent in her collages is that the machine which is symbolic of disposable, ephemeral culture has pushed her to explorations of the most ancient patterns and to an aesthetic of archival permanence.

Her discovery of the machine led her to papermaking. She wanted a substantive texture to support the delicate transfer patterns and finally arrived at a heavily starched 100 percent rag stock that she treats with calcium carbonate. Her collages hang against the white paper like tantras. Their layers of intricate border patterns lose their particular cultural origins in the final harmony of design and color, which consciously owe something to the geometries of Vermeer as well as to Hong Kong,

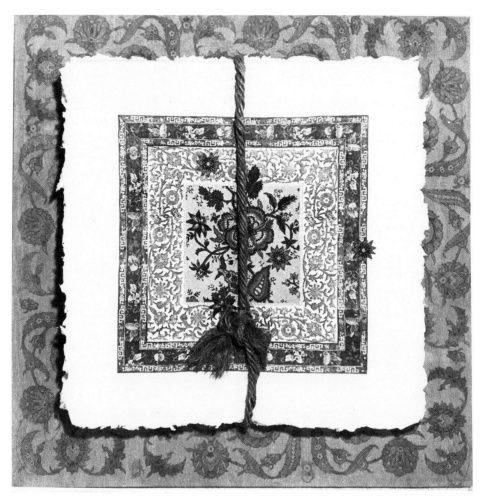

46 Charlotte Brown: *Woodland Garden* (1982). Photocopy transfers on handmade paper with plywood and rope, 32 × 32 × 5 in. Collection of the artist.

Indonesian, and American textiles that enter as embroidered ribbon. Brown designs from the printed papers and fabrics she has made in preparation for a composition. She cuts her separate pieces with a simple mat knife and pastes them to the mount paper with Jade 403. The final statement is an accretion of relationships that shift from the meditative center in concentric borders like a prayer rug. The largest of her paper tapestries is, in fact, a collage "rug" designed to be displayed on a floor.

Recently, in piling her newly made papers on the studio floor, she became fascinated with the sculptural quality of the stack with its rippling deckled edges. From these she began to compose three-dimensional pieces, binding heavy stacks together with braided rope and making collage cover sheets that allude to the magic of sacred tomes. Thus the photocopy becomes the illuminated manuscript. Pursuing the art of collage from its origins in papermaking to its future as machine-made artifact, Brown reiterates in her work the continuity of process intrinsic in the medium.

FRITZ BULTMAN

Fritz Bultman, who was born in New Orleans in 1919, began making collages in 1937. His early work, fairly small, included found objects and showed the influence of the constructivists. When he studied with László Moholy-Nagy at the New Bauhaus in Chicago during 1938, collage assumed a central and serious position in his art, which also included – and still does – drawing, painting, and sculpture. He continued to pursue collage in New York and Provincetown from 1938 to 1941, when he studied with Hans Hofmann, a leading proponent of abstract expressionism. At the beginning of the same period, in 1938, the collages of Juan Gris exerted a very particular and lasting influence on him. He found in them an ideal sense of transparency, of one form created by another. This is a quality that Bultman still admires and that informs his own shapely collages.

Not only transparency, but concealment plays a concrete role in Bultman's manipulation of form: "I like being able to add and change. In collage you can cover up and forget what's under there." Yet his large shapes are so assertive and bold that the viewer is hardly aware of a "covering up." Indeed, they appear to be so unified and spontaneous in conception that one is even less aware of their slow, accretive evolution to final form. In part, the impact of their spontaneous rhythms and contours is a legacy of his association with Hofmann and the New York School, which deflected his emphasis from collage to painting during the '40s and '50s, but their fluidity Bultman himself attributes to the influence of Matisse's cut-outs. By contrast with these, he distinguishes his own forms as begun "from a center outward, rather than working on the confines of a sheet of paper." To Bultman, these dominant shapes present themselves so insistently that a single form may be recurrent for a year or two. "Before and After," for example, began as a small piece, then triggered a whole series of much larger variations.

Bold, emotional colors essential to these variations are in fact the essence of Bultman's collages, though form and the recurring imagery of shape are always there. He prepares his own colored papers by painting whole books of Windsor and Newton bond (Bk #34). He uses strong tempera colors, the only paint medium that expresses for him the energy and transparency of his forms. Thus a red shape emerges as he cuts forms from successive pages of the red book, layering piece on piece until the contour grows. Giant forms accrue from smaller ones; a blue curve moves through a black rectangle. He shifts the angle of a bend, extends a sweeping line, overlays a series of squares: "By adding piece to piece I find a means that gives me a collage of random shapes through random growth, like the sculptures I made out of pieces of wax joined one to the other."

Bultman's dexterity with long paper shears, developed in the '70s, is essential to this aesthetic. He cuts sensuous, perfect curves freehand. He also tears straight edges against a ruler, but loves the ripped edge of paper torn from a binder which he often flaunts against his curves.

Although some of his collages issue from preliminary sketches – often of a central shape – growth and refinement take place directly on his studio walls, where the pieces, tacked with drawing pins, are shifted to their final configuration. This happens over a long period of time, during which he may return to another half-completed composition.

"I really would like to glue my collages directly to a wall where they would function as colored flat reliefs." Instead, he has evolved a method of working his larger paper collages on the muslin side of PVA-sized cotton duck canvas. He has sometimes used the French *marouflage* technique, sizing his stretched canvas on the wall, then adhering the sized face to a second canvas. He also stretches larger, sized canvases to the wall, sizes the raw side again, which makes it firmer and encourages a stronger bonding of the paper, then works his collages directly on the canvas surface.

He flattens his forms to the canvas with a roller, then coats the shapes with a transparent layer of PVA which binds the composite parts firmly. After the adhesive has dried, he goes over the surface with a final layer of tempera color. The resulting collage is put onto canvas stretchers and hung directly on the wall or in a plexiglass box.

Because he conceives of his collages as independent configurations of form, he would ideally present them without the confines of a rectilinear frame. "What I aim for is a surface that is charged in *all* its parts, yet has no reference to the rectangle of a canvas." Though his paper collages have not been totally liberated to sculptural freedom, his adaptations of collage to stained glass carry even further the dynamics of surface with all its parts charged. He began to design for the medium in 1977, at which time his wife, Jeanne, an expert pattern cutter, learned the techniques of stained glass in order to execute his designs. Their most recent collaboration is a series of monumental windows (12′ × 47′) for the Fine Arts Center of Kalamazoo College, Michigan, where he has served as artist-in-residence. The windows correspond to a curved, back wall mural of paper collages that Bultman is completing with the help of art students from the college. For Bultman, who has always meant his collages "to be as illuminated as a medieval manuscript," the immense project realizes both this goal and the urge to press his paper designs to new extensions of reference in free space.

Even in paper, Bultman's collages have a prismatic intensity of saturated, light-filled color. They might be mistaken for magnified details of Oriental carpet patterns or Harlequin robes. The twisting curves, like tangled horns and antlers, break from pure geometry into organic allusion. The shapes fulfilled, to use Bultman's phrase, become contours that establish their "thingness" beyond doubt. *Color illustration IV*.

47 Fritz Bultman: *Before and After #5* (1982). Painted paper collage on canvas, 50 × 28 in. Collection of the artist.

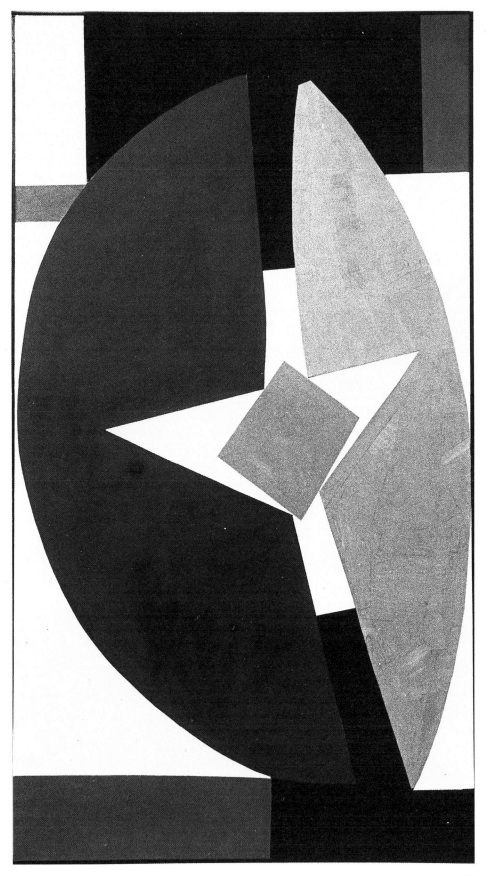

NANETTE CARTER

Born in Columbus, Ohio, in 1954, Nanette Carter moved to New Jersey as a child, then returned to Ohio to study art at Oberlin College. Throughout her studies she responded strongly to Oriental art and the Russian constructivists – Malevich, El Lissitzky – though she was not yet moved by them to collage. Later, in her training as a printmaker at the Pratt Institute, Brooklyn, she became "weary of the technical side of etching and engraving," and began to collage her own prints in revolt, as a way of achieving directness and immediacy. Her first collages were in black and white, a response partially to the values and lines of printmaking, and partially to the high contrast of winter landscapes.

She now lives and works in New York City. Her more recent collages in color have retained elements of landscape and seascape, at times giving the appearance of an aerial view of land and water.

While working, she listens to jazz, which she maintains has influenced her, and she deliberately refers to its rhythms in collage with such titles as "Syncopated Scape" and "Metronome."

But there are other sources of patterning. She recognizes the influence of African art, especially the incised markings of wood carving. And she is also drawn to the delicate quality of Oriental woodcuts. She has used her own woodblocks to print papers which she then collaged onto buff Arches paper. Recently, instead of working flat papers, she has taken to coloring, carving, and incising 4-ply acid-free board as her basic collage material. This she colors with Sakura Craypas or Sennelier pencils, cutting her elements with a woodcut knife, which she then uses to incise intaglio shapes. To refine the patterns, she may puncture holes with an etching needle.

Because she works with 4-ply board, her shapes often cast shadows, and in her strong lines of tension she is influenced by several figurative sources: ladders, bridges, waterways, and musical notation.

Her collages are based on recurring colors and shapes. The colors she often states in a color key, a map at the edge of the collage. Often beginning with a preliminary drawing, she builds a collage by working with two or three master shapes, colored to gradation and fixed in place with PVA. Then she puts down lines, tensions, paths to create a flow of motion around the surface. In a final leap they break the frame and extend beyond, "to show that there is still more life outside the form."

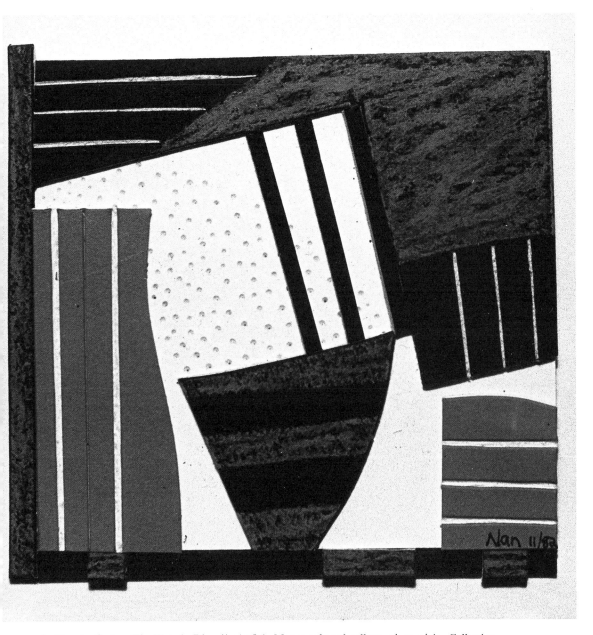

48 Nanette Carter: *The Water's Edge #5* (1982). Museum-board collage, $3\frac{1}{2} \times 3\frac{1}{2}$ in. Collection of the artist.

REGINALD CASE

Born in 1937 in Watertown, New York, Reginald Case was trained in painting and drawing at San Francisco State College and Boston University, where he received an M.F.A.

He came to collage in about 1975, attracted by a new world of subject-matter and effects that he could never have explored in conventional techniques. Although he studied art in a period dominated by abstract expressionism, still-life exerted a strong appeal on him, and in making still-life compositions he was drawn to taboo materials that violate traditional color harmony and taste. Almost in rebellion against the austerity of his training, he began to use fluorescent paints and household enamel, metallic surfaces, fabric, trimmings, glitter, and Mylar sheeting. These he set against cut images borrowed from popular magazines and the work of earlier artists that he admired. Even the borrowings violated his training, which he shed progressively as the collages evolved.

In his first explorations he would project a collage composition onto canvas and paint from it. Finally, the direct quality of the collage textures led him to abandon the painting altogether and turn to collage as the final expression.

Despite what he calls his "outlandish" materials, the glitter and the trim, Case's collages are formal statements. Beyond the initial jolt of their intensity, they are figurative pieces that derive from American folk art with its patterned geometries, repeating stencils, family trees, and dolls. In the *naive* he finds a "wonderment" that stands in opposition to contemporary abstraction. "Western tradition," he argues, "had obliterated pattern; collage gives it back." In his collages, particularly, pattern dominates so strongly as to eliminate empty space. He rejects altogether the white background. His most recent pieces cover even colored areas with total patterning, like the face of a pinball machine.

Enchanted as a youth with model railroad sets and movie facades, he returns to these in the collages, where the imagery often centers on American fantasy figures like Annie Oakley, Humphrey Bogart, Buffalo Bill, and Jean Harlow. Always in Case's collages there is the idea and formal organization of the stage. In recent work he has built the collage into a relief surface, extending the stage to a further, three-dimensional realization that sometimes includes miniature marquee lights.

Despite the subject-matter, his collages are not nostalgic or sentimental. In one series he chose to explore the Holocaust, setting German figures from the military and music hall against complex patterns of *Jugendstil* rugs, stained glass, furniture, and fragile butterfly wings.

In these and all of Reginald Case's collages there is an iconography of twentieth-century life that explores the patterned imagery at the roots of popular culture.

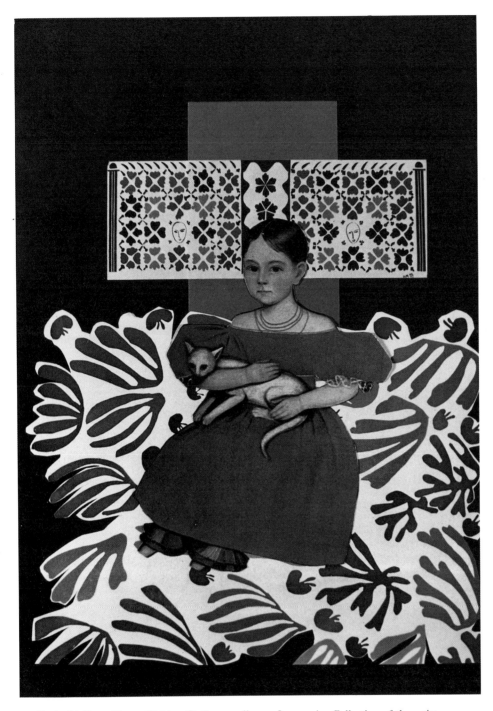

49 Reginald Case: *Young Girl* (1976). Paper collage, 18 × 13 in. Collection of the artist.

ANDE LAU CHEN

Ande Lau Chen was born in Lanai, Hawaii. She obtained a B.A. in art at Colorado State College and an M.A. at Columbia University, where she studied Oriental brush painting with Dong Kingman. She also studied Oriental art in Honolulu and Japan. Though she began as a watercolorist, the abstract gold leaf paintings of Tseng Yu Ho were a decisive influence that led her to refine her structural compositions by the use of collage. For the past twenty years collage has been her principal medium.

Her recent "collage-paintings" depict landscapes in Oriental perspectives. As the collagist explains, her scenes are viewed from above and not from eye level. The effect is particularly striking in her expansive vistas of mountain ranges stretching into water and clouds. These monumental four-panel collages are based on Oriental screen paintings. They originate in photographs or sketches that Lau Chen makes from the elevation of a small aircraft flying over the California or Hawaiian coastline.

Once she has formulated her essential scene, she then sketches it about one-third of its projected size. Her stretched canvases are then double-sized and, once dry, painted with background color. Her next step is to transfer the original sketch blown up to size onto the canvas. She does this by grid drawing, at the same time correcting the proportions that accurately define her perspective.

For each form in the collage – a mountain ridge, a cloud – she cuts a separate pattern out of plain white paper. The template is then set against a chosen piece of colored *washi* paper, and using a wet brush technique she tears the paper shape along the water mark left by the tracing brush line. This method allows her to make full use of long fibered papers like Unryu, which leave a particularly feathered edge when torn wet.

Her forms are then crumpled to give the impression of geological mass and shapely crevasses. Using an air brush, she emphasizes the contours with spray acrylic paint. Each piece is worked on the floor, looking down, away from the canvas, until its total form is complete. Then it is set in place on the canvas and glued with acrylic gel. After all the overpainting is completed, the finished piece is sprayed with acrylic matte varnish, or a combination of matte and gloss when she uses gold paint in the canvas ground.

Under the surface a tranquil cloud of Natsume or sea of Moriki stretches far away. All is "Shibui," a Japanese aesthetic she describes as not too much, not too little, but elegantly and simply right like the papers themselves.

Her commitment to the papers has led to other explorations of collage style. In one series she combines woodcuts from hundred-year-old Noh drama books with handmade Hawaiian *tapa* sheets, mulberry bark, Yucca, coconut leaf, and fig bark papers. Combined with ultimate simplicity, the collaged papers are worked with pure rice-starch paste.

Lau Chen's involvement with handmade papers finally led her to study papermaking in Japan, Hawaii, and California. In a number of abstract pieces she

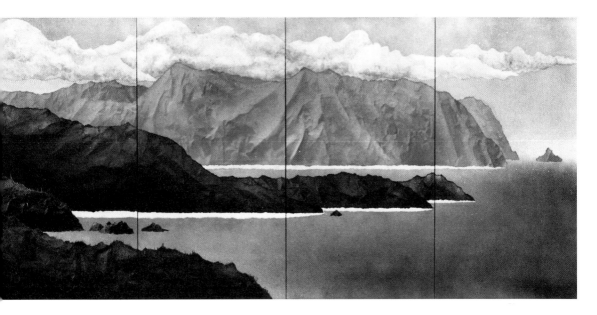

50 Ande Lau Chen: *Windward* (1983). Japanese paper and mixed paint media on canvas, 43 × 93 in. Collection of the artist.

collages directly with wet pulp, flinging dyed pulp from different vats onto the screen and producing collages from a multiple couching of sheets that are then dried together under weighted boards.

Even in this group, the elements of simplified poetic landscape associated with the painter Milton Avery filter through her own background and training in Oriental art. Her work is deliberately faithful to her Asian–American origin: "Seeking new materials, new insights, new techniques," she seeks a collage style that reveals "much serenity and harmony in untrammeled nature."

BUSTER CLEVELAND

"One day I took a perfect roll of film – 36 exposures and every frame perfect. From that moment photography ceased to be a challenge. I needed another form."

The search for form led Buster Cleveland (b. 1943) back to collage, a medium he had explored from childhood and which he has worked at now for nearly fifteen years. In the intervening time, he studied at the Chicago Art Institute, then lived in California and Italy. He turned to stamp art and mail art, making small collages in bound notebooks, photocopying them and sending them out by the hundreds. By this route he encountered Ray Johnson, John Evans, and a host of others.

Cleveland's bold images cut from product wrappers, postcards, and magazines are often subdued with delicate watercolor washes. Working on bond or graph paper, he uses water-soluble Pritt Glue-Stick adhesive. Against his pasted collage elements, he also juxtaposes rub-ons, decals, photos, matallic foil papers, and stamp images which he both makes and collects. The solemn and the scabrous bump into each other, like dada clowns that tickle and shock. In his iconology he is a sacrilegious saint puffing a Lucky Strike in benediction over a nude torso. His posture is *kitsch*, with a playful sense of bad taste and a genuine love of the popular cultures – Italian especially – from which he conjures his imagery.

Influenced also by the constructivists and futurists, Cleveland's work is technically "designed" and is as strongly formal as figurative. Still, at the center of the riot and humor, as well as in their composition, the collages generate energy from the subversive politics of dada. Cleveland's collages are global for a reason; they are popular and "democratic" in their borrowings from mass-media imagery most overtly because they are statements against rich establishment art. That is also the reason that Cleveland selects his own direct-mail audience as an alternative to conventional gallery viewing.

Cleveland's Italian maestro is Cavallini, the dada impresario, whom he contrasts deliberately with Leo Castelli, the king-maker of contemporary blue-chip artists. Almost in front of Castelli's New York gallery, Cleveland set up his "Limousine Show," dealing from the sidewalk and serving champagne and cherries to passers-by. This "Limousine Show" made a statement about the economics of both limousines and art.

The essential richness of Cleveland's work comes from travel. Once, on a train trip across Canada, he made a collage each day, based on the things he found along the way. Collage is his diary, his "visual travelogue."

51 Buster Cleveland: *Joan in Italy Stamps* (1982). Paper and aluminum foil collage, $8\frac{1}{2} \times 11$ in. Collection of the artist.

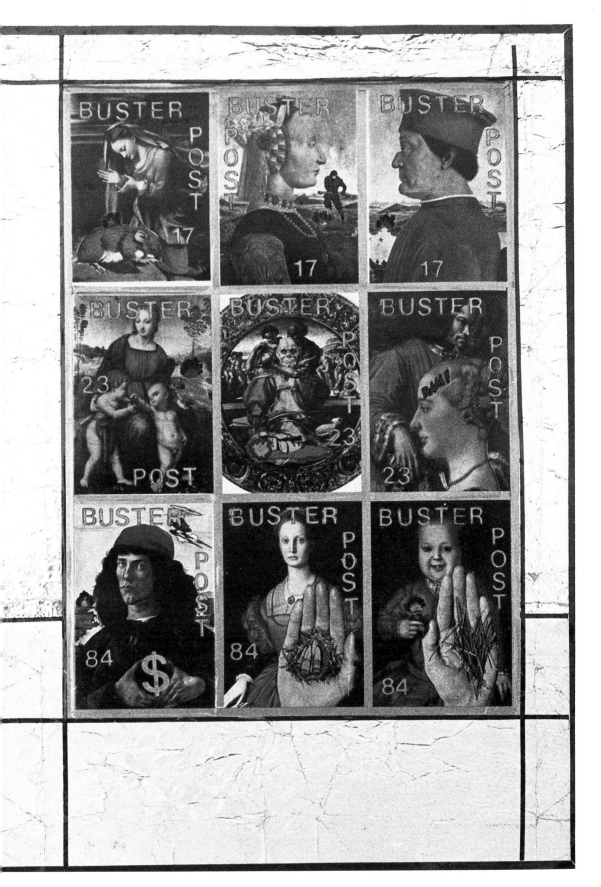

ROBERT COURTRIGHT

Robert Courtright approaches collage like the master-builder of medieval walls. His individual personality seems to dissolve into the vast and powerful anonymity of the facade itself, which is his landmark.

One can see that architecture, and especially the soft round arches and bleached red building blocks of the Romanesque, has had a seminal influence on his work. His decision to leave the Art Students League and New York's captivation with abstract expressionism led him to Rome in 1952. There, the campaniles and facades of Romanesque architecture became the subject of his fascination and the decisive impulse that turned him toward collage as a medium. The buildings were, in fact, themselves collages – walls compounded of the walls of yet older buildings, with their fragments of stone and half-erased inscriptions grafted onto new structures. Courtright began making collages based on drawings of these buildings, and gradually their imagery receded into abstraction. What remained was the medium itself, collage based on the skill of making paper walls.

Even the shape of paper has, for Courtright, a post and lintel feeling, and the cleanly torn edges that define his planes are the lines of the draftsman. His collages, his walls of paper masonry, set plane against plane in a close harmony of monochrome that is their mortar, their binding unity. Courtright's colors are cobalt, red earth, apollonian sun – drenched in southern light. Born in Sumter, South Carolina, in 1926, he remains a man drawn to southlands: to Rome (1952), to Antibes (1953), to Provence (1958), where he lives most of the time in the village of Opio in a house among bleached stone walls.

But between the solid stones of the Romanesque and his collage transformations, there is a striking difference. Through his originality and controlled technique, Courtright dissolves architectural geometry into a weightlessness that is almost ethereal. His collaged surfaces are like ruffled sheets of water; they curl slightly and catch the light's reflections. They are sundials, changing as the sun moves across the sky and over the water, illuminated at noon, darkening at evening.

Yet despite their Mediterranean saturation and values, there is something profoundly urban about them as well – like the famous Jungian dream that takes the dreamer through a labyrinthine house of architectural styles down to the earth floor of his primal human roots. If Courtright's walls absorb the history of Roman building, their monumental scale makes a suggestion of skyscrapers inevitable. They also appear to be weightless, floating above the grid plan of the city. In their repetition of windows they are like Courtright's collages, especially at dusk, when the mauve and blue light of evening plays against their gray and black exteriors. Recently, Courtright has come to live again part-time in New York, and one can sense the influence the city has exerted on his work.

An earlier attraction drew him to the paintings of the English artist John Piper, whose work often depicted English church architecture in the context of a certain

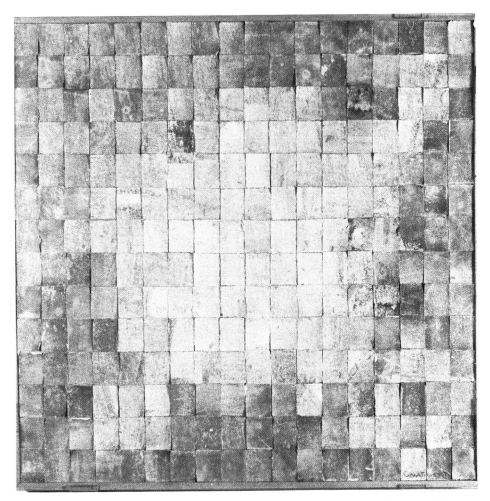

52 Robert Courtright: *Untitled* (1976). Paper and acrylic paint, $13\frac{3}{4}$ × 14 in. Courtesy Andrew Crispo Gallery, New York.

romantic mood. In Courtright's collages, too, there is an element of romanticism, expressed as a quiet contemplation, a gathering of tranquil intellectualism in which planes of being are brought to perfect balance.

This effect is achieved not only by his pure geometries, but by his pure labor as an artisan working his papers to perfection. His earliest papers had their own history related to architecture. They were posters torn from Roman walls and scrubbed to achieve a patina. Now he achieves a similar effect from magazines and newsprint. First he soaks the paper and places it on glass, against which he rubs it with brushes and sponges to remove all but a suggestion of lettering. Then the paper is soaked again in a protective wash of acrylic white, which serves as a barrier against pollution and decay as well as creating a color ground for the gouache or acrylic that he finally applies to the dried paper. In this painstaking way, he paints other papers, from thin cigarette sheets to heavily textured corrugated stock. Recently he has begun to make paper himself.

He continues to experiment with translation of collage into print editions, with photoetching, with typographic elements, all new ways available to refine and enlarge the surface vocabulary of his elegant constructions. Yet, despite all conscious manufacture, he is greatly concerned with the chance gradations of color in hand-painted papers. Tone suggests placement in the subtle rhythm of a monochrome, and as he shifts the puzzle pieces, emphasis gives way to composition. Sometimes he adds emphatic marks of his own, applying India ink to the back of a paper and allowing it to bleed through to the surface. From French house painters he acquired the technique of applying paint with a punctured drum roller, which creates a dappled effect like hammered aluminum.

Like any master artisan, he is concerned with the protection of his materials, sealing the treated papers with acrylic and backing them onto gauze tissue with PVA (Jade 454). The whole collage is preconceived to the size of a carpentered box and composed within the framework of its architectural housing. To secure each element, he uses only dots of adhesive (PVA) at strategic stress points so that the paper squares retain their natural curl and play against each other like sculptural effects of a grand mosaic.

Even Courtright's most abstract collages are expressions of human will, in their modestly understated patience, mastery, and grandeur. On a more intimate scale, human expression itself has been Courtright's subject in a powerful series of *papier mâché* collage masks. These were originally inspired by children's masks that he discovered in Nice in 1970. Though his transformations still include all the naivete of uncensored feelings, they are hardly childlike. They register emotion more primal than primitive; they are universal symbols belonging to the collective unconscious rather than tribe or place. Courtright's masks, like his walls, are universal frames of human reference, potent with the arcane magic of half-buried language that provokes the viewer to meditation. *Color illustration V.*

PAUL COVINGTON

Paul Covington is one of the few collagists who works principally in black and white. The paradox in his preference is striking since he came to collage through Josef Albers' color class. Discarding the scientific treatment of the color spectrum as inapplicable to an artist, since spectrum colors do not exist as pigments, Albers involved his students in looking at colored scraps of paper in the real world. "These," Covington remembers, "we used to shift around and from the process I came to collage, which seems to me a medium in which the final image comes from rearrangements, from changes of mind. I think of collages as orchestrating rather than delineating."

The emphasis on orchestration leads Covington to a formal, architectural view of collage, and in his figurative works the massive volumes of architectural space are themes and images. His pictorial sources are old newspapers and magazines. Frequently the texts themselves function as a framing device, set against an image suspended in the middle. The image, central and often architectural, is isolated and

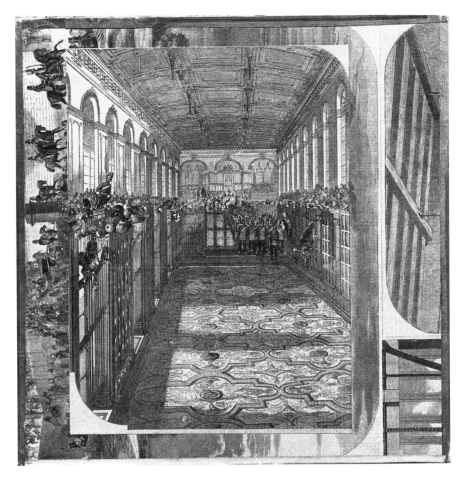

53 Paul Covington: *Airborne* (1979). Paper collage, 13 × 13 in. Collection of the artist.

appears floating. Thus, in one, a building of considerable measure and solidity appears to be weightless; in another, the ribs of a gothic vault fold into a labyrinthine ball. "The spatial image should be complete. For me, collage requires the kind of construction that goes into the planning of a building. I admit, I have a preference for geometry."

Covington's geometric structures require some architectural planning beyond imagery. He backs the images onto heavy board and these he mounts onto wooden stretchers (13″ × 13″). The final effort is selecting the right paper to cover the frame and finish the geometry of the image. The whole process may take him several months. He has also completed a square series designed to be housed inside a box that is collaged.

In all, his work is extremely private, not esoteric but instilled with a sense of perfection on a small scale. The eye drawn to a torn edge is deceived into forgetting that a tiny figure floating down the nave must have been cut with a fine blade and shifted to that space. Working with scissors and razors, he tricks us into this fragile world. Though he cites both Anne Ryan and Joseph Cornell as important early influences, Covington's work is free of overt allusion. The architecture is his own and his finished collages with their seeming weightlessness appear to be the work of a restless juggler caught at the moment of balance.

SARI DIENES

Sari Dienes, née Chylinska in Debrecen, Hungary, 1898, was brought up in Budapest and studied dance and philosophy in Vienna and Paris. She married Paul Dienes, a mathematician-philosopher and poet, and moved to England. Dienes worked with Fernand Léger and André Lhote in Paris; in London with Henry Moore; and she was also assistant director of Amédée Ozenfant's Academy in London.

In 1939 she arrived in New York on a trip. The Second World War prevented her return to England, and so she remained in New York, teaching at Ozenfant's, Parson's School of Design, the Brooklyn Museum Art School, and her own studio.

At the age of 86, Sari Dienes is a flourishing practitioner of "Creative Re-Use," a phrase that she used as the title of her May 1982 exhibition at the A.I.R. women's cooperative gallery where she is an active member. In the context of Zen Buddhist philosophy, which she has practised for the last twenty-five years, she defines absolute reality as a sphere without circumference where the center is everywhere. For her, art is the process of giving form to an insight of that reality, and since her center is everywhere, the art she makes is without limiting circumference. She deliberately does not concentrate on anything, but has worked for decades in collage, assemblage, drawing, bottle and bone constructions, and poetry. She developed a method of making rubbings (*frottage*) with inks and rollers which she applied to Indian petroglyphs as well as to the sidewalks of New York.

Her collages, particularly, are poetic ideas organized from the substances of every day. She works with unique materials, using a hot iron to bond elements onto map-backing fabric. This is her usual adhesive material. The visual elements themselves are ingenious, and include cuttings of her own curly hair, the rinds of grapefruit, used coffee filters, and the lint from her electric drier – all covered in a thin netting that conjures peculiar romantic illusions.

Yet her work is not nostalgic; indeed, she has always been in the avant garde, which she still outraces, making new collages of colored photographs, photocopies, Mylar foil, and shredded papers run through a laminating machine. These long banners she hangs in the window like new-wave stained glass.

She is consummately of this age and, having studied mathematics and philosophy, asserts with pleasure that "the big banquet today is not art, but science." She embraces with comic and poetic delight the materials of her age and by their use offers an art that is "humanity's stand toward the world."

54 Sari Dienes: *Untitled* (1980–81). Mixed media under net on map-backing fabric, 37 × 72 in. Collection of the artist.

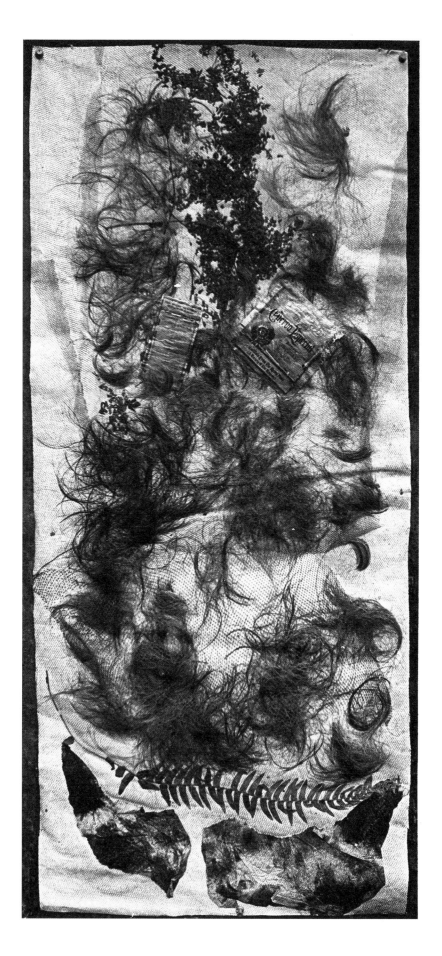

WILLIAM DOLE

It was with deep regret that we received the news of William Dole's death during the writing of this book. His wife, Kathryn, and his daughter, Deirdre Dole Golani, have been most kind in providing us with the information necessary to complete our discussion of his work.

Born in Angola, Indiana, in 1917, William Dole grew up in a Midwestern town isolated from the experience of art. His first direct encounter came at fifteen, when his mother took him to the Chicago Exposition of 1933. There, he was so impressed by what he saw at the Art Institute that he began to study art, and soon after entered Olivet College (Michigan) as an art major. At the same time he took a minor in English literature; words and their poetic essence must have seemed a separate language from his early painting, but the visual and verbal were later to share a common ground in the unity of his collages.

The shift in medium from oil painting, watercolor, and drawing began in Florence, where, in 1956–57, he traveled on sabbatical leave from the University of California at Santa Barbara. In a secondhand bookstore, he happened on a portfolio of assorted papers, some contemporary, others from the nineteenth century: archaic maps, handwritten bills, letters, and ephemera, marbled sheets, and Japanese paper used to make artificial roses. Their fragile textures and the mystery they provoked led him to mount them on watercolor paper and to work them into paintings. But the architecture of words and shapes in their two-dimensional configurations also opened up to him the medium of collage, which from 1958 was his chief vehicle of expression.

Like Gertrude Stein, whom he once met at Olivet, he saw in his papers the meaning of themselves. If "a rose is a rose is a rose," to be considered for what it is, then Dole's typographical fragments and colored spaces also demand to be perceived in their particular integrity. Like Stein's statements, they lead us by their mystery and grace into a suggestive inner life. Often the words or phrases are elliptical or incomplete. Foreign and ancient words appear like esoteric signs among others we understand, and the play of shapes, calligraphic letters, faded inks patterned among blocks of vivid color wash involve the viewer in an energetic dance across the page that is a purely non-linear counterpoint to the way we usually read.

In his thwarting of linear movement and logical comprehension, there arises a poetical statement. If we could, by chance, understand the foreign words, fragmentary diagrams and symbols, the poetics would be lost. Even the English words, because they are taken out of context and rearranged like elements of concrete poetry, take on a new mystery. By deliberately organizing patterns of suggestive language, Dole appears to compose secret telegrams for us, the viewers. We come away from Dole's collages with the unconscious idea that his message was intended solely for us. Though we may not understand their cryptic message, we are nevertheless consoled by the receipt of it and by its awakening of our imagination to a new play of words.

Moreover, from the chaos, the Tower of Babel that man has written, Dole constructs a harmony of intelligible design. His collages represent the very antithesis of those linguistic fragments presented by Schwitters as junk, intended for their shock value as anti-art. Instead, Dole revitalizes the surviving fragments with a power to communicate the essential magic of language that distinguishes human endeavor. His titles often underscore his respect for the documents by which man transmits his purpose: "Writ," "Decree," "Adage," even "Vernacular." It is significant that Dole worked consciously with the librarian's materials of conservation: "I have borrowed my technical procedures from the ancient craft of bookbinding in the use of adhesives, and I use, with rare exceptions, rag papers and Japanese and Chinese papers. When I color them I use water-colors . . . ."* Like Borges, who refers to the library as a metaphor for cosmos, Dole's collages interpret language as revelatory of cosmic form.

In constructing that form, Dole worked like a lyric poet, waiting, brooding, searching for the exact counterbalance of texts that would give the poem its wholeness. Therefore, he often worked on more than one collage at a time, awaiting the vital unity. Sometimes the key is color, the touches of red and blue by which a "Writ" revives oblique patriotic allusions, the sacramental reds of the Holy Word, romantic washes of pink and orange, or gilded reminders of alchemical transformation. Even the space itself, the blocks of paper set down among the characters, assert their just proportion like the spaces between Kepler's perfect solids.

Dole's collages have often been compared with music, but they seem more justly compared with the music of the spheres than with earthly melodies. For in the harmony they impose on fragmentary knowledge, they pay tribute to the place of the written word in cosmic design. Their structure is their decipherment. *Color illustration VI.*

---

*Quoted by Gerald Nordland in *William Dole Retrospective, 1960–1975*, p. 10; from an original statement of 1964 cited in *A Retrospective of William Dole*, Santa Barbara: Art Gallery, University of California, 1965.

RUTH ECKSTEIN

"Somehow, most of my work turns into collage," Ruth Eckstein observes. Born in Nüremberg, West Germany, she received her art training in New York at the Art Students League and the Pratt Graphics Center. Since her first exhibition of collage in 1960, the link between collage and printmaking has been her hallmark.

Often the collages begin as elements of prints. That is, the papers she uses in her collages are the discarded remnants of her print editions. "Sometimes," she explains, "only a particular color area or texture can be saved." In all her work she is sensitive to both, manipulating colors and textures of subtle gradations. In fact, she conceives and executes the prints as collages, using the layered effect of intaglio and relief printing, as well as the actual introduction of separate collage elements.

"Superimposing another plane over the original one makes it more three-dimensional, slightly more tangible, slightly more *real*." She works her prints mainly on Dutch etching paper and handmade Japanese Kochi, creating a textured effect by printing segments over vinyl floor tile and by *frottage*.

In collage, her preference is for the torn edge, though she cuts too. The collages, backed onto Dutch etching paper or other printing papers, are all worked with casein adhesive. Many of her best collages introduce photographs, kaleidoscopic images made from multiplying and reverse printing the patterns she deliberately shoots with her miniature camera. Although the photographic elements are the most figurative components of her collage work, they too become abstracted, geometrical reflections as they are taken out of their original contexts. Eckstein's collages give the impression of ancient imagery: monoliths, Cycladic stones, Oriental characters, or at their most complex the near-symmetry of tribal rugs.

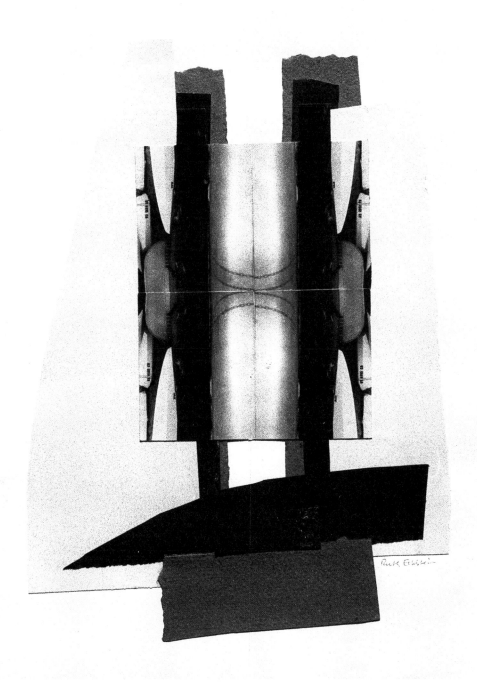

55 Ruth Eckstein: *Lift Off* (1978). Reflections Series no. XVIII. Photodyes and paper on Arches, $21\frac{1}{2} \times 17\frac{1}{2}$ in. Collection of the artist.

EVELYN ELLER

Born in New York in 1933 and trained at the Art Students League, Evelyn Eller has been working in collage since 1954, when she was a Fulbright student at the Accademia de Belle Arte in Rome. Italy suggested to her the power and rhythm of landscape, which is still a major element in her collages, even in the most abstract pieces.

Sometimes she starts from a photograph or the memory of a place. "We take trips all the time; travel is important to me, but I don't work on the trips." Later, without previous drawings, the masses of land and sky or sea present themselves as colored patterns. The impact of successive landscapes is most prominent in her *Impressions from the Window of the Adirondack Express*, a fold-out collage book that expands like a strip map to expose the inner journey frame by frame, with all its subtle changing tones. Its format is reminiscent of the ancient *oribon* and *tsuzuri-toji* accordion-folded books of Japan and China.

"I paint a lot of my Oriental papers with oils and acrylics diluted to a wash. This way I can achieve the exact tone I am thinking of." Sometimes the colors and textures pre-exist. She uses Unryu and Moriki, preferring long-fibered Japanese papers for their suggestions of grass or stony earth, and dyed colors for their resistance to fading. In her own tests on color, she has found that oil-painted paper is particularly color-stable.

In using large, fragile paper elements, she likes to work her collages two or three simultaneously (sometimes as a color or size series), allowing the ideas and the papers that compose them to settle awhile before the final commitment that requires adhesive. She builds up the image and pastes as she composes, working at an easel and stepping back to view the composition as a painting. In a literal sense, she works by hand, rarely with scissors, more commonly tearing her lines along a straight edge or simply with careful fingers making the jagged pattern of mountain or road. Even in the final laying down she spreads the adhesive (Jade 403) along the paper edges with her fingers as often as with a brush, leaving the central spaces free to breathe with changes of humidity. Recently she has turned to bookbinding techniques, using toothpicks in the application of adhesive and the bone folding tool as a smoothing instrument. Her work is backed onto Ingres or other large 100 percent rag papers and hinged with acid-free tape. Most are large and her impulse is to expand them further.

"I have come to diptychs and triptychs as a way of expanding the limitations of scale that paper by its nature generates." The large pieces, like her collage books, present themselves as visual narratives. Influenced by the view of space in Oriental scrolls, her collage perspectives are touched by the receding horizon line that suggests infinity.

Led to Oriental papers by Oriental thought, she sees in collage a medium for expressing universal ideas and defining her own particular, lyrical voice.

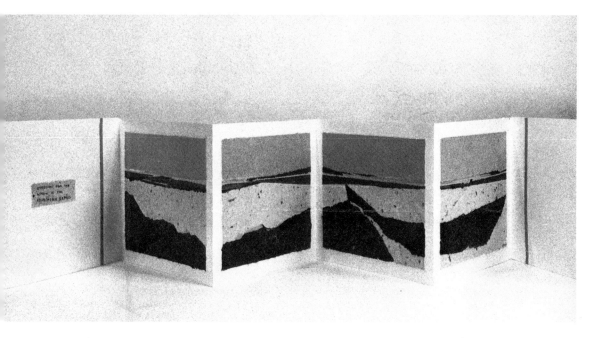

56 Evelyn Eller: Collage book, *Impressions from the Window of the Adirondack Express* (1982). Japanese paper collage on mat board. Collection of the artist.

JEAN-LOUIS ESPILIT

Jean-Louis Espilit was born in Ginestas (Languedoc), France, in 1943. He studied painting, decoration and ceramics for several years at the Ecole des Beaux-Arts in Toulouse. In 1966 he decided to make his home in Paris, and in order to survive he became an assistant model-maker and an illustrator for a firm of architects. In 1972 he determined to devote his full time to art; he has been a collagist since 1969.

Espilit's collages are constructed with natural fiber handmade papers of Japanese, Tibetan, Nepalese, or Indian origin. The works evolve very purely from the lines and folds of the fibrous textures. A frequent visitor to India, he invests the papers with allusion to the worn and shredded garments of simple poor people, which are dignified by use.

Handling and wear are elemental to Espilit's aesthetics. First, the paper that he has selected is coated on the reverse side with a layer of white or black gouache. Once this has dried, the paper is turned over and is ready to paint, stain, and dye with inks, gouaches, or even a medicinal umber brew made from crushed walnut husks. When he cuts, it is with a wet string or small handsaw to accentuate the natural fibers of the papers. And when he pastes he uses acid-free bookbinder's paste (Flexiplé). Cutting and pasting are both kept to a minimum, precedence being given to the paper itself as it comes to unfold its meaning.

Accident is very important in Espilit's collages, for it creates a language of its own, a personal communication of shading, an interplay of light and dark shadows that falls on his papers like a state of calm. Espilit pays conscious homage to the paintings of Nicolas Poussin and Caravaggio, and in his collages one can sense the painter's concern with the study of falling light. Espilit has, in a sense, abstracted landscape to pure shadow. His calm dusks melt into each other, throwing highlights on a single color – red, blue, ochre – that surprises us with its intense emergence from the buff and shadowed page.

In order to achieve this interplay of shades, Espilit soaks, unfolds, rubs, and scrapes the sheet of paper as he paints and dyes its surface. His method, immediate and tactile, gives rise to the accidents from which his language emerges. His most definitive marks are his "tailoring," the linen tapes that he hand-stitches with cotton thread. They are fragile reminders of the folded cloth that is his inspiration. The thin lines of cotton leave their poetic tracks on his collages like the mystery of unraveled mummies or fossil herringbones in a crust of earth.

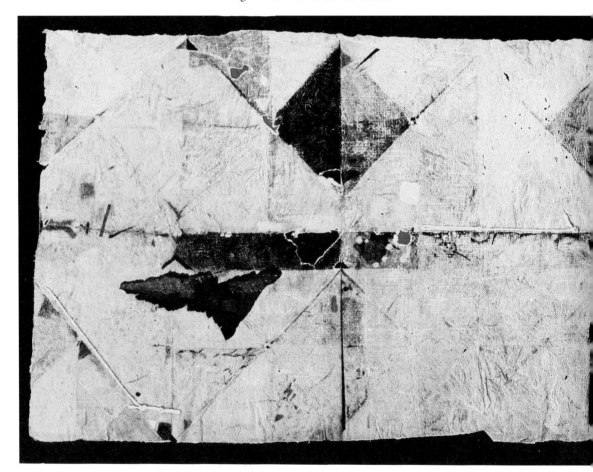

57 Jean-Louis Espilit: *Untitled* (1975–76). Gouache, collage and white string on Nepalese paper, 25 × 19 in.

JOHN EVANS

John Evans was born in Sioux Falls, South Dakota, in 1932 and received his M.F.A. from the Art Institute of Chicago in 1963.

He has been a collagist since 1964 and still feels compelled to complete a collage every day. His working method is to compose directly in the interleaved pages of acid-free Permalife paper in French (Aclé) spring binders. Thus, over the years, he has made eighty books of collages, most of them measuring two months of his life. Though one page may trigger the next by continuing to employ fragments of the same jigsaw puzzle or the same shade of blue, each collage is unique, with the integrity of a diary or journal entry.

Having now lived in New York for many years, John Evans finds his materials from the scraps of the city. His collages are constructed from a *pot-pourri* of everyday articles: fabric, labels, postcards, photographs, discarded or lost letters, even mementoes stretching back to the First World War and earlier. Correspondences

58 John Evans: *March 13, 1981*.
Permalife paper and ink, 8½ × 11 in.
Collection of the artist.

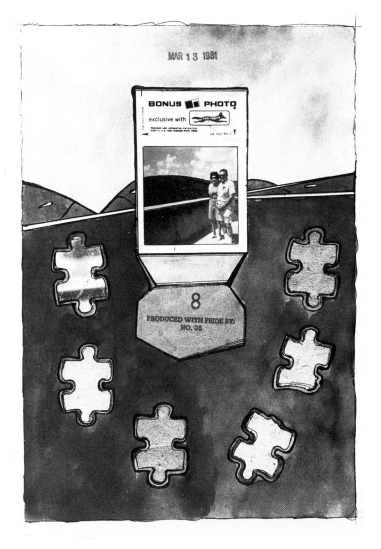

between the present and the past play an important role in his creative imagination. As a conceptual idea, correspondence motivates his use of letterheads and rubber stamps, and his involvement in mail art.

The actual construction of his collages recalls the building of skyscrapers, the skeletons laid bare. The collages are built in such a manner that they appear to take off from the page and stretch up. More often than not, Evans adds printing elements to his collages, as well as watercolors, so that the finished pieces give the vague impression of modern-day illuminated manuscripts. At the bottom of most pages are a row of duck heads which he calls "Ursuline Ducks" in homage to the writer Ursule Molinaro.

All Evans's collages since 1975 are pasted with Jade 403 onto $8\frac{1}{2}'' \times 11''$ Permalife paper. His transparent colors come from Dr. Martin's and Luna inks, which he applies with brushes. Evans's distinctive work can be viewed as separate collages or as a personal journal of his involvement with New York City. The separate collages reflect his moods and his ideas about the environment in which he lives. Each breathes like a separate life, like a separate day defined by its tension, action, humour, or tragedy. Every day is a collage for Evans and every collage captures his shifting sensibility.

SUZI GABLIK

Although Suzi Gablik was born in New York in 1934, she has resided in London since 1966. She obtained a B.A. from Hunter College, New York, in 1955, studied with Robert Motherwell, and spent a summer session studying art at Black Mountain College. The author of several books on art and a noted critic for many magazines in England and America, she has been working in collage since 1958.

Her work is figurative, set in an imaginary and evocative world reminiscent of Eden before the Fall or continents before discovery. In many of her collages dense with wildlife, isolated human figures appear, either as primitive species among the animals or displaced persons lost in such a wilderness.

In her landscapes Gablik often conjures a surreal vision, partly from mingling black and white with color images, partly from a radical alteration of proportions and natural environments. Berries and flowers grow as large as animals and starfish huddle together abnormally on *terra firma*. In one collage, a lone motorcyclist appears among a flock of sheep, goats, and cattle like a misguided messenger lost from a Kafka dream.

Gablik's images for her collages are usually magazine reproductions. These she cuts with scissors and adheres to canvas with PVA. Over the photographs she spreads Dorland's wax as a resistant barrier against oil paint. This is important because she extends the image or landscape with oil paint additions in the style of the photograph. In this manner she is able to bring disparate images into a unified composition and fuse them by the skillful deception of painting. Once the collage has been completed, she coats it with a polymer matte emulsion that serves as a protective seal and further emphasizes the unity of her visionary habitats.

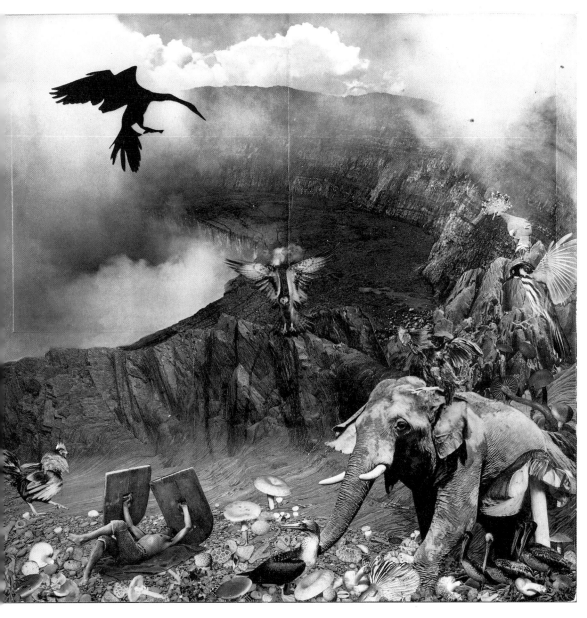

59 Suzi Gablik: *Tropism* (1968–72). Oil and collage on canvas, 24 × 24 in.
Courtesy Terry Dintenfass Inc., New York.

ESTELLE GINSBURG

Born in St. Louis, Estelle Ginsburg trained as a journalist at the University of Missouri. She came to art in her late twenties, first as a painter strongly influenced by the broken planes of cubism. It was the line in cubistic patterning that caught her attention, and her early paintings, heavily textured and colored, received definition from the hard edges of tape that she began using as a decorative medium.

The application of tape transformed her earliest paintings into collage. To paint she added sand, fabric, and other elements of applied design, which magnified in importance as she came under the influence of Schwitters. Perhaps her most important discovery was that she could, in fact, "paint" with paper itself, cutting freehand or traced designs with scissors or X-acto blades, and working directly with paper textures in collage. Today, she works with PVA adhesives and polymer acrylic medium, sometimes using the medium itself to create a hard, gemlike surface.

The formal patterning of her collages is still defined by the precise, thin lines of tape that are her hallmark. Within the hard edges, color and design explode in fluid opulence. Her work is figurative, a still-life saturated with the yellows of sunlight, eggs, and lemons; a crowded boudoir where women lounge among their silks and mirrors. The scenes, still touched by the fragmented planes of cubism, seem perfectly controlled despite their immense energy and profusion of design. The total luxury of texture and color remain under the tight control of filigree lines, which create an effect like mosaics or Persian miniatures.

Ginsburg's methods of composition are most unusual for a collage artist. She often works from live models or three-dimensional still-life arrangements. Sometimes she works in a sequence of media: drawing, watercolor, collage, and painting – all based on the same original composition. She also does three-dimensional polychrome sculpture composed of collage elements, in wood, paper, fabric, and plastics.

Some of her collages have also been inspired from vague and blurred newspaper photographs. These she dramatically translates into well-defined areas of figure and bright color, like her *charcuterie* of hanging red meats. Her large, abstract collage landscapes are composed of many hundreds of repeating images, both visual and verbal. And in a series of collage portraits based on classical paintings, she combines pieces of colored prints and decals with stark patterning in black and white. Her collages are a world of labyrinthine surfaces where her figures seem to dwell in self-assured elegance. *Color illustration VII.*

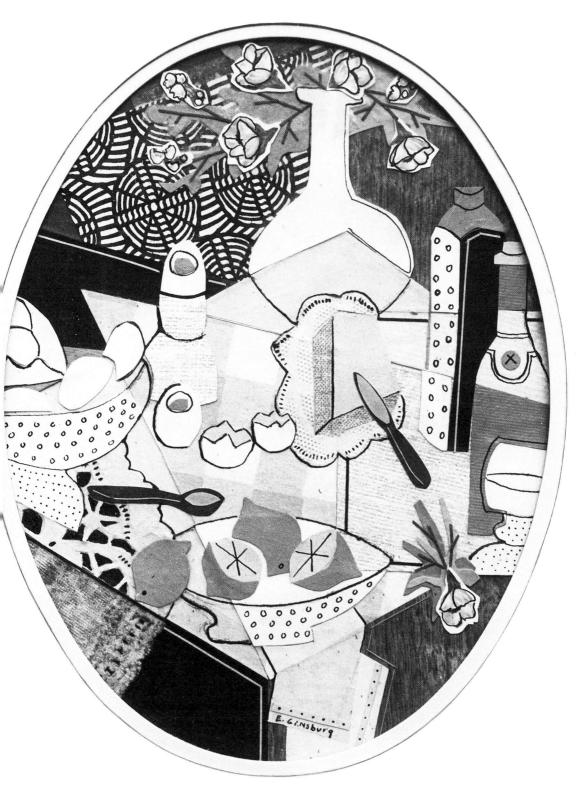

60 Estelle Ginsburg: *Breakfast* (1982). Paper collage, oval 7 × 9 in. Collection of the artist.

EMIKO GOODNOUGH

Emiko Goodnough's collages began five years ago when she was assisting her husband, Robert, with his blue cluster paintings. The "perseverance and faith" evoked by these paintings led her to make collages in newspaper, which seemed, despite its starkness, to generate a color of its own. Later, she began to collage with colored and patterned papers in a style that is personal and emotive.

Collage, she found, gives her a power to concentrate in creating "one harmonious feeling," a practice of exercise and energy that helps her clarify ideas for future paintings. She was first trained as an artist in Japan, then in New York at the Fashion Institute of Technology and Parsons School of Design.

Unlike her paintings, which evolve slowly through laborious methods, the collages are worked in intense hours of concentration. She cuts her papers with scissors and working one collage at a time may reorganize the composition of varied shapes over a period of days before pasting it down. The medium is, for her, compulsive, therapeutic, almost contemplative, in the sense that her harmonious abstractions aim to resolve chaos into satisfying order.

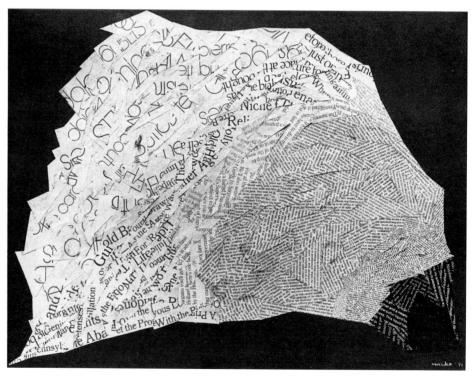

61 Emiko Goodnough: *Collage with Newspaper* (1977). Newspaper collage, 15 × 20 in. Collection of the artist.

ROBERT GOODNOUGH

They are intended to be like nothing – neither the flight of birds nor slivers of glass. They are simply a flutter of shapes that form spontaneous patterns in the collages of Robert Goodnough.

In his earliest collages the shapes pressed into dense clusters that alluded to cubism and were subject to the tug of gravity. The shapes themselves, Goodnough recalls, owed some debt to brontosaurus, whose skeleton he first encountered in 1952 at the American Museum of Natural History in New York. Its primal form and strength he refined to a triangulation of scales, building its backbone in small metal sculptures. The angular shapes remained and still assert themselves in his latest collages. Moreover, the paradox of brontosaurus – its weight and agility – became the conceptual fulcrum of his collage compositions that balance lyric movement against gravity.

Goodnough is also influenced by Bach and Mozart, and describes his shapes as more related to the purity of musical notes than to visual imagery. One collage, designed for the 1976 Mostly Mozart Festival at Lincoln Center in New York, illustrates the release of his shapes from gravity. In the collages of this period weightlessness exerts its own counterforce, and the pieces, once densely magnetized, become separate elements hanging grouped in free space, like individual ideas with their isolated integrity.

Goodnough's history as a painter led him to collage first through his attachment to abstract expressionism, then his commitment to dissolving the rigidity of cubism. Born in Cortland, New York, his earliest studies at Syracuse University suggested collage as a medium of fluidity and freedom. There his teacher, George Hess, cut up his students' drawings as a radical demonstration of breaking up canvas surfaces. In 1952, when collage first intensified as a shaping influence on Goodnough, its main effect was on his painting, helping him to clarify geometry and strength, the lesson of brontosaurus. From flat and sculptural collage studies, Goodnough expanded his two-dimensional space into a representation of volume and solidity. His abstract language, evoked in shapes and colors, was at once formal and emotive. In a sense, it was the fusion of his training under Ozenfant and Hans Hofmann – the formalist and the liberator.

In the '50s he worked his collages mainly from dime store paper, glad that smudges of glue remained as a visible testimony to the energy and immediacy of creation. By 1961 he was experimenting with raw canvas shapes applied directly to plywood. Composing spontaneously, he then painted over the forms that emerged, adding shapes by accretion. Even today, he contrasts the immediacy of his collages with the elaborate preparation demanded by paintings worked with masked color fields. Yet despite the apparent differences, his work in the two media is connected, beginning with the essential ideas that present themselves as geometries of thought. Both the collages and paintings, moreover, have shared in his shifting

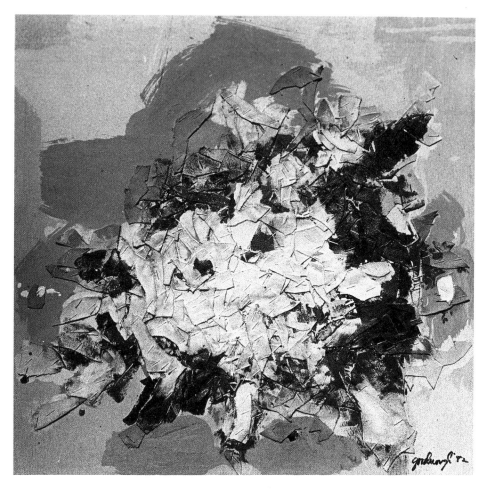

62 Robert Goodnough: *Collage Painting number 12* (1981–82). Acrylic and oil on canvas stapled to wood, 20 × 20 in. Collection of the artist.

experimentation with color. In one period he has worked them in strong primary colors, at another time in muted tones or pastels. For a while in 1970 he made austere, elegant studies of white on white.

In composing canvas collages, he sizes his background with acrylic medium, which he also brushes over the separate shapes stapled to the canvas. The recent work from 1979 includes canvas pieces that have been painted in layers of different colors allowed to drip in a "wet look" effect that came to influence his paintings.

At times, he admits, collage gives him ideas for painting; the thought process is often so close as to produce a series quite deliberately called "collage paintings." These employ stapled canvas shapes in the context of painterly brush strokes that sweep over the collaged clusters in close harmony. *Color illustration VIII.*

KLAUS GROH

Born in Nysa, Poland, in 1936, Klaus Groh lives and works in Edenwecht, West Germany. Collage has been his primary medium for the past fifteen years. It is the medium he finds most conducive to equations between art and reality.

His optimistic view leads him to approach magazine photography with gusto, looking for manifestations of life, sensuality, and the visual similarities between seemingly disparate images. Magazines, he asserts, turn "second-hand reality into a 'second reality'." By tearing and juxtaposing figures and landscapes, he reinforces parallels between dancing bodies and trees or people in different contexts poised alike. Gestures interest him as archetypal forms, gestures of seduction, pleading, love and fatality. Word fragments that emphasize the gestures give his collages certain political overtones, though almost antithetical to those of the dada photomontagists. Whereas the latter fragment images in protest against meaning, Groh's deliberately placed fragments impose a logic of harmony based on relativity as an imaginative philosophy.

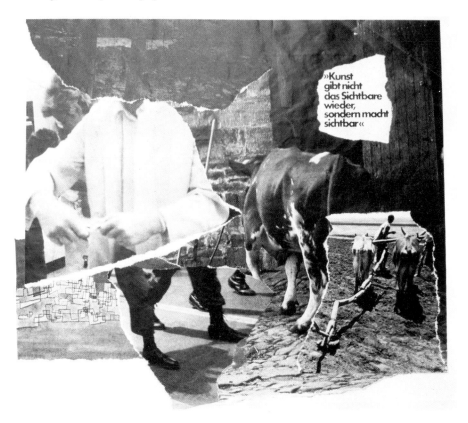

63 Klaus Groh: *Untitled* (n.d.). Magazine paper collage.

NANCY GROSSMAN

Nancy Grossman's reference to her constructions as "physical equivalents for painting – that is, for the illusion of making marks with a paint brush" – may also apply to her collages. The physical "mark" includes pressing and soaking her collage papers and hand-coloring them so that they are unique arrangements made from unusual materials.

In her New York studio, she spends months making paper forms. The accumulation builds to a chaos of materials, from which she then chooses papers; piecing these together creates the structure for the new work. One assemblage series resulted from composing papers whose surfaces were made from rubbings of objects in her working space.

The collage papers, many of coated stock, are soaked in aniline dyes, which they accept in accidental ways. Because the aniline is alkaline, her coloring technique is also a beneficial treatment for acidic papers. After hours or days of soaking the papers, she allows them to dry, examining the chance dye patterns that gather in folds and run across the sheets.

The papers she chooses for a collage are first resoaked. Then, holding the wet papers, she brushes them with PVA. The adhesive is applied to both of the wet pieces intended to fit together, and with her hands she presses and smoothes them firmly to secure the bond. Thus the collage comes together like a jigsaw puzzle, and before it dries to shape she removes unnecessary pieces of underpaper so that it achieves a perfect flatness. The forms are pasted onto a permanent masonite backing, which she constructs, as Bearden does, with pasted sheets of brown paper to distribute the tension evenly.

Her methodology hinges on a challenging dialectic. She makes paper shapes that are attractive for their separate identities, then recreates them as a more complex unity through composition. Simply by evolving, as she says, "after a certain point, the work takes on its own life and makes itself." Sometimes this process generates a number of related works, the one growing naturally from the other.

The organic quality of Grossman's collages also derives from a tactile sensibility combined with her landscape and figurative subject-matter. The landscape contours and the seamed torsos are alive with muscular implications and nervous energy that render even her flat collages sculptural.

Born in New York in 1940, Nancy Grossman obtained her B.F.A. degree from Pratt Institute in 1962, studying with Richard Lindner, who, she remembers, "tricked students into doing their own work." She found her way to collage in Venice in 1962, when the need to work pressed her to make use of ticket stubs, wrapping papers and engaging scraps of her travel. In her latest collages she has returned to found papers, with their diverse markings, which she has saturated with strong colored dyes. *Color illustration IX.*

SATISH GUJRAL

Satish Gujral's paper collages have the transparency and shimmering colors of Indian silk. Red, pink, ochre, orange and purple are comfortable together in his stylized compositions, as they are in classical Indian painting. His patterning also alludes to familiar Indian iconography with its peacock feathers, swirling circles, and energetic hunt scenes set in the blues and greens of landscape. Gujral fills his space profusely like the gardens in miniature painting. A statuesque female figure seated in profile on a bench strikes a classic posture, with her mythical bird perched on her knee.

Like Picasso, Gujral expressively isolates the feminine form into geometric components. In this way he discovers a link between the traditional and the modern, for while his figures allude to classical painting and even painted wooden folk dolls, their freedom is contemporary and personal.

Gujral's paper collages, composed on a cardboard or plyboard base, are made from torn papers that include bright opaque papers, thin colored and white tissues, as well as pieces torn from magazines and advertisements. He works them with the polythile adhesive Fevicol.

The sculptural quality of these paper works have suggested to Gujral a dimensional expansion of collage surfaces into wood, leather, shell, and bead compositions which render the powerful presence of mythical figures such as appear on ancient temples.

Born in 1925, Gujral studied in Lahore, Bombay, Mexico, and New York, and has exhibited internationally. He lives in New Delhi and works with equal facility in paint, leather, glass, ceramics, metal, and wood. Since 1964 he has made wide use of mixed media. *Color illustration X.*

JOAN HALL

From childhood Joan Hall collected Victorian images and obscure objects that today remain the basis for her collage work, which combines textures and often juxtaposes objects against flat design. This particular combination comes to her from a variety of sources, beginning with her parents, since her mother was a painter and her father a sculptor and photographer. From her training at the Brooklyn Museum School and the Pratt Institute, she turned to set design, first as a student at the Julliard School of Music, then in her work with The American Mime Theatre and The Netherlands Ballet Company.

The dramatic impact of textures and images is at the core of her work, which makes her successful as a commercial illustrator. For her, collage has an international currency comprehensible from Paris to Brazil, and she sees no major separation between her public and private work. It only depends on "whose problem you're solving, yours or theirs." In all problem-solving, she invests a certain element of surrealism, encouraging people to "see this fantasy as if it were a reality and dream a bit." Her dreams drift onto record sleeves and through the pages of the *New York Times*, *Horizon*, *Vogue*, and *L'Express*. One appeared on the cover of *Time*, a complex box depicting the Carter presidency like the memorabilia of Joseph Cornell, whose influence remains inspirational, though she strives more consciously in her work to fuse old with contemporary iconography, including even electronic parts.

Her most private box-collages, by contrast with her dense assemblages, seem almost covert. They investigate dimensions that are provocative and frustrating. A series of wrapped packages, her "Parcel Project," is composed of three-dimensional small collages, each with torn wrappings that admit a glimpse of scenes "indigenous to the return address." Since 1971, she has been experimenting in illusions which are composed of paper, mirrors, lenses, wood, and twine.

Versed in illusion, she strives in all her work for unity – to obscure the seams and arrive at a visual whole. She works in paper with a combination of scissors and X-acto knives (#11 blade), using PVA for her private collage work and rubber cement for commercial pieces, acknowledging that these images are intended to achieve their permanence ultimately as photographs.

To see collage as a stage in the development of a photo-image is an important conceptual development of the medium, one Hall shares with other collage illustrators, such as Jim Harter, as well as with artists like Ray Johnson who are concerned with recycling their imagery. Collages transformed to photographs are returned full circle to the public domain, where, in magazines, they become sources of imagery for future collagists to cut out and reassemble.

For Joan Hall, a collage must move "very far back and very far forward" in space and time. While her textures achieve the spatial dimension, her images move as far back as her oldest sources and as far forward as a future which may borrow her imagery for new creations.

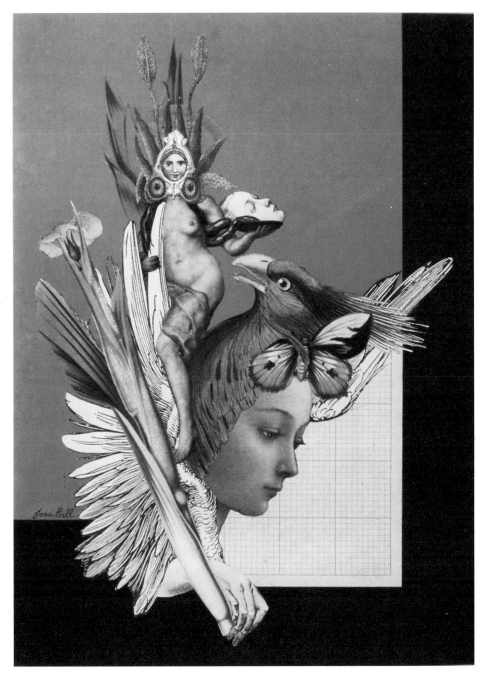

64 Joan Hall: *New Ingenue* (1982). Magazine paper and paste, 12 × 16 in. Collection of the artist.

JOAN HARRISON

Joan Harrison's intimate collages interpret reality as if through a dollhouse window. Indeed, she traces her motivation to childhood constructions – cut-outs of figures, rooms, and products taken from magazine illustrations and rearranged into two-dimensional still-life fantasies. Like Joan Hall she saw the work of Joseph Cornell while she was a child. He has remained a steady influence on her collages, though tempered by her keen interest in Japanese prints and in fictions, such as the storytelling of Donald Barthelme.

Like Barthelme's, her work has a strong mythological dimension in its narrative. Her "cow" series, for example, interpolates the animal figure with exotic female riders, starfish, and enigmatic writing. Designed as elusive emblems, the collage elements are controlled by a tense color key. She consciously introduces color elements that should not work, forcing them to comply with surrounding papers by an overlay of fine pencil drawing.

The desire to control and subdue is also felt in her box-like frames which surround the emblematic figures. Often she uses these to create the illusion of a containing room, suggesting walls, a floor, sometimes penciled shadows. In one series of collages, her comic theme is the nightmare dream house, where cherry pies turn to Spam, televisions grow ominous, angelic wings, and punished children have their heads replaced by apples. Her imagery in these comes from magazines of the '40s and '50s, but rather than referring nostalgically to a specific time, they convey an idealized world that is out of control. Her smiling repairmen are not what they seem; their products make drastic alterations, and happy homemakers "want to rip off their aprons and get exotic."

In all her work, breaking out of control is a persistent theme and is related to her choice of medium. Collage is particularly important for its expression because pictorial sources imply a strong reality, the reality of the photographic image. In collage she is freest to tamper with scale and relationships. People, animals, and objects often pop up and break out of her boxed-in spaces, expressing an element of structural liberation that is not possible with real photographic frames.

Her collages, which are visually very formal and controlled, nevertheless explore liberation in their method. She works intuitively, surrounded with still-life works. The pieces, cut with sharp sewing scissors, are pasted with PVA applied directly with her fingertips. She also transfer-prints magazine images. The picture surface, soaked with lighter fluid, is turned face down in place on the collage and rubbed to achieve a reversed, positive image.

Harrison's collages, influenced by photography, are indeed closely related to her own photographs – hand-colored gum bichromate prints – which arrange people and objects in still-life compositions.

Born in 1950 on Long Island, New York, she received her B.A. and M.F.A. from C.W. Post College, where she currently teaches silver and non-silver photography.

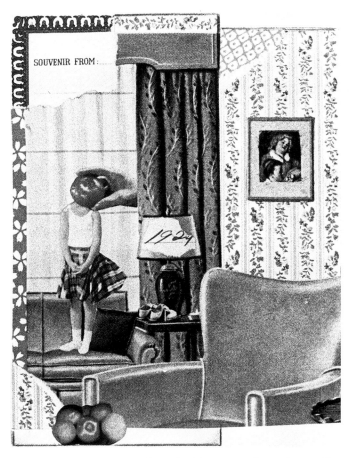

65 Joan Harrison: *The Punishment* (1980). Paper collage with pencil drawing, $3\frac{1}{2} \times 4\frac{1}{2}$ in. (Actual size)

JIM HARTER

Jim Harter began photomontages for musical concert posters in 1970. Under the spell of the late Sätty's book, *The Cosmic Bicycle*, he turned for sources to nineteenth-century engravings.* The discovery coincided with his cultivation of hallucinatory experiences, and his black-and-white collages became linked to visionary perception. "In a sense," he argues, "collage is alchemy; transmuting the lower into the higher, the base material into the magical, through the power of creating relationships." The initial quest for imagery transformed Harter himself into a source. He edited six collections of public domain engravings for Dover Press, to which contemporary collagists are greatly indebted.

Harter's personal alchemy transforms and integrates his divergent sources into a completeness that is stark and arresting. He works with small scissors and an X-acto knife (#16 blade) for precision. His compositions are often symmetrical, like mirror images. In their imagistic concern with time and space they become universal, escaping their Victorian origins.

Harter seeks out the highest quality images from his nineteenth-century sources and touches up the blemishes with a Rapidograph pen and white acrylic paint, applied with a fine brush. At times he has the images photographically enlarged, using a film negative for better reproductive quality.

In his manner Harter takes off from Max Ernst rather than being influenced by him. Instead of fusing human and animal forms, Harter frequently plays them against one another in distorted scales that owe something to Magritte. He also plays off violence and control, as in "The Primal Symphony" from his unpublished book, *Hymn of the Infinite*. Here and elsewhere, his isolated forms stress the simplicity of the collage. By doing this, he comes close to the mystical intention behind his work. His special sense of reality allows us to raise the question: where have we witnessed this scene?

Harter's work is all the more astounding considering his vocation as a commercial artist. He has turned the imagery of surrealism into negotiable currency, illustrating contemporary magazines and science fiction. Both his visual imagery and his published compendia have infused black-and-white collage illustration with vital spirit.

*Sätty (Wilfried Podreich) was a seminal figure in collage as applied to poster art, media, and book illustration in San Francisco during the '60s. He was born in Bremen, Germany, and schooled in architecture, engineering, and design. Despite his technical training, the liberating fantasies of surrealism exerted a stronger influence on him in the aftermath of war. He pursued the fantastic and grotesque in his four published books of collage illustrations: *The Cosmic Bicycle*, *Time Zone*, *The Annotated Dracula*, and *The Illustrated Poe*. Sätty had completed 300 illustrations for a collage history of San Francisco when, at the age of 42, he died of an accidental fall in 1982.

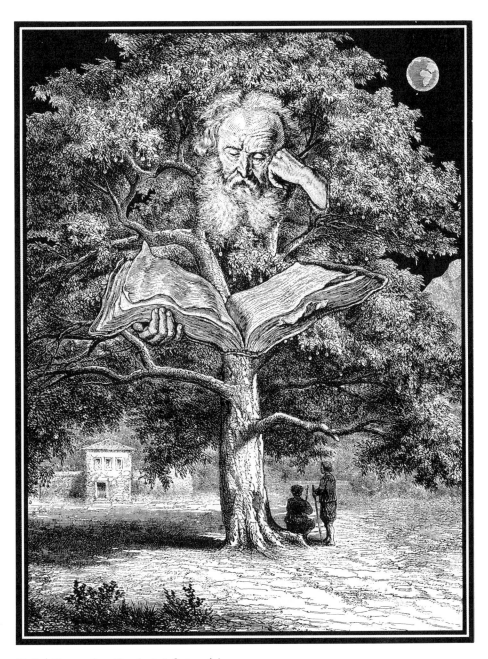

66 Jim Harter: *Poet Tree* (1982). 8 × 10½ in.

PHOEBE HELMAN

Although Phoebe Helman has won her reputation as a sculptor, she has, for the past twenty years, spent a great deal of time constructing collages which deserve as much recognition as her other work.

Helman was born in New York City in 1929 and studied at the Art Students League and Columbia University before taking her B.F.A. from Washington University, Saint Louis, Missouri, in 1951. Apart from her formal training, she maintains that her mother had a great philosophical influence on her life and work. Her mother was a suffragette, an activist, anarchist, and organizer of the Amalgamated Clothing Workers Union for many years after witnessing the Triangle shirt waist factory fire, March 26, 1911, in which 154 women were burnt to death.

It is transparently clear in her collages that Phoebe Helman herself is an anarchist, which accounts in part, perhaps, for her attraction to the medium. In the true spirit of collage, she is involved in facing chaos and bringing order to it. Deliberately breaking surfaces in order to construct anew, her work is an emphatic assertion of the anarchist philosophy that one cannot create without first destroying. As she collages she builds and fragments simultaneously, taking perpetual revolution as a fundamental aesthetic.

Helman consciously chooses to work in muted earth tones keyed to the dominance of black. It would be incorrect to read any particular political statement into her work. No dogmatic viewpoint is stated, but a certain engaging emotional tone is clear. It is not bitterness; it is not violence, but rather a sobering reflection on the social and political disorder one confronts in the world. Often her statement is poetic, for she questions the contradictions around her and in her work.

Angularity is her specific subject in a series of collages constructed from etchings. In working as a printmaker she found the surfaces too flat, and motivated by the impetus to pull them forward into the room, she began to cut through layers and build up complex patterns of triangles. Though working with minimal forms, she multiplied them to provocative angles of thrust, arguing that "more is more" and to be enjoyed for its intellectual surprises. These layered collages are mounted on pH neutral Fome-Cor with mat pins that have been pasted in place with Jade 403. They convey the impression of a restless architecture that hovers in space.

In her most recent series Helman has been influenced by the architectural theories of Frank Lloyd Wright and Robert Venturi. She does not box or frame these collages; rather she allows them to float freely attached to a wall, so that her work becomes a statement of non-restrictiveness, a statement that questions authority and demands freedom.

She builds these very large collages from pieces of acid-free architect's paper backed with fabric. Working directly on the wall, she begins with a "foundation" that she covers in acrylic modeling paste. Once this has dried she surfaces it with a layer of gesso and begins to paint with black and gray oil sticks and turpentine,

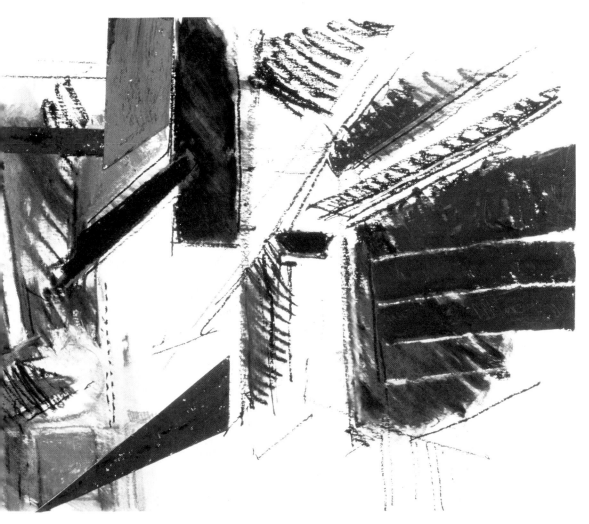

67 Phoebe Helman: *Untitled* (1977). Collage, oil stick, muslin-backed rag paper, 24 × 36 in.

rubbing the mixture into the surface. From other papers worked in the same fashion, she cuts forms and adds them to the foundation as structural overlays, adhering them with modeling paste. Gradually the collage takes shape and grows subtle. In one area she rubs and washes out paint to discover lights; in another she scratches through to white ground with a blade or mat knife. The aggressiveness of her work is felt in the flexible textures that she handles firmly – drawing, building reliefs in modeling paste, working over to unveil nuances.

HELEN HOIE

Helen Hoie is an abstract artist who first turned to collage in 1968 as a way of doing color studies for large paintings. In these she depicted with realistic accuracy the translucent quality of folded Oriental papers. The edges, the texture and fiber of the papers became the quintessential subjects of her paintings.

But the collages also took on a life of their own, and though she continues to make some as preliminary sketches for her "realist abstract paintings," most of her time is now spent making collages for their own sake.

Hoie interprets collage as a dynamic medium of free-flow. In her artistic background it is related to her study of piano. "Just as musical compositions have grace notes, *allegrettos* and *fortissimos*, so do my collages." Sometimes her tones are keyed to color, sometimes to fragments of musical notation that become a physical presence in her compositions. And like the grace notes, choice lengths of thread often embellish the papers, underscoring their lyrical movements.

A kind of "chamber music," her collages also belong to the chambers of the sea. She likens their undulating rhythms, especially in the darker pieces, to the gravitational drifting of the tides. Like buoyant seaweed or pulsing urchins, the papers appear to float in an ephemeral underwater universe which she associates with contentment. The imagery is not figurative or deliberate; quite the contrary. But in her art, abstraction is a manifestation of reality linked to the natural world. Much of her association comes from the summer months that she spends with her husband, a watercolorist, near the ocean on Long Island.

Her collages are very much a product of walks on the sand and the free associations they generate. In composing, her starting-point may be a background acrylic color that she paints on 4-ply rag board. It may also be a "nugget," a fragment of shaped or colored paper that triggers a suggestion. Usually tearing her papers, she begins to compose layers of melodic lines built outward from the center. Most of her papers are tissues that attract her by their transparency. Others are handmade textured papers that she collects in traveling.

She pastes the pieces with PVA or acrylic gel medium and uses a roller to bond them flat. Unlike most collagists, she permits her composition a kind of organic growth uninhibited by form. The form comes later, in the same way that it often does for the photographer whose final composition comes in cropping. Hoie works with triangles of mat board which serve as flexible borders. She shifts them over the collage surface, studying the multiple alternatives until she settles on the one that finally satisfies her. Thus her collage is an editorial imposition of form on open creativity.

Born in Leetsdale, Pennsylvania, Helen Hoie lives and works in New York City.

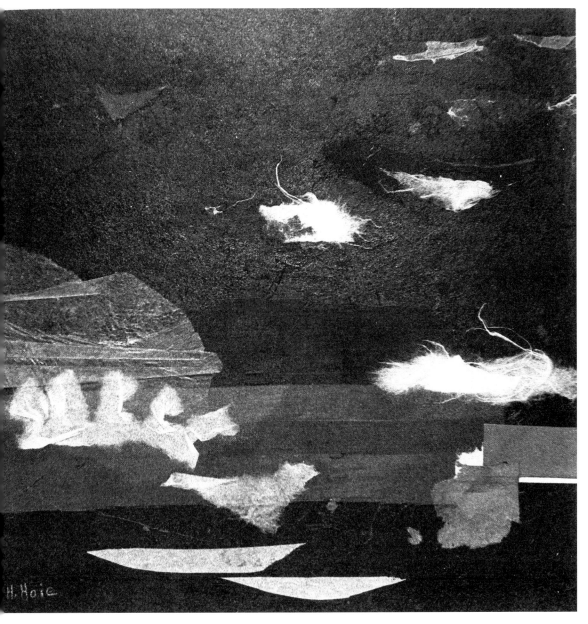

68 Helen Hoie: *Wanderer* (1981). Japanese paper collage with string, $7\frac{7}{8} \times 7\frac{7}{8}$ in. Collection of the artist.

JAMES JACOB

James Jacob's collages are densely compounded images that convey a sense of oblique narrative. Like city walls covered in successive layers of half-obliterated posters and markings, they give the impression of urgent public messages rendered obscure by time and concealment.

Their provocative obscurity has its roots in the influence of dada and surrealism. Like the dadaists, he employs fragmented language, sometimes even Chinese and Spanish, for its assertive but allusive relationship to surrounding images. Because he takes his figures from magazines, newsprint, books, photographs, and photocopies, they are strongly connected to our sense of spontaneous media and we perceive them with political overtones.

In combination with discernible imagery, Jacob uses paint and colored pencil drawing, often in strong diagonal lines that read like the effacement of graffiti associated with a clash and confusion of cultures. Jacob achieves this seemingly impulsive quality with great care. His images, cut with an X-acto knife, are mounted on rag-board with dextrin "Yes" paste and spray adhesive. The successive layering of image, language and drawing creates a spatial approximation of the covering-over characteristic of urban iconography.

Jacob, who was born in Brooklyn in 1951, lives in Albuquerque and teaches at the University of New Mexico.

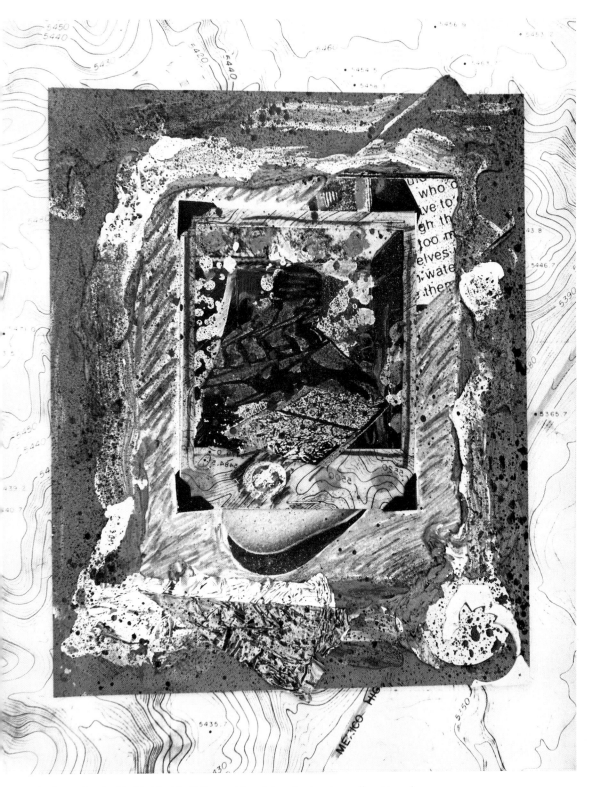

69 James Jacob: *Untitled* (n.d.). Collage with paint and colored pencil, 9 × 12 in.

RAY JOHNSON

Ray Johnson points at the scratches carved in his worktable and says, "These are the story of my life; these are the places to which I've traveled." His collages, worked at constantly seven days a week, are the maps of his voyages, which he sends abroad like clues to a buried treasure.

Among his earliest collages is a 1955 "Elvis Presley" made of a magazine image, overpainted with tempera, brushed with inks and mounted on cardboard. He eventually noticed that it was three times the size of a business envelope, and he began to cut others of the same size in thirds, mailing pieces of his collages around the world. Thus, the archives of his early work exist in other people's letter files.

Long before he began cutting up his work, he had already begun his "New York Correspondence School," which today remains an international generator of collage in mail art circulation. A few of the oldest envelopes survive from 1942 or '43, painted with cartoon-like drawings that anticipate his most recent silhouette series and are still a reminder that the essence of Johnson's work is social communication.

He chose collage for the messages because even as a student he never liked canvas with its stretchers and bulkiness. A native of Detroit, Michigan, he was trained in commercial art in a technical high school before attending Black Mountain College, where Josef Albers and the collagist Jean Varda exerted some influence on his early work. Above all, he "liked the feel of cardboard and the smell of glues and pastes." His preference was always for flat materials and mosaic-like chips or tesserae. In his early painting period he used De Kooning's recipe for white lead paste as an adhesive to put paper on board. (He now uses PVA and backs onto chipboard.)

He worked these boards to standard size ($7\frac{1}{2}'' \times 11''$), making boxes of a hundred collages which, since the 1950s, he has been showing at private viewings intended for specific people. The presentation form has a certain parodistic element to it, announcing Johnson as a dealer of anarchy as well as a dealer of art and suggesting that the two might be interchangeable.

From the beginning he has been drawn to pop stars, whose personalities merge in his work with everyday scraps of the tragicomic world. He creates a patchwork of unrelatedness that nevertheless composes a puzzle-piece collage of reality. If we believe that nothing can be salvaged from this ephemeral civilization, then Ray Johnson's gentle, mocking dadaist collages nudge us with humor that serves as a safety valve. This is important because his collages offer to interpret our fragmentation not as a frightening reality but as healthy play.

The dada roots are still alive in Johnson's work, and with the dadaists he shares a gift for verbal and visual puns. Once in 1955 he made a collage that used an engraving of a cave. Quite by accident he later discovered a Joseph Cornell collage of 1933 that used the very same image. The coincidence struck him so profoundly that he has determined to generate a new series based on transformations of the cave, multiplying its contexts and allusions.

"It's the nature of my work to shift everything around," he says, picking up a frame filled with chopped-up pieces of old collages that were added through a hole at the back in 1976. As the frame turns, the pieces fall, tumbling like shifting pieces in a Cornell sand box. He calls the work, "Let it all hang out, 1968." Not only in this collage but in all his self-annihilating, self-disposing, self-mutating, self-packaging work Johnson toys with civilization. They are his counter-products, answers to the machine-made world – answers which also ask questions. They bring home the point: How much is art worth? How long should it last? Who puts a value on art?

In a sense Johnson's collages formulate a protest against the art establishment, its current vogues, its inflated prices, its self-importance, its quest for permanence. At the same time they confront society with artifacts that are well-made, for Johnson takes extraordinary care in the construction of his collages. For the last seven years he has devoted himself to a major portrait series based on silhouettes of East Hampton artists and writers and other celebrities. He begins each one with a pencil sketch that he transforms into thirty to forty ink drawings, then reduces them to use as collage materials. In the final composition, the silhouette becomes a three-dimensional "documentation of shape," a kind of formal record. He used a similar manner of documentation in his very earliest collages, on which he drew the shapes of his other collages as a sort of visual filing system. Johnson's latest silhouettes, mounted on illustration board, are sandpapered and gently abraded to give them a soft edge and scuffed surface. They are consciously "worn" in the making, worked over with ink, embellished by his characteristic mosaic elements, backed on masonite and housed in frames. A contradiction of transience and permanence, his collages are the memorabilia of a still living age, a cross-index of the people and objects by which we can define this culture.

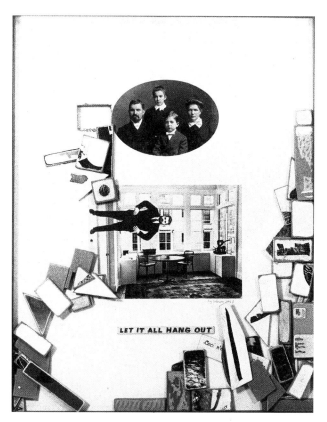

70 Ray Johnson: *Let It All Hang Out, 1968* (1968–76). 18 × 14½ in.

ERIKA KAHN

Born in Berlin, Erika Kahn was trained in painting at the Art Students League and attended design classes at the Pratt Institute, Brooklyn. At California State University, Northridge, she received a B.A., specializing in printmaking, and then took her M.A. at California State University, Long Beach.

During the resurgence of papermaking in Northern California about ten years ago, she became involved in this craft and has been exploring paper as art ever since. For the past six years collage has been her principal expression. She currently lives and works in Santa Monica.

Kahn's collages hang free-floating on silk and linen stretchers. Inspired by a diversity of folk art, she translates to paper the suggestive rhythms of handwoven tapestries and folded kimonos. Divested of particular tribal origins, they refer to universal forms of ceremonial ornament.

Her designs convey first the symbolic power that she attaches to paper itself, and then the triumph of human achievement in making it. She makes many of her own acid-free papers and deliberately selects others made by craftspeople around the world. Working them with inks, oils, acrylics, and watercolors that she applies with brushes or rollers, she conceals the white surfaces beneath her floating colors and textured designs. Some of the patterns are from etchings of her own invention, others are transferred impressions of lace and brocade. The irregular shapes of her organic geometries reflect the influence of folk traditions. So do her dense and vibrant colors, that carry the implication of festive textiles.

Like fringed textiles, her papers show off their elegant edges. Working directly with her hands, Kahn tears and folds her papers, rejecting altogether the intrusion of cutting implements. To secure the collages she works purely with methyl cellulose or rice-starch paste. The process, like the finished piece, pays homage to ancient traditions and cultures.

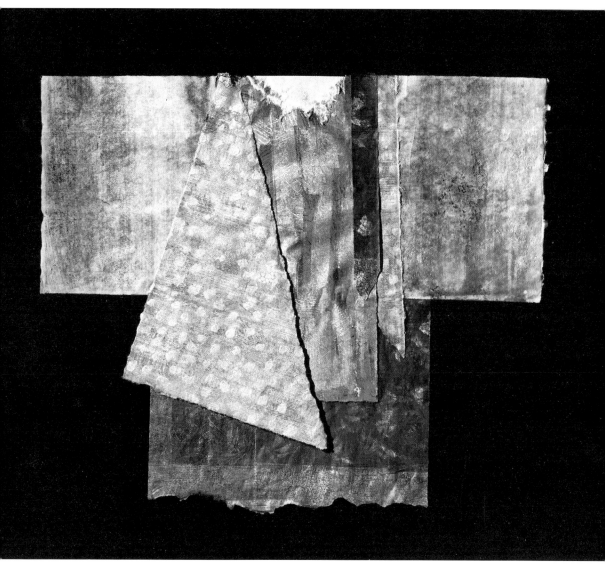

71 Erika Kahn: *Fragment Series 1982*. Handmade paper with mixed media, 23 × 25 in. Courtesy
Elaine Starkman Gallery, New York.

MARCIA GYGLI KING

Marcia Gygli King was born in Cleveland, Ohio, in 1931. She studied at the Corcoran School of Art in Washington, D.C., and the University of Texas at San Antonio, where she took an M.F.A. in painting.

As a painter, King gradually developed a style of "sculpture-collage" that introduced "cantilevered elements" – floating dots and discs – to the surface of paintings. Her more recent work in New York has shifted to large figural collages in mixed media.

The origin of these forms is the Mexican *piñata*, a colorful *papier-mâché* animal shape associated with festivals. King's animal forms combine this allusion with reference to Texas ranch dogs, whose muscular energy and movement she sculpts in relief styrofoam and acrylic modeling paste on the surface of her gessoed canvas. The imagery still emanates from the Southwest. To the surface she collages pine bark chips, *ristras* of chili peppers, and large paper shapes, conspicuously more dynamic and abstract than the trees they often suggest. Her papers are adhered with modeling paste or acrylic medium and sometimes stapled to the surface in order to permit the edges to curl.

King works in pure paper collage as well as mixed media collage on canvas. Often the paper work serves her as a model for the larger composition.

"Part of the purpose of my work is to play off the different media against each other." To this end she incorporates raw *papier-mâché*, sculptural relief in various media, flat or impasto surfaces painted with acrylic color, along with her diverse and unusual additions. Sensitive to durable materials, King continues to experiment with new media that enrich the organic play of surfaces.

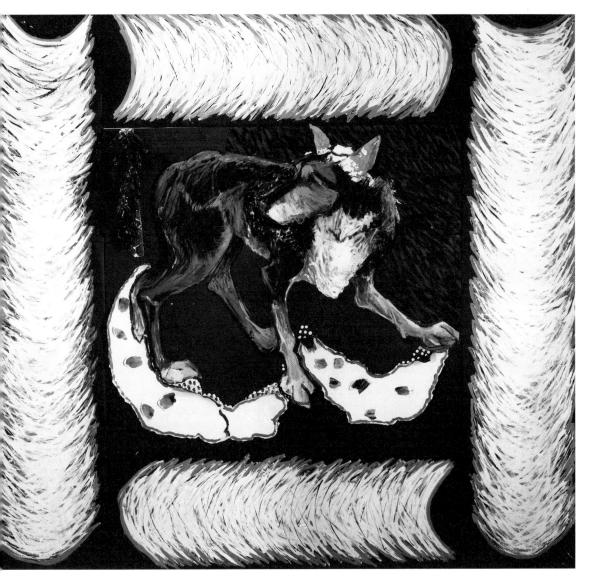

72 Marci Gygli King: *Child Queen 5 panels* (1983). Mixed media collage, 9 ft. 3 in. × 11 in.
Collection of the artist.

STEPHANIE KIRSCHEN-COLE

The collages of Stephanie Kirschen-Cole bring together two distinct traditions of handling the medium. The tags, string, and particularly postage stamps that she uses in conjunction with the torn edges of envelopes and wrappings refer clearly to the aesthetic of collaging found papers, traceable from Schwitters to Motherwell. For these materials she has established a new context, setting them against the densely colored and textured sheets that she makes by hand, and that belong to a different collage aesthetic linked to papermaking.

Kirschen-Cole's cotton linter papers gain their originality from her unusual additives: book pages, computer cards, torn postage stamps, and coffee grounds that surface as a texture in her rich acrylic colors. She applies color to the top surface, and for subtle effects also pours color into her pulp. She also utilizes the floating edge of the deckle against the ragged tears or square cuts of her paper patterning.

The collages vary greatly in scale. The small works are often not larger than 18″. Her large pieces, worked to dimensions of 5′, are composed on linters $\frac{3}{8}''$ thick to achieve firm support.

For deliberate contrast Kirschen-Cole may set her found materials against the handmade paper color fields. She cuts into the work, layering elements over and under. While she sometimes pastes her fragments, she prefers to stitch the work together, using thread lines functionally as well as aesthetically, in the fashion of a banner or quilt.

Abstract geometric patterning is even more pronounced in the collages made of her own papers, sometimes in conjunction with fabrics, worked in squares and hexagons and often framed in elaborate multiple borders. Indian painting, from which she takes her titles, has clearly been an influence on these as well as Amish quilts.

The Tantra concept of duality/unity consciously governs her fusion of found and handmade papers. In yoking diverse materials into compositional unity she has also brought together frequently disparate traditions of collage.

Stephanie Kirschen-Cole was born in 1945 in New York City. She studied art at the University of Maryland where she gained a B.A. and an M.A. She also studied at the Maryland Institute of Art where she obtained her M.F.A. She has been doing collage since 1973.

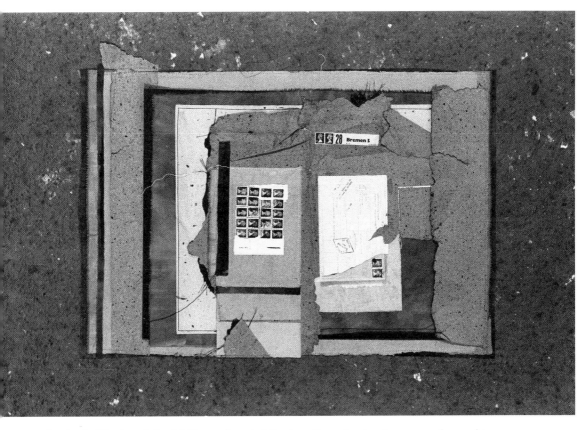

73 Stephanie Kirschen-Cole: *BB/Bremen* (1977). Mixed media on handmade paper, $52\frac{1}{2} \times 35\frac{1}{2}$ in.

JIŘÍ KOLÁŘ

Jiří Kolář was born in 1914 in the Bohemian town of Protivim, now part of Czechoslovakia. In his early days of writing poetry, Kolář discovered Marinetti's book of poems, entitled *Mots en Liberté*, which must be considered a turning-point in his life as a creative artist. Not only the revolutionary language and subject-matter of Marinetti's work strongly appealed to Kolář, but also the futurist typography, which left its permanent and distinctive mark on his later collage style.

It remains essential to view Kolář as coming to collage through poetry and experimental typography. In a sense, the futurist experiments were a revival of the baroque "pattern poem," a seventeenth-century vogue for making poems assume the shape of their subject on the printed page. George Herbert's "Easter Wings" is a perfect example that leads eventually to Kolář's "Butterflies." Although the futurists were less concerned with imitating concrete objects, their patterns did explore new discoveries about light, sound, motion, and energy as physical realities conducive to poetic shape. In Marinetti, Kolář found whole pages designed as a pictorial image, a complete visual plan in which the typography played a double role as text to be read and as a non-verbal statement of emotive energy.

The futurists influenced Kolář first as a poet. It was not until the late 1930s that visual art, particularly collage, became his chief mode of creativity. In this shift he does not cite the futurists as his prime model, but the work of Schwitters, El Lissitzky, Ernst, and then certainly the Czech collagists Voskovec, Preissig, Štyrsky and, above all, Jaroslav Hašek. The change, however, came under pressures more difficult and complex than merely artistic influence or attraction. It might be regarded as going back to the theme of "mots en liberté," and his painful discovery of ambiguity in language that led to betrayal instead of freedom.

Kolář himself describes the experience as one of being *forced* to seek "orbital, non-verbal expression for poetry." In part he suffered from a sense that words betrayed him. From one point of view he had, perhaps, exhausted the single dimension of language. But there is also a political implication in his consciousness of betrayal. The great disillusionment came in the wake of the Second World War and the repressions of the Soviet occupation. With many of his friends, Kolář suffered directly. He was imprisoned briefly in 1953, and lived through a dark period of Czech history until his move to Paris, where he now lives and works.

Although he abandoned poetry in his collages, he carried his poetry along with him, making the printed word the essential field of vision against which his images and objects assert their manifest freedom. In the most profound way, his collages are linguistic expressions, "pattern poems"; and even if he had never suffered a "betrayal" of words, they would be a natural stage of Kolář's poetic evolution.

Kolář's work belongs to a transformational reality. His collages are inspired less by an aesthetic of beauty than by a need to redefine, make new, revitalize the pictorial immediacy of language, and in that sense they are collages that issue from ideas. He often begins with ordinary objects – an apple, pears, kitchen utensils – covering them in cut-up texts, musical scores and art reproductions that force them into a new plane. He calls them *Chiasmage* in reference to the Greek X, which implies both their classical intention and the crossing of disparate images. Structurally they are reminiscent of the crossing patterns in Alexander Pope's couplets, which allow him to compare the breaking of nature's law and a china jar in a single breath. Kolář's implied comparison of objects and texts render the objects poetic and the language concrete – also in the same breath.

In all his collages, Kolář asserts the strength of purpose by which he has regained control of the words that betrayed him. Sometimes he shows us the foundering world, in the *crumplages*, for example, which distort architecture and space as if in a hall of mirrors. But the formal patterning of the distortion re-creates the space with new cohesion, renders it metaphoric, fluid, and like futuristic space full of electric motion. The same is true of his *rollages*, which slice and elongate static images so that they stretch to fit new dimensions. Likewise, he has remade images from the history of art, cutting them open and interleaving them so that unrelated ones share the same integral space. It is this unique combination that triggers off our associations when confronting his work. A butterfly constructed from a reproduction of an Ingres picture still remains a butterfly, but it is a butterfly that mimics art. Further, one thinks of a collection of butterflies in dusty cabinets, faded and lifeless, pinned to cork linings. Even the most magnificent collection of butterflies causes a certain twinge of regret, a feeling of life betrayed. How much more wonderful to discover Kolář's innocent butterfly – not a faded, dead one pinned in a cabinet – and imagine it flying around with the natural ones.

In Kolář's collages life and art are subject to constant poetic comparison. This is achieved by the solidly based ideas that inform his work. His solidity and even classicism extends to his techniques as well. Kolář works with old papers in the manner of a conservator, employing starch pastes and methyl cellulose, always in particular combinations related to the texture of the paper and stability of color on the printed surface. He cuts with razors and scalpel, pressing the pasted fragments as long as necessary to produce the firm adhesion and clean edges that give his images a polished, definitive quality.

If he began collage with the need to force words into new poetic expression, he succeeds also in forcing inherited images to join language by entering new relationships. For a collagist who constructs principally with ideas, there cannot be one style of collage; the more he thinks about his work, the more the pool deepens, the wider becomes his circumference of freedom. Thus Kolář extends his "mots en liberté." *Color illustration XI.*

SHIRLEY KRAMER

Shirley Kramer's collages began twenty years ago from an impulse to manipulate texture and space within a spontaneous organization that suggested movement. The approach was then and still is totally unpremeditated. But her earliest work, incorporating color areas, sewing patterns, old maps, tissues, and a variety of papers, seems to her in retrospect to lack a strong connection to any human reference: "People and symbolism became progressively important to me, and I began to integrate torn fragments of photographic images in the tissue layers and pigment that carry the implications of space."

Space is Kramer's dominant theme, the physical unknown, which she links by her imagery to the occult inner caverns of the subconscious. From a distance, her large collage canvases give the impression of shadowy vortices, abstract blocks swirling in motion around a focal point that is the source of light. As the viewer moves toward that point, fragmented figures emerge: a sacramental hand, a seated scribe, an ancient cave, part of a coiling snake. These half-glimpses are so elusive that the figures – often tiny against the masses of color form – merge into the pigment and crumpled textures of the tissue. The unity creates an impression best described as a kind of "abstract surrealism" that investigates another sphere of being.

Kramer came to identify this place through the writing of the Jungian Max Zeller: "Images happen to us. They make up the tapestry of our inner life, surround us as our inner world, and silently talk to us in their picture-language, the language of the unknown background" (*The Dream – The Vision of the Night*).

Kramer's images, however unconscious in origin, are technically elaborate in construction. She works on large canvas, masonite, or upson board, which she surfaces with gesso. Over this layer, she brushes Liquitex medium in patches as she builds up saturated layers of tissue in dark earth tones. The imagery asserts itself without her precognition, and slowly, sometimes over several months, she completes a collage in this manner, making tissue veils for her half-concealed imagery, over and around which she paints with Fezandie-Sperrle powdered pigments mixed with Liquitex.

The twilight of uncertainty is the latest extension of her theme. The new series of paper, plastic, and automobile part collages is executed on a small scale, set in deeply recessed frames. For these she covers the background papers in gray acrylic spray paint to symbolize "the hour of dawn where everything is gray and slightly terrifying." Disturbing fragments of human and mechanical forms arouse from the whole series the question she has made the title of one piece: "What are we handing our children?"

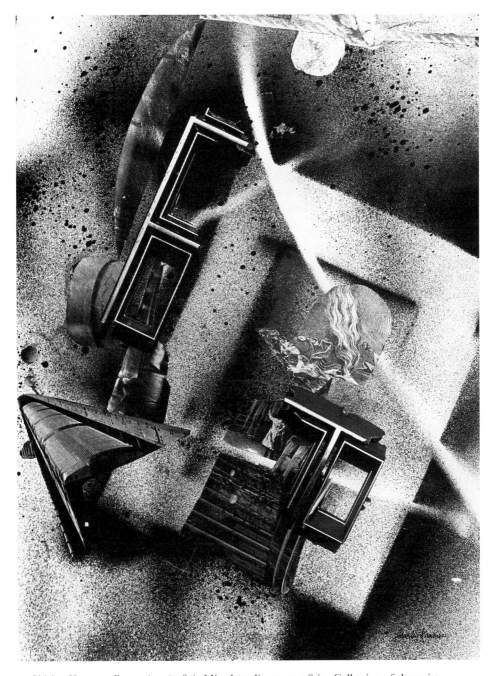

74 Shirley Kramer: *Emanations* (1982). Mixed media, 13 × 18 in. Collection of the artist.

IRWIN KREMEN

Irwin Kremen, born in Chicago in 1925, came to collage by a long detour. He studied writing rather than art at Black Mountain College, took a doctorate in psychology years later at Harvard University, and not until 1966, when he was past forty and a professor at Duke University, did collage assert a profound claim on his imagination. At the instigation of a friend, he had begun a fabric collage; and shortly afterward, in Switzerland, on visits to an old acquaintance, Italo Valenti, he was powerfully affected by the unity, intensity, and integrity of Valenti's paper collages. Once home again, Kremen threw himself into playful experimentation, using "materials with abandon,"* and he also began to paint. On a sabbatical year in Europe in 1969, he chanced on some weathered poster papers whose painterly surfaces, irregular edges, and colors of subtle beauty stirred his sensibility, and ever since he has annually hunted these "unduplicable papers, experienced papers that have been in sun, in rain, in dust, in snows, covered with the dirt of the city." They have become his staple material.

Kremen's way of working, refined over many years, strives for unity in *composition* and durability in *construction*. He describes his process – from the collection of the paper through the continual sorting and selection of it, the twisting, tearing, cutting, trimming, snipping, folding, wrinkling, patching, scraping, and cleaning – as a search for the whole that defines for him a collage of his kind, non-representational but integrated within itself. In that search he is directly responsive to the sheer appearances of his materials, to their subtle color and surface qualities.

Kremen organizes and joins his materials by techniques that require meticulous precision, the more so as he has rejected – for both aesthetic and conservational reasons – the direct application of adhesive as a bonding method. To minimize buckling and ruffling, to maintain integrity of edges, to avoid a pasted-down look, and to lessen the potential for rupture of paper from thermal change, Kremen has worked out a method whereby he hinges his collage elements – even minute fragments – to each other and to the backing museum board.

Kremen's first step after arriving at a compositional whole is temporarily to hinge the collage elements in place, using acid-free glassine tape. Next he makes a life-size photographic reproduction of it. This allows him to disassemble and reassemble the elements at will with the aid of fine measuring calipers that keep deviations from the original to fractions of a millimeter.

From the life-size photo Kremen now makes a tracing that shows the position of the collage elements. On this tracing he makes a schematic diagram as he hinges the papers together permanently, marking this template with the exact location and type of every hinge employed. The hinges vary in kind, by size, shape, and, to some extent, function. He uses float, bar, and bridge hinges depending upon various

*All of Kremen's remarks are from "Why Collage? An Interview With the Artist," a dialogue with Janet Flint in *Collages by Irwin Kremen* (Washington, D.C.: National Collection of Fine Art, 1979), pp. 15–31.

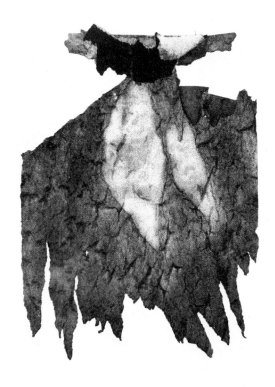

75 Irwin Kremen: *Presently Untitled #1* (1983). Paper collage, $8\frac{1}{2} \times 6\frac{1}{4}$ in. Collection of the artist.

factors such as the hinge's location, the materials being joined, and the relief quality of the edges involved. He makes these hinges from Japanese papers of differing weights – Usumino, Kizukishi, Kanaryoshi, Kizuki-Oban. The PVA (Elvace 1874) is his adhesive. Kremen fashions small instruments from the finest gauge stainless steel, to aid him in laying down the hinges in locations out of manual reach and to effect the desired tightness of crease for his float hinges. Using microelectrodes, he can, under magnification, affix the smallest flakes with minute dabs of adhesive.

Once the collage is completed, Kremen deacidifies it using a method taught him by James E. Kusterer, Jr., former chief chemical engineer at the Barrow Laboratory. Kusterer's procedure, a vapor process, can penetrate closed books, and can consequently be applied to a many-layered work. Conscious of preservation and permanence, Kremen is currently working with Hugh M. Archer, of Dearborn, Michigan, to develop a sealed time capsule frame that will display collages behind UV filtering plexiglass in a medium of inert nitrogen to prevent deterioration of the deacidified papers.

SAM LADENSON

Sam Ladenson was born in Philadelphia in 1927. As far back as he can remember, art has been his natural inclination. After military service during the Second World War, he decided to remain in Paris and study at the Beaux-Arts. Later he continued at the Pennsylvania Academy of Fine Arts from 1947 to 1951, working in watercolor and gouache as well as oils.

Ladenson's present-day abstract collages date back to the early 1960s, when he began to incorporate found papers and cut-up canvas into his paintings. At first these appeared as isolated references, but gradually they began to dominate the paintings. Within recent years he has been painting largely within the context of collage.

His principal materials are tissue papers, paper towels, brown paper, and shopping bags, which become greatly altered by his transforming process. The method is related to his sensibility as a watercolorist. To prepare his papers he frequently takes a large glass jar and places absorbent paper toweling or other porous, soft papers in the bottom of it. Over them he crumples colored tissue papers; then he pours water into the jar so that the dyes from the tissue color the other papers and mingle together, often giving the appearance of marbling. He sometimes works with the papers while they are still wet.

In order to make a collage Ladenson tapes a piece of heavy watercolor paper to a mounting board, which he sets on an easel. He brushes the paper area with acrylic gel medium and sets his collage pieces into the adhesive. His porous papers absorb the medium; his wet papers can be manipulated into position with a brush, and he deliberately encourages their colors to drip. In this manner he builds layers of transparencies, also working over areas with paint to achieve particular colors that are not inherent in the papers.

Ladenson conceives his collage technique as painting with paper, and he has come to prefer collage for its freedom and rapidity as an emotive medium. Despite this, his procedure is elaborate. Once the papers have dried in place, he brushes them over with a second layer of acrylic gel, and when the surface has hardened, he rubs it with sandpaper. This smoothes the wrinkled areas and sometimes reveals small particles of an underlayer which enters the composition as a catalyst of tension between dominant forms.

He sees his present work as expressing the whole gamut of emotions from joy to hostility. Ladenson often composes while listening to classical music, and the emotion expressed in his collages has a kind of musical intensity. He is particularly drawn to the music of Richard Wagner, whose *Die Walkyrie* he has interpreted in a suggestive landscape collage.

The shapes that most intrigue Ladenson are "primeval" in the Wagnerian sense, like boulders and monoliths. In the collages these forms predominate, but not always as independent areas, since he frequently obliterates sharp edges and encourages a greater subtlety. The finished pieces, generally small, have an intimate quality that

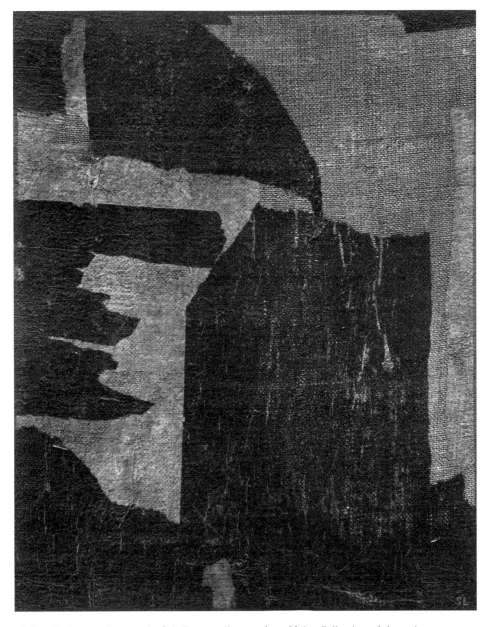

76 Sam Ladenson: *Looming* (1983). Paper collage, $11\frac{1}{2} \times 8\frac{1}{2}$ in. Collection of the artist.

comes from his personal rendering of emotive color. Sometimes he heightens them with a final acrylic layer, added just before he edges the collage with a painted color border and mounts it onto acid-free rag board.

DALE LOY

Dale Loy came to collage in 1972 when she was working on her M.F.A. at the American University in Washington, D.C. Initially, she was attracted by the immediacy it contributed to her painting. It also added edges and textures, what she calls "a toothy quality," that derives from materials that have been subjected to time and wear. Collage elements expanded her abstract vocabulary to include frail textures and colors paled with age, which she simply could not achieve from paint on a brush.

From the beginning, she intended to "use collage as a purely abstract element in abstract paintings." She began also to study the medium and came under the influence of Kurt Schwitters and William Dole. "I continue to think of my work as painting even though the pieces may consist entirely of collaged elements, with minimal traces of brush-applied paint. I do this because I use the materials solely for their gestural, textural, and tonal qualities, never for any polemical or connotative value, as collage materials have frequently been employed in the history of art."

In fact, she works deliberately to "subdue the informational qualities" of her materials, obscuring or inverting words. This is especially interesting considering her earlier vocation as a journalist. The formal is what mainly interests her; she is, as she puts it, "struggling to find the containers."

In this search the scale of her work is both very small and large – up to nine feet. Her collage paintings of both extremes (which she works at simultaneously) combine torn papers with acrylic paint. Even here she mingles the new paint with cracked scrapings lifted off the palette. She mounts her small pieces onto Rives BFK 100 per cent rag paper with acrylic medium, sealing the old papers into the composition with matte varnish for preservation. Her large works are made on canvas, using the same adhesive and coating materials.

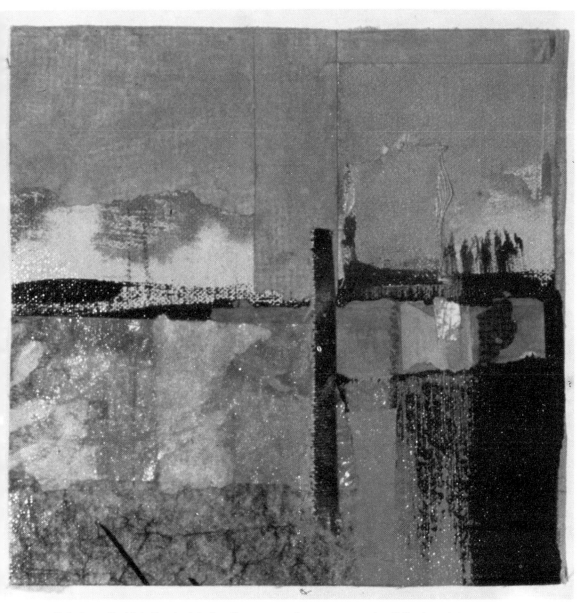

77 Dale Loy: *Untitled #12* (1981). Acrylic, paper, and canvas, 7 × 7 in. Collection of the artist.

LEO MANSO

Leo Manso's collages are landscapes of a metaphysical world. They allude to mysterious strata of the earth's altering crust in the Kathmandu series, and to time and place in the *Variazioni Romani*. The images themselves, physical only by implication, issue directly from what Manso calls, "collage ideas." They are ideas of transformation, ideas that "dematerialize the material world by ranging in unexpected associations – physically, aesthetically, and psychologically."

Born in New York in 1914, Manso studied at the National Academy of Design, the Metropolitan Museum of Art, and the New School for Social Research. By 1939 he was established in a New York studio and by 1947 began working summers in Provincetown, Massachusetts, which was rapidly becoming a center of the avant garde. There in 1952 he helped to organize "Gallery 256", and later in 1958, with another artist, Victor Candell, he established the Provincetown Workshop School.

He refers to his early work, with its powerful infusion of seascape light, as "abstract impressionism." The phrase deliberately separates him from the expressionist trends of the New York abstractionists and emphasizes other aspects of his receptivity: to Cézanne's intellectual structures, to Turner and Blake for the passion of their vision, to Matisse and Bonnard as colorists, to Caravaggio for making blackness a living presence. This is only one gathering, one layer. His idea of color as a conveyor of mood and light also has roots in a study of Persian miniatures, Sung painting and Tantric art, with its particular fusion of organic energy and strict geometry.

Manso's collage expressions of Tanka and Tantra occupied him from 1962 to 1973. In 1973 a trip to the valley of Kathmandu decisively altered the structure of his work. The immensity of the physical location could neither be represented nor captured in its sublimity. This recognition caused Manso to abandon large rectilinear landscapes and to seek large scale in the miniature. He began to work in microcosmic circle compositions that shift from the sublime to the beautiful, from overpowering immensity to particularized encounters of the earth's crust.

Manso's collages are extremely tactile and conscious of their basis in physical materials. He works with found papers and fabrics that he hand-dyes himself. Many of his most exquisite materials come from books and bindings, many centuries old, which he found during the last three years in a Roman flea market while he was working at the American Academy. These he treats with sacramental austerity, often isolating them in strict composition in the finished piece. Manso almost never doctors the surface of his found papers, but allows them their own transcendence in the aesthetic context. Their expressive formality, somehow engendered by the material itself, is experienced simply as unity. Of late, the compositions often float in black space, with references to the influence of Caravaggio.

Manso aims in his collages not at pictorial representation, but at a synthetic rendering of highly charged states of feeling. He works without preconception,

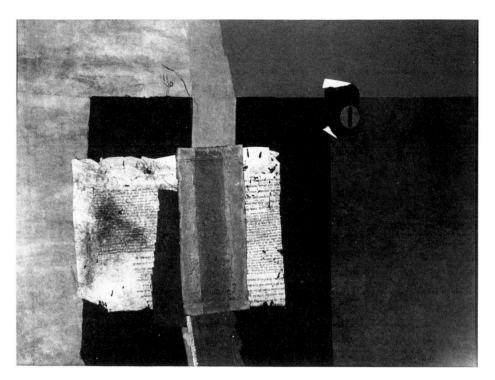

78 Leo Manso: *O Roma* (n.d.). Paper collage, 19 × 25¼ in. Collection of the artist.

stimulated by the contrast between torn and cut edges, sometimes burning or scorching elements to heighten the tension. His strong central compositions emerge against a ground of Fabriano paper. Carefully he tacks the collage pieces together with PVA, and when the composition is structurally complete, he turns it face down to tear away unnecessary material so that it can be pasted flat to stretched canvas. Using PVA, he covers the back of the collage with adhesive. Then he applies the same adhesive to the area of the canvas where he has traced the shape of the collage. Now, using a hot iron, he bonds the two adhesive surfaces together, using a heat/pressure dry mount technique.

Manso's collage techniques and ideas extend also to printmaking. His newest development is a series of prints based on collage and allowed to develop by chance in the printing process. The material sources of their imagery, found papers and textured string, create a *trompe l'oeil* belief in their authenticity, and Manso introduces real collage fragments to tease comparison further. Thus cultivating perpetual transformation, Manso continues to evolve as a collagist filled with enthusiasm for tangible manifestations of a spiritual world.

FRIEDRICH MECKSEPER

Friedrich Meckseper's work has been called a *Raritätskabinett*, a "curio cabinet" of delicate and humorous mechanisms. They owe their inspiration, in part perhaps, to his training in mechanics at the Robert Bosch Company, where he apprenticed before studying art at the State Art Academy in Stuttgart (1955–57) and the State Hochschule in Berlin (1957–59). Born in Bremen in 1936, he had his first major exhibition in Oldenburg in 1960 and has since shown widely throughout Europe, in America, Australia and Japan.

Meckseper's principal reputation is in oil painting and etching, which he executes in the clean, distinctive manner of an Old Master turned surrealist. Space and volume are his recurring themes, often depicted in imaginary geometries and volumetric solids. His landscapes and still-lifes are planes marked by abstract vectors that whimsically intersect observable reality.

Meckseper's invention has a strong Galilean component, the quality of an inventor and applied scientist who revels in discoveries of phenomena. His metaphysics is physics, and nowhere is this more apparent than in his collages, many of which are made with lilliputian parts of old typewriters, cogs, and pocket watches that can actually be wound up. They move and purr lightly, also with a certain mystery, since he frequently removes the hands and leaves time completely to the imagination. It is clear that he believes not only in the idea behind the piece of work that he is constructing, but also in the technical skills of the hands necessary to create a jewel. He is firstly an artist, but also a superlative technician. There is a German saying that Leonardo da Vinci would have been just as great if he had lost his hands. Meckseper refutes this by implying the value of hands to execute ideas.

His imagination is often stirred by old bookplates and scientific drawings, which he reinterprets by collage inventions. An antique cartographer's rendering of longitude and latitude reminds him of human fantasies about the round earth, and he pastes over the south pole a hapless man falling to his doom.

In Meckseper's collages mechanics turn the cogs of myth. His playfulness recalls the lighter mood of surrealism; his fantasy machines enjoy an idealized, harmless precision that is a wish in perpetual search of fulfillment. *Color illustration XII.*

CLAYTON MITROPOULOS

Clayton Mitropoulos's collages are strong, vital emblems of human endeavor. They celebrate the fire fighter, choreographer, swimmer, and architect in energetic shapes that define their professional lives. "The Fire Fighter and His Dog," for example, are epitomized by heads, hands, and hose in a patterned geometry, almost a stencil or template of their basic forms.

Mitropoulos sets these central, purely colored shapes, cut from Toyama paper, against an Arches cover stock background in black, gray or neutral. The image begins with a single dominant form, which he tears against a straight edge or cuts with scissor or blade.

Often, as in "The Fire Fighter," the shape is emphasized by white lead pencil guidelines that give it a sense of architectural reality. Typically, he shifts the image, offsetting it from the ruled lines, so that the shape appears framed in lines of tension or energy. He also uses pastel drawing and secondary forms to complete the collage,

79 Clayton Mitropoulos: *The Firefighter and His Dog* (1982).
Paper collage with pencil drawing, $13\frac{3}{4} \times 19\frac{1}{2}$ in.
Collection of the artist.

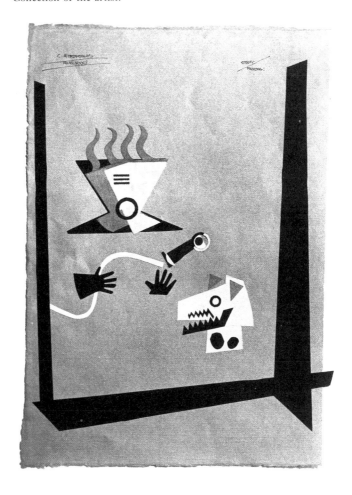

which he adheres with acrylic gloss medium, finding it a stronger bond than the matte.

The finished collage reads like a blueprint, and indeed Mitropoulos uses the medium as a blueprint for paintings and his cut-out masks that render the central imagery of the collage. Yet despite the fact that his collages lead to paintings, the collages themselves are constructed of acid-free materials with a conscious consideration of their permanent life apart from the paintings.

Mitropoulos was born in New York in 1953. More a product of his independent study and apprenticeship than of his training at the Maryland Institute, College of Art, in Baltimore, he is a meticulous technician committed to classical techniques and materials in oil painting and collage. In his imagery he shows the influence of the Russian constructivists. His particularly American sensibility relates as strongly to machines as to Indian geometries and petroglyphs. He brings them most perfectly together in the simplicity of his collages.

ROBERT MOTHERWELL

"The Tearingness of Collage," a title that he gave to a 1957 piece, has the quality of a *leitmotif* in the work of Robert Motherwell. The definitive spokesman for abstract expressionist painting, Motherwell has continued throughout his prolific career to work in collage with a passion for the torn edge that is as decisive and spare as his elegant *Open* paintings.

In some respects his work in the two media is complementary. Painting, particularly before the advent of fast-drying acrylic, has been for him a slow art conditioned by revision and the sheer size of his canvases. His collages have always been freer and more spontaneous. By contrast, too, with the universal forms of his paintings, the collages are more intimate vehicles into which he can interject associative fragments of his private life as an artist and a man.

Motherwell's private life, particularly his intellectual life, has an important bearing on his collages. Born in 1915 in Aberdeen, Washington, he studied from the age of eleven at the Otis Art Institute, Los Angeles, then at the California School of Fine Arts in San Francisco. At Stanford University (B.A., 1937) Motherwell studied philosophy. From there he went to Harvard, where he specialized in aesthetics under Arthur O. Lovejoy and David Prall, who encouraged him to continue in Paris the research of his thesis on Delacroix's journals. Motherwell's European trip in 1938 led him to the French symbolists, with whom he came to identify so strongly that he accepted Joseph Cornell's revised title for one of his collages, "Mallarmé's Swan" (originally "Mallarmé's Dream"), as a symbol of his affinity with the assault against pure space. Perhaps more than Mallarmé, the ideal world of Baudelaire's "L'Invitation au Voyage" invited comparison with Motherwell's space. The poem depicts a place of order and beauty in a balance of sensuous calm ("*luxe, calme, et volupté*").

The French sensibility is pervasive in Motherwell's collages. In one series (1959, 1960, 1973) the wrappers of Editions Gallimard (publishers of his avowed heroes Valéry, Gide, Proust, Breton, and Camus) were deliberately employed in connection with the literary associations conjured by their logo, *nrf* (*nouvelle revue française*). The Gauloise packet on a field of Motherwell blue (*l'azure*) is positively a hallmark of his collages, but he is also drawn to French wine labels as concrete symbols of taste and sensibility.

The other side to his European passion is his romance with death, and above all Spanish death. This began perhaps as early as 1937 when he heard André Malraux speak about the Spanish Civil War at a San Francisco rally. *Elegy to the Spanish Republic* became a preoccupying theme from the forties on (No. 1, 1948), with variants that took him to "A Little Spanish Prison" (1941) and aroused a passion for Lorca, bulls, and blood. Mexico also evoked his enthusiasm; in collage it expressed itself in the search for "Pancho Villa, Dead and Alive" (1943).

During Motherwell's first visit to Mexico in 1941 he began a friendship with the artist Matta, who introduced him to surrealist theories of "automatism" that were to have a shaping influence on abstract expressionism. His emphasis at this stage on ovoid forms and the primitive figure – like his Pancho Villa – links him more to the lyrical plasticity of Matta and Miró than to the mainstream of surrealist dream imagery.

The early collages constructed in this spirit have a certain density that Motherwell was to prune drastically through the next two decades. The ovoid and linear rectangles associated with the early collages shifted to the *Spanish Elegies* as controlling black shapes; the collages meanwhile became progressively defined by the isolation of torn forms. In "The Tearingness of Collage" (1957) the complexity of layers is still apparent, but by 1960 he had begun to eliminate and reduce to the single wrapper and a concentrated, personal shape against a ground of expressive paint.

The isolation and control of his collage papers on their spare color grounds is the basis of Motherwell's elegance. Often an envelope or brown wrapper with its confluence of folds, tears, and printing governs the relationship of vast space. There is a cosmopolitan longing to travel implicit in his diverse fragments gathered from Dublin, London, Geneva, Germany, Turin.

The romantic longing is perhaps part of what draws him to music. In the 1970s his identifying wrappers became associated with fragments of musical scores and with unprinted colored and white papers. Their clean tears imply a negative space against which to read his salvaged wrappers.

The papers must also be read against the paint, with its general strokes, vehement splashes, oblique calligraphy, and feathered edges. Motherwell has always made collages concurrently with painting, and like his paintings their space often takes on the characteristics of a wall, which Motherwell perceives as a symbol of modernist aesthetics. Unlike most collagists obsessed with walls, he never conveys in his "tearingness" the feeling of décollaged posters or the implications of found wall patterning.

Over the years his collages, like the paintings, have gone through some material revisions. His earliest work in both forms used Permanent Pigment oil paint, in the collages oil on Strathmore paper backed onto heavy board. Casein, gouache, and tempera were also used in some of the earlier collages. From about the mid-sixties he shifted to faster drying acrylics, and in the seventies a heightened consciousness of permanence brought about other changes. He replaced commercial colored art papers with his own colored rag papers, which he painted in acrylic. He also began to have wrappers and other image papers printed and sometimes enlarged by hand lithography on rag paper. Finally, he shifted from an assortment of adhesives to the copolymer Jade 403.

For Motherwell, collage is part of a perpetual voyage of self-discovery and refinement. It is an intellectual "Grand Tour" through philosophies and civilizations whose thought and artifacts are distilled in the "tearingness" of original edges. *Color illustration XIII.*

80 Robert Motherwell: *Dublin Collage* (1975). Collage and acrylic on canvas, 72 × 36 in. Courtesy M. Knoedler and Co., New York.

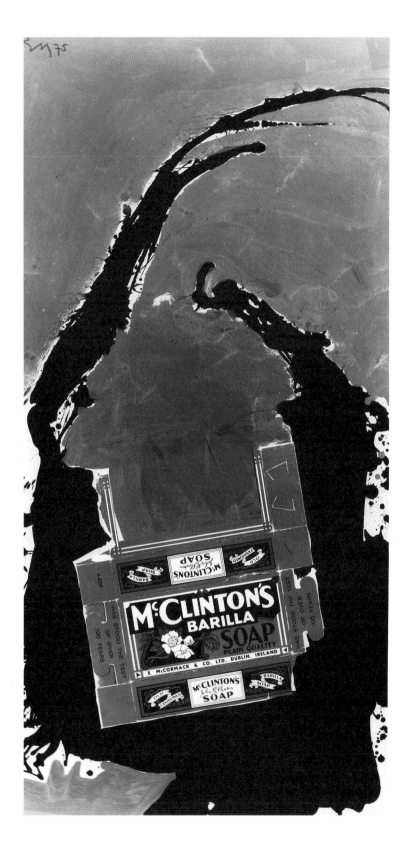

JOAN NEEDHAM

Joan Needham was born in 1935 in Philadelphia. For the first twenty-five years of her artistic life she was a printmaker, and it was not until 1981, when she studied with Laurence Barker at the Barcelona Paper Workshop, that she turned to handmade paper with collage.

From printed images on paper she has consciously shifted to pigment-colored imagery embedded directly into the paper or overlaid geometric forms adhered with methyl cellulose. Many of her collages are three-dimensional, like her "Window Shade," which alludes also to the sails of square riggers. Her principal material is acid-free 100 percent linen and cotton rag which she manufactures and colors herself, most recently with the collaborative assistance of the Dieu Donné papermill in New York.

Her durable papers are intended to have an architectural strength. They can be folded, twisted, and tied into assertive, permanent contructions. In making collage Needham cuts with scissors and mat knife, but she also tears the paper with her hands for particular effects.

She endeavors to convey in her collages the purity and strength of the actual papers themselves. Thus the material directly inspires her collage forms, which often incorporate her embossments and etchings.

81 Joan Needham: *Window Shade Series 1* (n.d.). Handmade paper collage, 36 × 36 in.

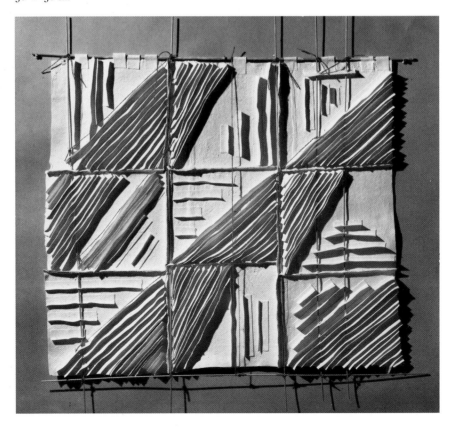

VALERY OISTEANU

Valery Oisteanu was born in the U.S.S.R. in 1943. He emigrated to the U.S.A. in 1973 and now lives and works in New York City. As well as being a collagist, Oisteanu is a poet, and he maintains that he is a poet/collagist in the dadaist tradition, having published three books of poetry illustrated with his collages since 1974.

Still very much concerned with the intercutting of word and image, he uses both dadaist and surrealist techniques, such as *décollage*, *fumage*, and his own version of *frottage*, which he calls *rubbage*. Instead of floorboard and stone rubbings, à la Ernst, Oisteanu's rubbings involve picture and word stamps, both commercial and home-made. This device, used by Schwitters to make typographical compositions, has regained popularity among the mail artists, and Oisteanu generally credits the influence of Ray Johnson. Extending the technique, Oisteanu prints his rubber stamps on clear slides which he then projects during "body collage" performances. He also prints the slides as photocopy images to be cut up and used in other paper collages.

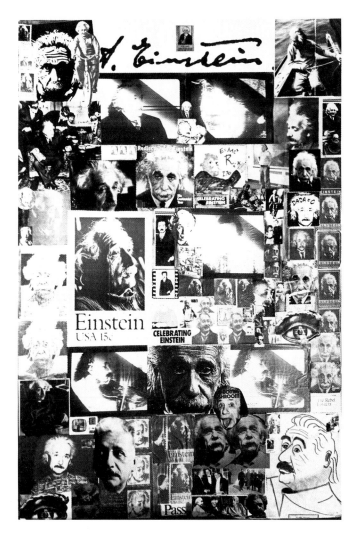

82 Valery Oisteanu: *Hundred Heads of Einstein for Albert's Centennial* (1980). Paper collage, 60 × 80 in. Collection of the artist.

Stimulated by media imagery, Oisteanu often makes collages of photographic prints derived from video and television images. Extending into media performance, he also does collage projections, using multiple slide projectors in combination with music, dance, and poetry. Some slide imagery he captures in photocopy color collages made by printing sandwiched slides as a single image. The life of these can be extended by lamination.

There is no new material to which he is not responsive and no form of collage that he has not attempted. He has pressed home the need for a healthy society to admit a certain anarchistic philosophy. His art supplies that need.

Before emigrating to the U.S.A., he was mainly influenced by black-and-white word cut-out collages, his own form of concrete poetry. He dates his color work from his move to America in 1973. "Coming here was like a mental explosion. The color seduced me." These colors – of photos in magazines – he explores in every way and recently in commercial work for a variety of magazines.

For his conventional cutting he uses an X-acto knife with #11 blade, and pastes with Jade 403 on paper, using O'Glue for photographs and hard materials, Pritt Glue Stick for repair work.

JOHN O'REILLY

John O'Reilly was born in 1930 in New Jersey. He received a B.F.A. from Syracuse University in 1952 and an M.F.A. in 1956 from the School of the Art Institute of Chicago. Although he was trained chiefly in painting and sculpture, he turned to collage as his primary medium and has been a collagist for the past twenty-two years.

The turning point was a fourteen-month trip to Spain, which awakened his interest in collage. While his earliest pieces were abstractions, the impact of Old Master painting gradually shifted him to a new subject-matter and voice. The voice is humorous, the gentle humor of a respectful parodist in love with the originals.

O'Reilly turns to Old Master figures with a strong sense of narrative. He sees an Ingres nude in the context of her nineteenth-century setting, then visually transposes her to a modern boudoir where she seems equally at home. For a moment the contrasting image disrupts our sensibility and provokes laughter. But the real shock is the perfect consistency of color, movement, and form that makes it natural for her to occupy this new space. By virtue of O'Reilly's careful organization and prevailing wit, we come away from the collage with a sense of the timelessness of art and design.

Thus the humor of O'Reilly's collages moves us to a perception of the universal, and in this his theme is comedic rather than satiric, emphasizing the common foibles of the human species. A nude draped on a chaise longue might be any fatigued man's dream. The fact that this nude is Boucher's and her bedroom of a much later age is a compliment to the persistence of the dream, which in O'Reilly's collages is interpreted as a kind of Freudian wish-fulfillment.

In spite of the disparity between figures and landscapes his imagery is congruent. Unlike the surrealist's use of juxtaposed images to disorient and disturb the viewer,

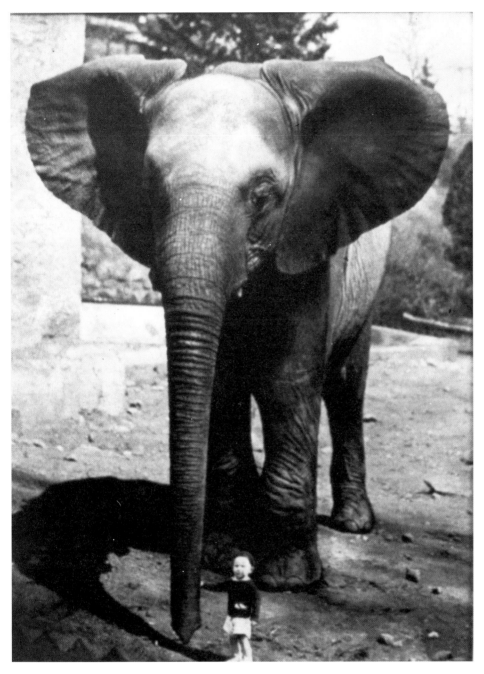

83 John O'Reilly: *Self Portrait with Elephant* (1977). Paper and paste, $7\frac{5}{8} \times 10\frac{3}{8}$ in. Collection of the artist.

O'Reilly's unique world appears to be a natural order that *could just be possible*. In an unusual self-portrait collage, for example, he has taken a photograph of himself as a child and placed it beside that of an elephant. The child, holding the trunk, is totally dwarfed beside the disproportionately gigantic animal. Only after searching for what is unusual do we realize its gentle absurdity of exaggeration and the truth it conveys about the peaceable kingdom that might exist in the absence of fear. O'Reilly's feeling for the naive and unconstrained imagination is perhaps deepened by his twenty years of work as an art therapist.

He maintains that he can only work with materials that he understands and loves. Therefore he relies mostly on reproductions of Old Masters from illustrated art books, magazines, and prints. He uses a medium pair of scissors to cut out his images, which are remarkably delicate and clean. He then pastes the images together with acid-free methyl cellulose wallpaper paste. With his fingers he first smoothes the paste over the back of his image; then he brushes it to achieve an even surface. Using only his hands, he presses the work flat. The collage is then mounted and framed on acid-free board. *Color illustration XIV*.

ALFONSO OSSORIO

Alfonso Ossorio was born in Manila, the Philippines, in 1916. Even at an early age he craved to become an artist, and his sympathetic parents raised no objection, providing that he graduated from a university. At his father's wish, Ossorio obtained a B.A. (1938) from Harvard, where he studied art history at the Fogg Museum. Further training was at the Rhode Island School of Design under master-carver John Howard Benson.

In many artists, childhood memories can have a profound influence on their mature work. Memories and visions remain in the unconscious and at a later stage of development, as Henri Bergson claims, the trap door opens and the artist collects these floating images and distills them in his work. Ossorio's childhood memories continue to play a sacramental role in his art. At the age of eight, he was sent to a Catholic preparatory school at Malvern, England; then to Portsmouth Priory School in Rhode Island, which was organized and run by Benedictine monks. Here religion deeply influenced Ossorio, who, recalling the Benedictine motto "labore et orare," says in later life, "I worked and prayed."

The icons of Christianity are still inherent in his substances and his surfaces, whether they are the cut-up Mass cards and Christmas cards that are recycled in collage or the ink mark devils and saints that he conjures from subterranean depths of belief. Their sheer plentitude is a kind of offering. Though his three-dimensional works, collages which Ossorio calls "Congregations," have earned him an international reputation, his flat collages, which are equally important, have for some reason been neglected. These intimate pieces have, perhaps, simply been dwarfed by the monumental scale of his overpowering work.

In Ossorio's collages on paper there is a baroque scheme of design, a religious feeling that mingles contemplation with *Angst*. Their compulsion preserves them from oddity, for the driving wish to express his vision of Christianity and draw nearer to God infuses them with an electric creativity.

In the "Victory Collage" (1966) figures appear crucified, dark, brooding. Similar to the drawings of children or primitive people, they float spread-eagle like universal self-portraits of fear and separation. Adam and Eve appear below a crow-like bird that carries an ominous egg. This figure, placed in the middle of the collage, reinforces the central theme of anxiety with respect to artistic and perhaps cosmic creation. Around the bird the primitive forms float in various stages of torment and foetal birth. There is little relief for the eye or mind until we come at last to the image of the Virgin holding her Infant. It is a tiny figure, but it is there to offer relief amidst this visual hell; and once we have found it we cannot fail to notice the word "Victory" above, as a signal of the struggle resolved.

Ossorio's collages on paper are personal in a way that brings the adjective "uncomfortable" to mind, but once we have understood their philosophy and read their construction, a religious and metaphysical truth shines through.

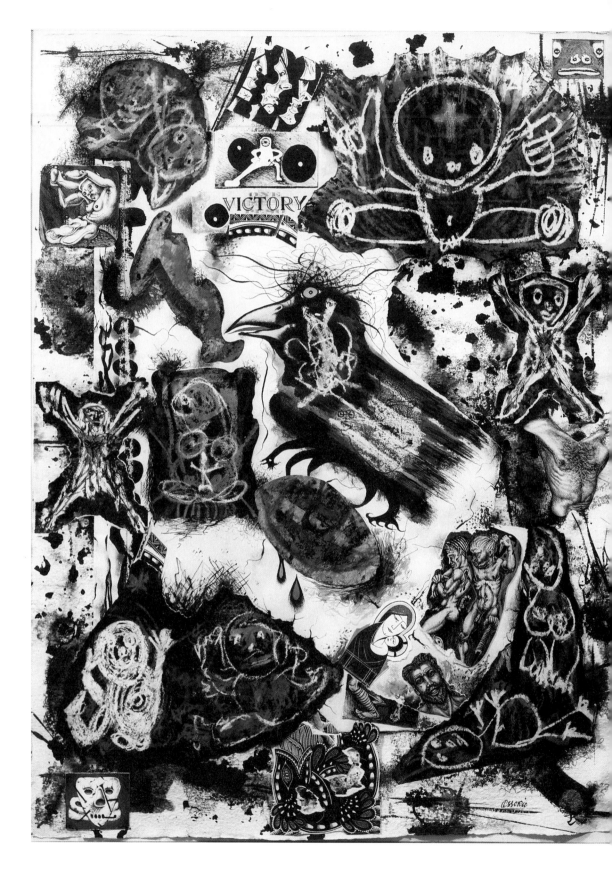

184

The collages are worked on handmade papers from Barcham Green, Whatman, Howell, and Oriental stock. In his works Ossorio often recycles his old watercolors, wood-engravings of the forties and Christmas cards, many of which he designed himself. The creative process had ecological overtones for him even before ecology became current politics. Along with foreign currency (like the Manila "victory" currency to which he is particularly attached) appear reproductions and photographs.

Through his manipulation, the diverse elements gather a strong romantic sense of organic unity. This is helped by the fluidity of his wax drawing (which he does both dry (cold) and wet (hot)) on the white paper. Using the wax resist technique, he brushes the surface over with strong color washes, adding India ink drawing, scraping through the wax in places in order to work the surface over from light to dark.

He pastes as he constructs, with no conscious preconception beyond a basic sense of direction. Thus the collage develops by accretion as a composite labyrinth of drawing and fragmentary elements that leave no space untouched. But in the *horror vacui* dense with liturgical texts and symbols, we arrive finally at a wholeness that is satisfying. Like the gem-encrusted surfaces of Gustave Moreau, Ossorio's collages are embellished myths, not invented, only discovered by art. To use his own words, they "allow the unspoken controlling impetus to work," to build in silence its totems of devotion and power. *Color illustration XV.*

84 Alfonso Ossorio: *Victory Collage* (1966). Collage and drawing incorporating the artist's earlier work, $34\frac{1}{2} \times 26\frac{3}{4}$ in. Collection Mr. and Mrs. Frederick E. Ossorio.

WOLFGANG PETROVSKY

Wolfgang Petrovsky was born in Hainsberg, near Dresden, East Germany, in 1947. He graduated as an art student from the Karl Marx University in 1970 and has worked in collage since 1973.

Petrovsky has been influenced by the German dadaists, and his collages are politically oriented toward German history in the twentieth century. They escape the clichés of political satire by their strength of visual arrangement, often a stark formality from which Petrovsky's interpretations of memorabilia emerge. Papers, maps, photographs, newspapers combine in compositions that generate sad ironies. These are the same feelings we get from desecrated scrapbooks and obliterated posters.

In collage Petrovsky structures walls of memory as backgrounds against which to read his portraits of the dead. On a ground of maps and documents, words give evidence of *war*, *revolution*, and *life*. In one corner the portrait of Rosa Luxemburg appears, damaged to symbolize her assassination. Petrovsky's "Memorial to Rosa Luxemburg" (1981) is part of his collage series *On German History*, in which he searches for the causes of the two World Wars. Petrovsky's personal attachment to Rosa Luxemburg as a universal figure is related to his identification with the working class and the Artists' Union, through which he has endeavored to raise the consciousness of history and social ideals of peace to be gathered from the ruins of tragedy. His attachment to history is rendered in the collages with a certain objectivity and distance that come from his training in graphic art and design.

Although Petrovsky works with ordinary papers gathered from the everyday world, he is careful to preserve them as best he can. For this reason he works on acid-free backing board, applying his cut and torn images with rice-starch paste. His pigments are acrylic and India ink.

85 Wolfgang Petrovsky: *Memorial to Rosa Luxemburg* (1981) from the series *On German History*. Collection of the artist.

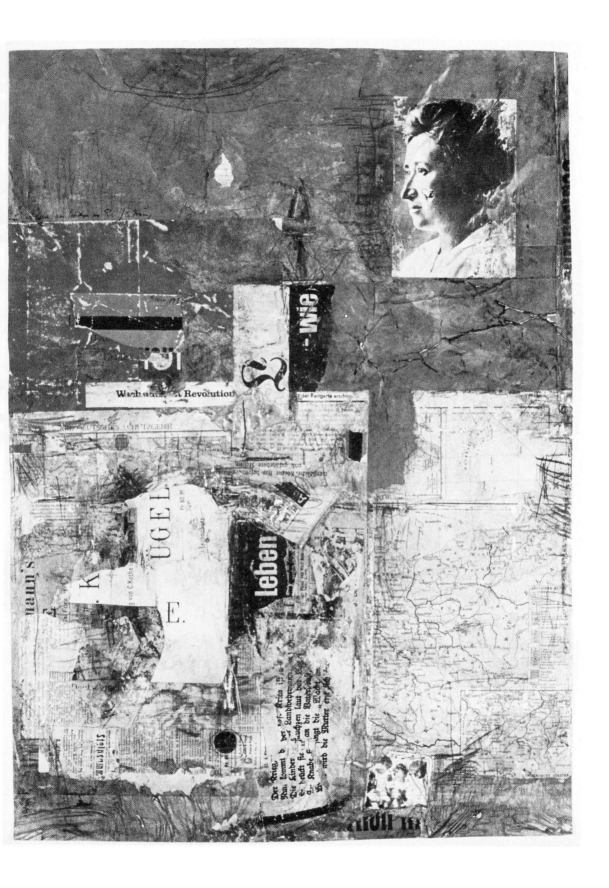

GEORGES PINEL

The imagery of surrealism is given classical structure in the work of Georges Pinel. His collages are like reliquaries, divided into multiple compartments.

Born in Algeria in 1949, Pinel views his collages as essentially dialectical. For him, the medium is a "fast, spontaneous, but precise way of putting ideas into visual perspectives." His alphabet of ideas is translated into colors, forms, and conceptual as well as figurative dimensions. Color is instrumental in establishing the dialectic, setting up gradations of mood for Pinel: "I know what red can make me feel and what blue can make me feel." These feelings he seeks to express in figurative work that draws heavily on classical figures to express universal themes such as melancholy, love, and sorrow.

Since he rarely plans out a work in advance, he surrounds himself with imagery, cutting and patterning by freely associative progression. Sometimes he works on several collages simultaneously, constructing and developing. The original idea often gives birth to a new one which necessitates the creation of a new work. In his patterning he may lay the collage out several times before pasting. He can always remember how the pieces fit no matter how many times he gathers them up. The amazing thing he notices is that the essential relationships rarely change. Each work has its own particular architecture, which is somehow predestined.

In a sense, Pinel views his work as sculptural. He likes to carve and considers the delicate work that he does with his thin, sharp barber's scissors a form of sculpture. The scissors is his main tool, though he occasionally uses a scalpel. Both precision and consistency of idea are important to him. He chooses his materials from offset color images in fine art reproductions and has spent considerable time aging papers in sunlight to test the durability of colors.

Though he is currently living and working in California, he chooses a German adhesive that he has to import. "Technicoll" is a multipurpose "crystal polyvalent" in acetone that is strong and yet permits paper that has been laid down to be removed quickly if necessary. Pinel works directly from the bottle, using a brush or fingertips to smooth the adhesive around the edges. His pieces are backed onto Strathmore 4-ply board and pressed with heavy books to insure an even bond.

Pinel's collages have the distinction of hard, brilliantly polished surfaces, which he achieves by successive layers of Varathane spray. He works on the collage as a whole with an anti-UV spray, then applies four or five coats of Varathane spray, permitting a 24-hour drying period between layers to avoid wrinkles in the varnish. This method, he finds, seals the collage image, intensifies the color tones, and protects it against atmospheric corrosives while creating aesthetically the sense of a varnished classical painting. *Color illustration XVI.*

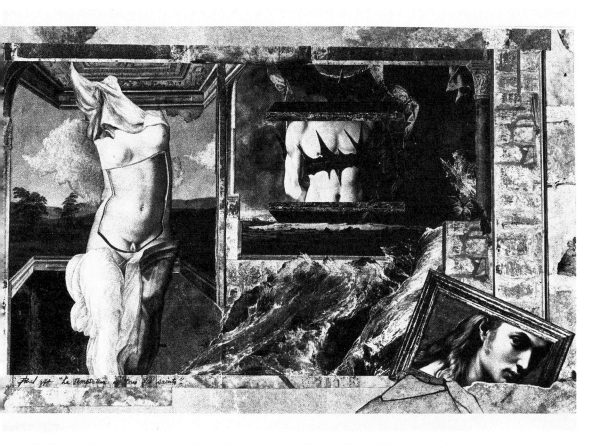

86 Georges Pinel: *La Temptation de tous les saints* (1972). Paper collage with spray varnish, 24 ×
18 in. Collection of the artist.

LILIANA PORTER

Liliana Porter was born in Buenos Aires, Argentina, in 1941. She studied at the School of Fine Arts in Buenos Aires and at the Universidad Iberoamericana in Mexico City. For the past eighteen years she has lived and worked in New York City.

Trained first as a printmaker and painter, she turned to collage for the conceptual use of the medium in exploring different levels of reality. The most immediate influence on her work is the writing of Jorge Luis Borges, whose mysterious inquisitions explore the idealistic view that the dreamed world is the only stable reality.

Porter's collages explore this haunting perspective. They are large paper still-life compositions in which objects and fragments of objects float in an illusionistic, almost empty space. The images are themselves deceptive. A book rests on an apparent, implied table. Superimposed on its open pages, a curled fragment of collage interposes a second layer of being. The torn edges make its intrusion obvious, yet the fragment contains the book's text and, resting on the surface, completes the image in such a way as to assert a "reconstruction," an ordering of a reality that is multilayered. The text Porter depicts is often *Alice in Wonderland*, a conscious metaphor for exploring the nature of a dreamed world.

The visual realism of her imagery also contributes to her questioning. Just as she quotes literary sources, she also alludes to the work of other painters, like Roy Lichtenstein, whose mannered still-lifes become borrowed images which she invests with a higher realism.

Typically on the first layer she paints and draws objects: vases, model ships (a metaphor for the voyage), geometric solids, crayons, brushes (the tools of deception). Then she superimposes photo-silkscreen images, sometimes painting a part of these or a second duplicate, emphasizing the mysterious looking-glass nature of reality. Her collaged fragments drift across the surface, intruding, juxtaposing themselves, organizing, completing patterns, exerting a tangible presence like dream commentaries on the waking world. Strategically tacked with PVA, the pieces curl white on white against the broad sheets of Arches Aquarelle. The poetic, often pale compositions seem at once firmly planted and hanging in open air, at once formal and free.

In Porter's work, collage is less a handling of substance than a plane of consciousness. Her paper surfaces provoke a desire to subvert illusions of solidity and representation.

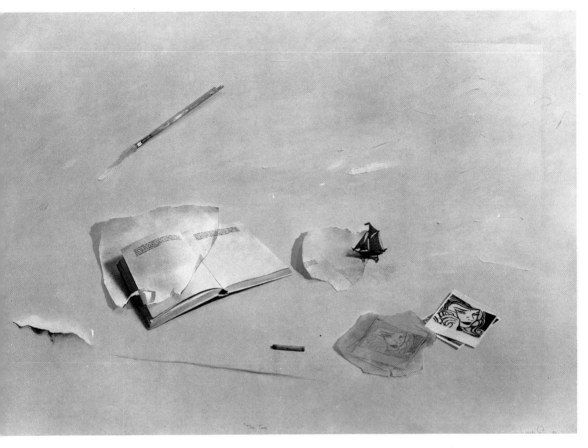

87 Liliana Porter: *The Tear* (1982). Acrylic, silkscreen, and paper collage, 40 × 60 in. Courtesy Barbara Toll Fine Arts, New York.

ELENA PRESSER

Born 1940 in Buenos Aires, Argentina, Elena Presser lives and works full-time as a collagist in Miami, Florida. After studying psychology at the University of Buenos Aires, she was trained in art at Miami Dade Community College and Florida International University, where she took her B.F.A.

Specifically inspired by Renaissance and baroque music, her collages are visual reconstructions of the Age of Bach. Drawn to the mathematical perfection of the music, her "manuscript" collages replicate the melodic flow of canons, fugues, and most recently the whole of the *Goldberg Variations*.

Each *Goldberg Variation* begins on a sheet of Spanish paper that she hand-colors with muted layers of pastel. Then, listening to the music that is the theme of the piece, she writes a spontaneous flow of calligraphic shapes that read like a "shorthand" of sensibility. They are in no language, and the indecipherable secrecy of the automatic writing acquires potent magic. Against the shapely script, Presser articulates a counterpoint of squares and numbers and/or letters. At times she cuts them from old sheets of pianola music paper, one of a variety of papers used.

With an X-acto knife, she excises minute pieces. Thus the cut scroll becomes another inversion of the theme. Each square is deliberately placed for aesthetic reasons.

She builds in layers, making pencil marks behind square holes; adding movable square chips of colored paper that slide along silver threads or hang from silken ones. Against her muted papers the squares of primary colors remind us that her music also belongs to the Age of Newton, who found the colors of refracted light. The labyrinth of her colorful notation conjures up the embellishing grace notes of the harpsichord. Her belief in music as an expression of perfection also has metaphysical overtones, like Kepler's belief in the music of the spheres.

Without conscious reference to either Newton or Kepler, Presser's collages nonetheless look like cosmological manuscripts as well as musical ones. Their vectors, circles, and numerology give them strong resemblances to texts of Renaissance science, which increases their fictive power. In fact, her manuscript research extends principally to Anna Magdalena Bach, whose notebooks she has transcribed in a long collage series. In these and her other musically inspired works, the mechanics of baroque thought are captured as intimate, private ideals. In structures she sees games, building a child's alphabet puzzle to symbolize the youthful spirit of Wilhelm Friedmann Bach, or burying her own signature in secret number combinations.

Her interpretation is very personal, combining perceptions, fantasy, and research in an unusual way. "All the facts and realities of my musical readings become distorted intentionally by my ignorance of music, and the freedom I have because of this ignorance." Thus she creates new symbols from the original. Presser identifies her personal quest for perfection and complexity of feelings with the glory of the

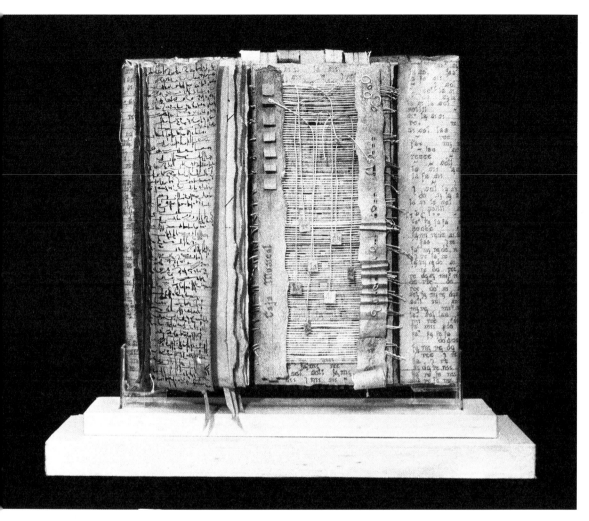

88 Elena Presser: *Caja Musical* (1981). Paper, pastel, pen and ink, silk thread, 8 × 8 × 1 in. Private collection.

music. She expresses the connection best by her meticulous care of construction. Her pastel grounds are worked to perfection even before they acquire overlays. She uses acid-free new papers and deacidifies her pianola manuscript papers with Wei T'o #10 spray. The collage is pasted with methyl cellulose and supported where necessary with heat-set Promatco tissue on gessoed Gatorboard. Like the music that is her inspiration, the finished pieces conceal their difficult problem-solving, exposing principally their joy.

ERIC QUAH
(Quah Kee Hiang)

Eric Quah (Quah Kee Hiang) was born in 1949 in Taiping, Malaysia. He emigrated to Australia in 1972. Having studied art first in Malaysia, then at the Caulfield Institute, Melbourne, where he gained diplomas, he now teaches art in Melbourne.

Quah started doing collages in 1973. Although he also draws and paints in oil and mixed media, collage is his main vehicle for expressing the flexibility of his impressions.

His collages are often scaled to a small size and saturated with lucid colors that refer back to impressionism and fauvism. Underlying his abstraction are traditional spaces: windows, intimate rooms, whose colors are keyed to the emotions of their inhabitants. In some cases his veiled layers lead to the portrait itself, and in these pieces Quah's figural drawing works in gentle stylistic counterpoint to his abstract order.

Quah's collages are, in every mixture of styles, extremely painterly. He generally works with acrylics, oil pastel, charcoal, and pencil on Arches-Rives or Fabriano paper. The collages sometimes make use of magazine fragments, theater programs, photographs, and newspapers, but they are composed predominantly of his hand-painted archival papers and acid-free tissues. His shapes combine tearing with the clean use of scissors, Stanley knife and scalpel. His adhesive is Aquadhere PVA. Painting and collaging simultaneously, he sometimes builds by interlayering the two techniques to create tension and visual effects. This is apparent in his piece called "Time," which is filled with the motion and the obliteration which he associates with American culture. Quah has worked and exhibited in New York as well as in Australia. Consciously endeavoring to bridge the east and west in art, he has quietly grafted on his Chinese upbringing the urgency of American media, the light of the impressionists, and Australian domestic interiors.

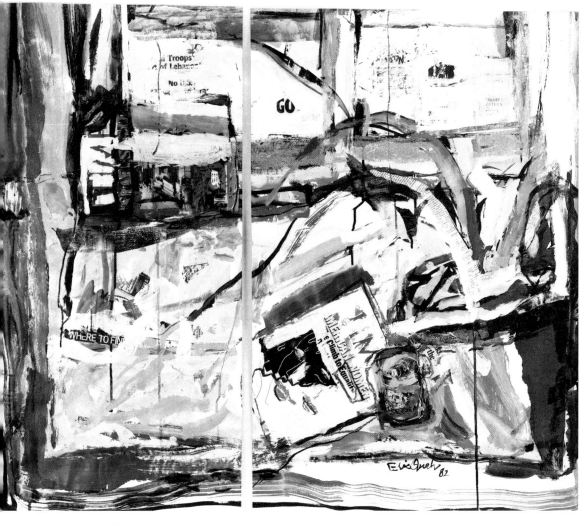

89 Eric Quah: *Time* (1982). Mixed media and paper collage, $42 \times 54\frac{1}{4}$ in.

ROBERT QUIJADA

Born in 1935 in Los Angeles, Robert Quijada has purposefully established his studio on the fringe of New York's garment district. There, among the discarded remnants, he discovers materials and visual ideas to be transformed by the process of collage.

Quijada views his work, begun in 1970, as a "celebration of the visual senses." In calling it "ceremonial," he refers back to his Mexican-American heritage, the complex designs of weaving, temple steles, and the Codex. But Quijada does not draw his imagery overtly from these sources. Instead, he works from "a refinement of what I've seen in the streets," streets where he frequently photographs the abstract patterns of drain, dumpsters, and cracked walls. These he interprets with elegance. Instead of rejecting the obvious symptoms of poverty and urban decay, he finds in them a source of beauty that he seeks to convey.

Quijada's sensuous collage-constructions are "natural artifacts" that beautify street ideas. His materials, too, come from the street, not only the fabrics but cast-off wooden moldings from a nearby theatrical set company. He transforms these into elaborate patterns that he sees as running through all aspects of nature – including human.

His collages begin with a specific idea that might be about color or form, often abstracted from his photographic studies. To execute this, he usually limits his color range for a series of about fifteen pieces, often emphasizing earth tones, grays, muted reds, or blues. Then with a combination of acrylic paint, wax crayon, and Rhoplex AC-33 (used to build solder-like textural areas) he paints canvas and fabric pieces with a variety of patterns that he will work into the overall design. Working on one collage piece at a time, he builds a compositional idea symmetrically, playing off an oblique counterpoint of asymmetry against the central division.

Despite the apparent simplicity of design, the composition is complex. Even his 1979 paper collage series involved seam-stitching as well as pasting linear fragments. His new canvas and fabric pieces are worked on stretchers, sometimes in multiple layers. He uses PVA adhesive for paper and canvas, and in these pieces wraps canvas around wooden elements which are nailed and pasted into place, and sometimes tied with twine which he hand-dyes in acrylic paint. Ultimately, despite their sculptural basis, Quijada's collage-constructions leave the viewer with an impression of flat surfaces made rich.

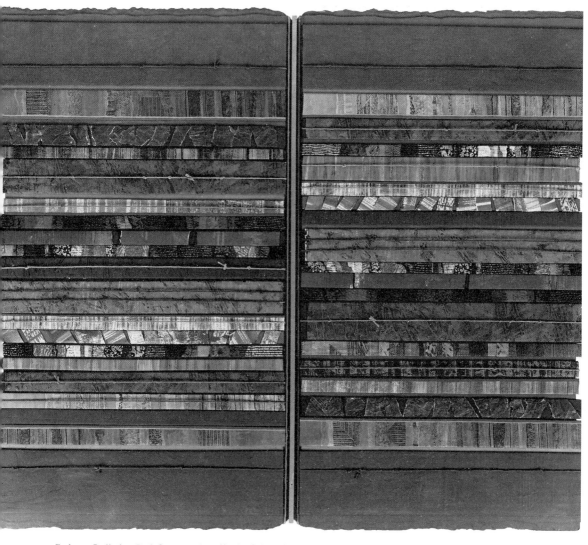

90 Robert Quijada: *Red Construction #2* (1982). Mixed media, 29 × 36 in. Courtesy Ericson Gallery, New York.

ROBERT RAUSCHENBERG

In 1986 Robert Rauschenberg is expected to complete *Quarter Mile Piece*, the longest painting ever made. His "whole earth catalogue" is a vast personal symbol of art's exploration and connectedness. Rauschenberg's explorations are launched from his remote satellite base on the offshore Florida island of Captiva, where he is a man at home in his native South.

Rauschenberg was born in Port Arthur, Texas, in 1925. After high school and a tour of duty in the Navy during the Second World War, he studied painting at the Kansas City Art Institute and for one year in 1947 at the Académie Julien in Paris. At Black Mountain College in 1948 he "worked hard but poorly,"* he recalls, under the discipline of Josef Albers and studied photography. Albers's color theory provoked Rauschenberg to questioning and revolt, which persisted in the self-color paintings done in the years (1949–52) that brought him to New York and the Art Students League.

The route from Black Mountain to New York was one commonly traveled by contemporary collagists, and on Rauschenberg the painter it left a distinctly material impulse which is felt in the collage *Black Painting* of 1952. Composing freely with color grounds, he began also to intrude material objects, insisting that they retain their identity. He called the paintings "combines," and beyond the associative gathering they began a reaping of the world for materials and images that would take him on global journeys.

In the early fifties he traveled to Italy and Morocco; then back in New York he began friendships with John Cage and Merce Cunningham, for whom he undertook stage lighting and design. Music became important to him in opening the possibility of making paintings as distinct to each observer as sound is to each member of a concert audience. Collaboration, another idea gathered from music, exerted an influence on his working style along with performance. Frequently he made his art in public and addressed it as an act of giving to special people.

The autobiographical gesture extended to his imagery, and the paintings evolved as encyclopedic collages that were diaries and inventories of his experience. Marshall McLuhan's announcement that "the medium is the message" (1967) was something of a belated proclamation for Rauschenberg. Over more than a decade he had already been investigating art as an extension of communication media.

In 1958–59 he happened on a printing process that gave him expanded access to the imagery of mass communication. By soaking newsprint and magazine images with lighter fluid and then rubbing them against a new surface, he found that he could make transfer prints and pile up iconography in a single plane without cutting. Using this new manner of *frottage* he generated illustrations for Dante's *Inferno*, interpreted in the political context of contemporary America. The same technique

*Andrew Forge, *Robert Rauschenberg* (New York: Harry N. Abrams, 1970).

afforded him an image base for his silk-screen paintings, begun in a deliberate effort "to escape from the familiarity of objects and collage."**

Escape from familiarity has led Rauschenberg through many circles of his own voyaging, and in recent years the circles have widened. The artist who once threshed the fields for useful junk has lately turned from the cast-offs of materialism to the origins of craftsmanship.

Sponsored by Gemini G.E.L., Los Angeles, he went in 1973 to the fourteenth-century papermill of Richard de Bas in Ambert, France. In 1975 Gemini sponsored a second trip to the famous Sarebai family of papermakers in Ahmedabad, India.

The Rauschenberg Overseas Cultural Interchange (ROCI) has become a public, even political activity that marks a new stage in his expansion of communications and collaborations. One message is peace. In 1983 a 150-piece retrospective of his art on a world-wide tour opened in Peking. A second message is mutual aid. The man who has endlessly pursued and symbolized art as a non-restrictive cultural expression has himself felt a need to experience and work with the most historically ancient root materials of art.

In this latest stage Rauschenberg has also revitalized his impulse to collage. In 1982, again sponsored by Gemini G.E.L., he made a trip to Jing Xian, Anhui Province, in the People's Republic of China. There, at the world's oldest surviving papermill, he collaborated in the making of 491 sheets that have since been constructed into seventy sets of paperworks.

Each of the China collages is supported on a thirty-sheet layered foundation of thin Xuan paper. The classical dignity of large relief Chinese characters molded in paper pulp and elegant pendants made from embroidered silk invest the collages with a ceremonial reverence that issues from the sense of place and people as well as from the paper itself.

On the same tour Rauschenberg shot eighty rolls of film, from which he made *Summerhill*, a 100-foot-long photomontage of daily life in China. He traveled on to Shigaraki in Japan to collaborate in producing a series of silk-screen ceramics at the Otsuka-Ohmi clayworks. Since then he has been to Sri Lanka and Thailand and continues to travel, making international relations of his autobiography and art. *Color illustration XVII.*

**Ibid.

MIRIAM SCHAPIRO

The flower is rooted in a heart, the heart entwined in a chain of quilted boxes that harbor the memory of women's work. Miriam Schapiro calls her collages "femmage," with sanctified allusion to the handwork of anonymous women whose sewing, needlework, appliqué, samplers, embroidery, scrapbooks, and valentines have gone unrecognized as art for centuries. Her work is a ritualized act of "repairing the omission, the historical loss, by bringing these women along" with her into the vital present of acknowledged personal creativity. In her art, the anonymous history of feminine decoration also becomes a major component of autobiography.

Schapiro, who was born in Toronto, Canada, in 1923, has been from her earliest childhood trained to art. Her father, an artist and industrial designer, taught her to draw by the age of six. She studied at home, and once she moved to the U.S.A. at evening classes connected with the WPA (Works Progress Administration). After two years at Hunter College, she transferred to the State University of Iowa, where she gained a B.A., M.A., and M.F.A. There, too, she met the painter Paul Brach, whom she married.

With Brach, Schapiro became involved during the fifties in the New York School attached to abstract expressionism. Like her training, the abstract perspective seems to her in retrospect a masculine point of view – spare, formal, and empty of decoration. Slowly, unconsciously at first, her work began to admit femininity. The earliest changes are reflected in her "shrine" paintings of the sixties, which progressively shaped formal space into totemic boxes housing personal symbols: iconic references to the history of art, an egg identified with herself, "unopened, uncracked," a silver mirror that encouraged reflections of self. The golden arch atop her "shrines" always had an "aspirational" significance, and it was clear that her personal aspiration included gaining acceptance for the feminine perspective in the male-dominated mainstream of traditional art.

She became receptive to decoration – the patterns of folk art that had intrigued her since childhood but were taboo in formal training. Now, with her own acquired formality, she could go back to them consciously, even politically, to fill the empty spaces of abstraction with a decorative sensibility. Her new goal was to "heroicize" feminine shapes and objects by presenting them as stately art.

From painting she shifted to collage, asserting the materials and techniques of decoration as a basis for her statement. "Being a feminist," she adds, "did not make me give up traditional training in form and structure." Indeed, the formal element defines her patterning more sharply. She has deliberately chosen "trivialized" objects for the formal circumference of her work: the heart, the fan, kimono, and house, establishing them as archetypal vessels of feminine meaning that she fills with complexity.

This she has pressed even to a monumental scale. Her "Anatomy of a Kimono" (1976) expanded, opened, embellished, and flaunted the architecture of dress in a

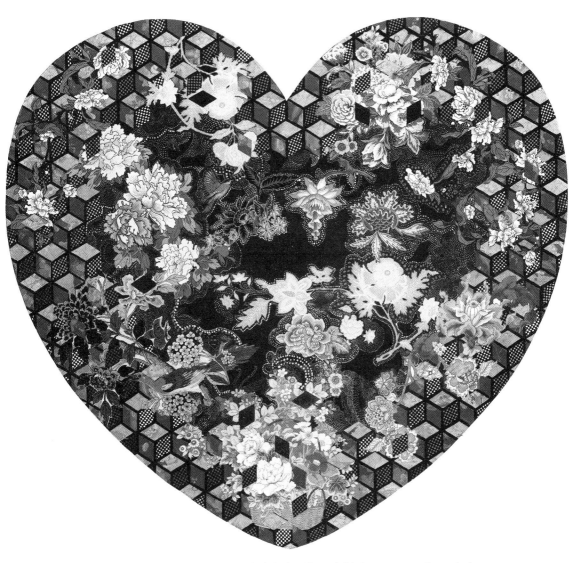

91 Miriam Schapiro: *A Garden in Paradise* (1982). Acrylic and fabric on canvas, 64 × 69 in.
Courtesy Lerner-Heller Gallery, New York.

"femmage" mural 52 feet in length, embracing an entire room. Although she does not typically work to this scale, even her smaller pieces expand the dimensions of intimacy.

Worked with paper, fabrics, and acrylic, Schapiro's collages pivot on a balance of form and emotion. She uses the hard-edge geometries of traditional quilt patterns deliberately against the curvilinear flowers and vines to establish this fundamental balance. Her studio has the look of a haberdashery – hundreds of boxes and drawers that organize her patterns and templates by color and form. She uses stencils and die shapes to cut her lexicon of building blocks. The solid colors are often cut from Color-Aid, but she also uses patterned gift wrap, Japanese Mingei, and papers of all sorts. Likewise she is a collector of fabrics, from new printed cloths of all textures and weights to old lace and needlework cultivated for the delicacy they arouse by contrast with bold flowers.

In making a collage Schapiro works without preconceived ideas. She composes from a diverse assortment of pre-cut geometric and floral shapes that she pastes spontaneously to her shaped backing paper as the piece progresses. Her choice of PVA (Jade 403) permits her to reverse the adhesive with alcohol if necessary, but principally she develops her interweaving of images with a view to their organic development, uncensored by revision. The smaller collages are backed onto Arches, the larger onto cotton duck canvas covered with acrylic gesso. The finished pieces, pressed under heavy weights, are also sealed with a four-layer protective coat of acrylic matte medium.

Schapiro's latest direction includes the use of enlarged photo silkscreen images of antique children's clothing printed on fabric. In this innovative pattern cutting, as in the whole of her work, she dignifies the ornamental dress of innocence.

DAVID SINGER

David Singer was born in 1941 in Bethlehem, Pennsylvania. Although mainly a self-taught artist, he did study for one year at Penn State University, after which he enlisted in the Navy as a radio operator. During his Navy junkets between California and the Far East, he began to devote his free time to studying art.

When he started montaging in 1965, it was in the climate of San Francisco's Haight-Ashbury period. Music flourished at the Fillmore West, and Singer made his reputation designing photomontage posters for its owner, Bill Graham. When the ballroom closed in 1971, Singer's poster work continued in a studio shared jointly with Sätty and another montage artist, Nick Nickolds. Over the past decade his interest has shifted to the sacred geometry and its mythic associations with eastern and western symbolism. This has culminated in a series of mandala prints and goddess images.

Mythic force and symmetry have exerted a continuous influence on Singer's work. His montages are not merely surreal; they have a strong visionary quality which avoids sheer caprice or fancy. The strength of imagery and profusion of intense color in his work are subject to an austere sense of composition, with the result that seemingly disconnected elements unify into an imaginative whole. If they appear to be dream visions they are more archetypal than personal, and that too removes them from surrealism.

Even the early work is akin to the mandala. Singer's compositional strength lies in his focal point of simplicity. His posters are often constructed on a powerful composite central image floating against a mysterious landscape: a fractured stone mask on a field of red pills; a silhouette crucifixion set on an auto junkheap. Capturing the mood of their time, his concert posters reinvest the familiar American landscape with the barrenness of a forbidding, alien world.

Yet, in all Singer's work there is a strongly implied spiritual dimension that relieves the desolation. Sometimes it is expressed by planetary space, otherwise by Christian or Oriental references. In one montage, entitled "Harvest," the Madonna and Child preside over scenes of lush plenitude and fertility. With the density of Dutch still-life and the intensity of a Samuel Palmer, the piece opens into idyllic scenes of Western farmers and dancing graces that retreat through arbors into distant space. Singer's perfect meld of color detail and complex formal balance tricks our belief in the unity of this paradise.

The conviction of unity in Singer's work comes from his skill. He works simply from color photography, composing a layout on the floor before fixing the image in place with spray adhesive. His tools are a pair of barber's shears for cutting large surfaces and small German scissors for fine detail. The fineness of his manipulation is conveyed by the final impression. *Color illustration XVIII.*

KLAUS STAECK

Since as far back as the Berlin dadaists during and after the First World War, Germany has always been strong in political satire. With the rise of Hitler in the 1930s the work of John Heartfield developed a savagery not witnessed before. The Heartfield/Herzfelde tradition is revived in contemporary Germany in the work of two brothers, Klaus (in West) and Rolf Staeck (in East Germany).

Klaus Staeck (b. 1938) published a catalogue that he calls a *Staeckbrief*. The pun on his name means a "wanted poster" and suggests the political thrust of his work. Staeck's enemies are enemies of the people: tyrants, aggressors, warmongers, powerful conglomerates, and the smug bourgeoisie. He directs subversive barbs at their complacency in satirical posters and postcards, which he began to make in 1960 during his training in law at Heidelberg University. A professional lawyer, Staeck has worked over the past twenty-five years as an artist on behalf of radical politics. Since 1970 his productions for Edition Staeck (begun 1965) have been in collaboration with the printer Gerhard Steidl of Göttingen, and he chooses to regard his prolific output as the work of a firm.

Advertised in his *Staeckbrief*, many of his political collages are based on puns or arresting discrepancies between language and image. The Oil Prince, for example, is a seabird with blackened feathers contaminated by an oil spill. The proverbial expression "at the center is always the man" he illustrated with a faceless head that has been replaced by universal consumer product stripes. "Nobody is perfect" shows Mona Lisa handicapped in a wheelchair.

Staeck is a generator of visual expressions for ideas of global significance. Even when he makes dadaist allusions, like his play on the much-abused Mona Lisa or his human bodies with grafted heads, he does so with great originality and visual clarity. His intent is to turn advertising against itself and reveal the inner horror. He cites John Heartfield as a primary influence on his work. Like Heartfield, Staeck emphasizes the isolation and distortion of his satiric victims. His collages are essentially visual parodies of advertising layouts.

His promotional literature too is a retaliation in kind against the political-industrial complex. Not only is he organized as a mail-order business for postcards, posters, graphic art, and books on social and political issues, he also has an instruction pamphlet for mounting a show of his work in public places. Staeck's neo-dada, well beyond game-playing, is a strategy of opposition complete with cut-out coupons.

92 Klaus Staeck: *Im Mittelpunkt steht immer der Mensch* (1981). Postcard,
$4\frac{1}{8} \times 5\frac{7}{8}$ in.

ROLF STAECK

Since 1976 Rolf Staeck in East Germany has also been involved in media collage satire, focusing on posters and postcards. To receive one of his productions is to receive a jolt. It is meant to spoil your breakfast, more perhaps than the daily news to which it is akin, for his images portray the violent and ironic implications of an everyday political reality that we have come passively to accept. Staeck makes clear in his imagery that there are no more sacred cows, only dying institutions that would profit from being led to the slaughter. He strikes at political and social injustice and at their poisonous roots in industrialism.

In one collage entitled, "Bitte Freilassen" (Please Set Free), a blackened town is depicted as dwarfed by huge, smoking, factory chimneys. Above the black-and-white image, in a blue summer sky, the imploring caption is printed in red, strongly implying the power of industry to blacken the world. In another postcard collage, "IKARUS made in usa," a dead American soldier, seemingly fallen from the sky, is draped over dollar bills. Behind him, his helmet and machine gun stand as a marker against the blackened, perhaps napalmed sky.

Staeck's texts, like exposé newspaper headlines, are aggressive with horror, threat, and disturbing truth. Text, together with composite pictures, creates a tension-field in the collages which emphasizes the bitterness and irony inherent in the modern world. Staeck's materials are photographs from newspapers, periodicals, and journals as well as his own photographs. In his art he returns to the media an editorial based on the reportage of fact.

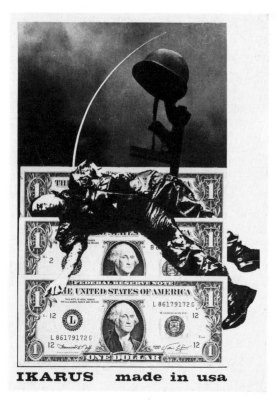

93 Rolf Staeck: *IKARUS made in usa* (1980). Postcard, reproduction of paper collage, in commercial circulation, $4\frac{1}{4} \times 5\frac{7}{8}$ in.

R. PATRICK SULLIVAN

Born on Long Island, New York, in 1931, R. Patrick Sullivan has been doing collage for sixteen years. "I came to collage through my first trip to Europe about twenty years ago. I was so impressed with the art and different life styles I encountered, that I collected souvenirs and shaped them into collages as a way of preserving the experience."

Since then, he insists, his collages have been influenced by Schwitters, Picasso, Ernst, and Cornell, though in his approach to found objects he has developed a distinctive style that is consciously directed to his audience. In one series, for example, he transforms figurative engravings into seasonal greetings cards that are photocopied and actually sent. These collaged emblems of Winter, Spring, Summer, and Autumn all carry elaborate messages appropriate to the time of year that is also represented by the landscape, allegorical figure, and cornucopia of surrounding objects.

Communication, the motive of these collages, is central to Sullivan's work. "Most people in our society," he complains, "are intimidated by art, by its obscurity. And this should not be." For them, he converts everyday objects into collages that lend a beauty to the recognizable. His series of paper bags, for example, employ ordinary brown sacks, some painted some plain, from which mysterious objects float out. Their simplicity is tantalizing, drawing the viewer into the magic of daily experience.

All his materials come from his immediate world: carbon paper, newsprint, photos and postcards, tickets, retrieved in a spirit of recycling. "Sometimes I

94 R. Patrick Sullivan: *Lady with Note* (1977). 8½ × 11 in.

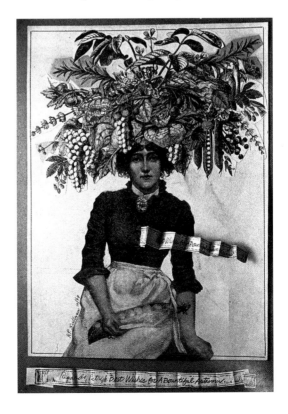

deliberately limit myself to things I have found in the street to prove that a picture can be discovered this way. I have developed an eagle eye for garbage dumps that embarrasses friends who walk out with me."

For Sullivan, who lives and works in Manhattan, the street is a source of powerful transformation comparable to theater. There is a strong connection in his work between collage and theater since Sullivan has designed theater sets and is also an actor. In each medium his goal is communication – to reach the audience through a heightened and disciplined portrayal of real life. It is appropriate that he has recently applied his collage aesthetic to portraits of real people, in which the central figure is represented by fragmentary clues and props gathered from the subject's belongings. All Sullivan's collages are, in a sense, like miniature stage sets manufactured to involve us in mystery plays.

He works with a cutting tool of the simplest type: a single-edged razor blade. Sometimes painting his materials, he composes one collage at a time, setting the final composition in place with spray adhesive.

WILLIAM TILLYER

William Tillyer was born in 1938 in Middlesbrough, Yorkshire. He studied at the Middlesborough College of Art for four years, the Slade School of Fine Art in London for two years, and spent a further six months studying with Stanley William Hayter at Atelier 17 in Paris. Since 1963, Tillyer has held many visiting lectureships from London and Bath to Brown University (Providence, Rhode Island) and the University of Melbourne where he was artist-in-residence in 1981.

Tillyer has gone his own way, working diligently to master his distinctive style and technique. At almost every turning, technique has had its special bearing. Tillyer works in paper collage, principally using Arches paper and Pritt Glue Stick. Fragments of his own etchings and drawings frequently serve him as collage material. In his latest print series he sometimes creates the illusion of collage and sometimes a genuine collage surface. His structured compositions have, in addition to their volume and balance, a primal urgency that comes from his bold, diagonal colored markings. Despite their abstract patterning, they have a figurative content which suggests a second layer of style and meaning.

It is not surprising that Tillyer has applied his collage technique of layering to work in other media: drawings, to which he has added collage; etchings, in which he has collaged metal and plastic elements directly to the plate using epoxy resins.

In collaging, Tillyer has experimented with subtracting as well as adding layers. In an etching, for example, he may cut an aperture through the plate (subtracting) at the same time collaging a different layer onto the surface.

The balance of aperture and layer is perhaps most personally rendered in his "mesh paintings" (1977–80), made by collaging elements onto a metal screen which becomes the frame and support for other systems of form and imagery. Tillyer also made a series of canvas collage paintings based on the Victorian terrace architecture of Melbourne, with its ornamental facades and cast iron punctuated by foliage.

The wire mesh frame has also served Tillyer as a collage grid for interior still-life studies. In these, as in his facades, the white wall visible through the mesh plays deliberately against the fretwork and colored collage patterns. In working these large pieces, Tillyer uses acrylic gel as both a paint medium and an adhesive. By the collage process he builds texture and color in an accretion of forms secured to the painted screen.

His most recent painting has taken him back to oil on stretched canvas. Here, as in the Australian group, he cuts the canvas away to expose the wall, which then becomes a plane of the work. Layering is as essential as collage is to Tillyer's energetic construction of vibrant surfaces that lure his viewer to the inner core. *Color illustration XIX.*

JOHN URBAIN

John Urbain has been working in collage for more than sixteen years. He came to the medium through a fortuitous encounter with the folds of a piece of cloth which suggested to him their potential for collage. But even this chance occurrence had roots in design and very consciously in the *matière* studies encouraged by Josef Albers at Black Mountain College. Much more than Albers's well-known color studies, the exercises in surface textures designed to cultivate the tactile sense were extremely influential on Urbain's work. "Through the combination of materials we become sensitive to the subtle transitions and transformations of surface qualities. . . . We use materials seen in everyday experiences, change their original form and discover they take on an entirely different meaning."

Urbain is particularly drawn to the textures of fabrics and leather, which he fuses into composition with papers new and old, wood, acrylic, and tempera paint. The response of the viewer is important to Urbain, especially the response to the materials and their transformation, a kind of delightful guessing game of surface textures and their origins in the *matière* study tradition.

At the core of his abstraction are dominant shapes – monolithic posts and lintels, or the strong circles of the sun and moon. The landscape of Block Island, off the coast of Long Island, has been a perpetual source of inspiration in these collages. From the place he often gathers a sense of time or simply a feeling that generates composition. Even people, or the circle of their eyes alone, lead Urbain to abstraction. "Sometimes I don't have any idea prior to composition. Then, the subconscious asserts itself. I take a piece of masonite and begin with a color, like raw umber, or a piece that feels right. From the color or form something will grow."

Since 1968 Urbain has also been involved with poetry, and as a writer strongly influenced by William Carlos Williams, he feels that poetry has enlarged his painting vocabulary. "In poetry you can write *behind* an image." The importance of the ground behind the image is strongly felt in his collages, where his assertive shapes play against deep areas of sienna, orange, purple, red, or brown.

In working with paper, he often scrubs found materials with color. All his papers are treated with acrylic matte medium gel as a protective overlay. His adhesive is Polybond BW-1283, a polymer developed for the Philip Morris Corporation. He uses this adhesive for cloth as well as the papers that he backs onto masonite.

A native of Brussels, where he was born in 1920, Urbain moved to Detroit, Michigan, as a child and has also lived in Philadelphia, Paris, and since 1953 New York, where he continues to explore life's textures and surfaces in collage paintings.

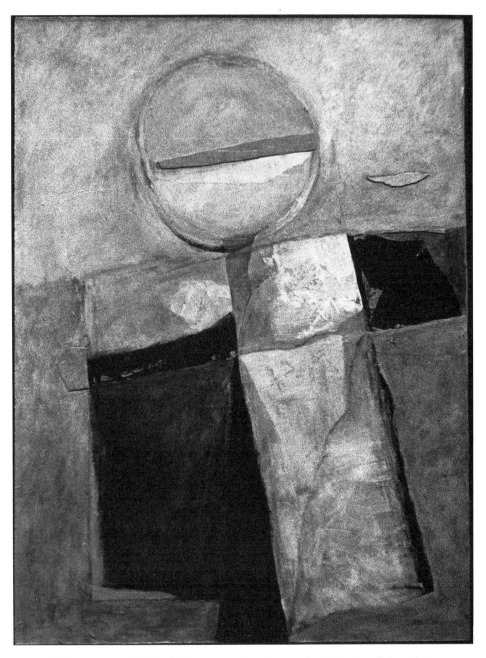

95 John Urbain: *Dancer C.U.* (1982). Mixed media, 48 × 36 in. Collection of the artist.

ESTEBAN VICENTE

Esteban Vicente was born in 1903 in the province of Segovia, Spain. As a young man he studied at the Real Academia de Bellas Artes de San Fernando in Madrid, where he was trained in the masterwork tradition. In 1925 he moved to Paris, but by 1932 the vitality of New York exerted a strong attraction on him. In 1936 he made the move, which introduced him to the influence of Demuth, Dove, and Ryder. Later Vicente became attached directly to the New York School by virtue of his overwhelming abstractions.

In the course of his career he has shifted across the whole American landscape, teaching in colleges and universities that include Puerto Rico, Black Mountain, Princeton, Yale, New York University, Columbia, and California; and he has been artist-in-residence from Boston and Des Moines to the Honolulu Academy of Arts in Hawaii.

He has never lost his European charm and personality. At eighty, he still acts and speaks like a Spanish courtier, but his artistic vision is charged with the quintessential abstraction of modernity. For Vicente, whose painterly style applies even to collage, the subject of art now can best be described as a refinement of sensations – mystery, the quality of being human. This, for him, is not related to specific "things," though it may contain a hint of landscape or interior. Since surrealism, he argues, there are no more movements of ideas. More than ever, the institutions that once supported art have dissolved, leaving the artist no longer a professional but an isolated being for whom the void is real. "You do what you do. If you do that with honesty and believe it, somebody will react." Vicente, who works throughout the year, divides his time between his studio in New York City, where he draws and collages, and Bridgehampton, Long Island, where he paints in the spring and summer months.

Vicente started as a painter in oils. He came to collage while teaching in the summer of 1950 at Berkeley, California. Isolated, without his paints but with a need to work, he cut up a Sunday color supplement and composed his first collage. This piece generated a later painting, and while he has since used collages as "sketches" for paintings, collage itself developed as an alternative medium that he pursues separately. "The material of collage," as he perceives it, "is given. You don't make it, you transform it. Paper is paper. It has a physicality that you use in that sense. Collage becomes like painting, in fact is a way of painting."

Many of Vicente's collages are executed on the scale of his large paintings and with a painter's frame of reference. He works on stretched, unprimed canvas, over which he pastes a layer of supportive backing paper. For all his collages the adhesive is organic starch, wallpaper hanger's paste (Foxpaste). He mixes the powdered material with water and applies the paste with brushes, finally flattening elements to the surface with a roller. His collage elements, cut and torn to achieve distinctive, complementary edges, are made from Japanese papers. Currently he has been

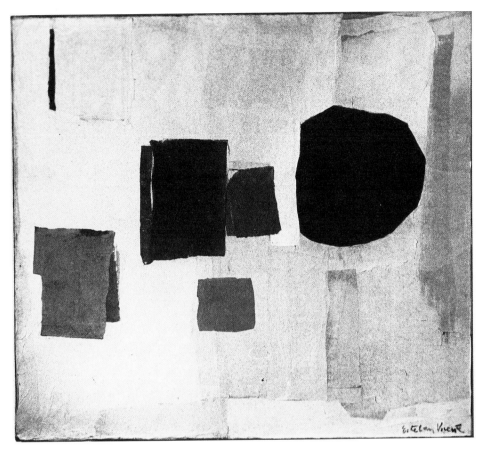

96 Esteban Vicente: *Untitled* (1982). Paper on canvas, 36 × 40 in. Courtesy the Gruenebaum Gallery, New York.

painting them with acrylic, completing a quantity of assorted colors in preparation to collage.

Each collage is worked, one at a time, to its final composition. As in painting, he often sketches in charcoal an underlying order, but the pieces are worked from sensation without preconception as he shifts the forms around with tacks in a process of evolution. Colors rich with shifting light play on the surface by contrast and gradation. Vicente has worked collages even in the high contrast of black and white, in complex rhythms of hard-edged shapes. In color too he uses the white edge of a torn paper as a statement of definition. But he also overlaps, blends, comingles shapes and grounds in a way that mysteriously defies horizon lines and discrete planes of being. His most recent work limits the spatial geometries to isolated rectangles with softened, curved edges and circles with surprising angularity. These floating abstractions of evocative color convey sensations gathered from life with philosophic calm.

CYNTHIA VILLET

For twenty years a resident of Barbados in the West Indies, Cynthia Villet has lived and worked formerly in England, Canada, Africa, and Israel. Descended from a family of painters, she studied painting at the Sir John Case School of Art in London and at the Vancouver School of Fine Art.

Her ideas are formulated from the interplay of color and the abstraction of classical shapes. The forms of letters, of Renaissance man, of transparent glass bottles have played a strong figural role in her investigation of resemblances. Interested in the relationship between illusion and reality, Villet has in the past five years made collage her primary medium. The shift came for aesthetic reasons, "including freedom" to design expressively from a variety of materials.

The materials include newsprint, stamps, flour bags, gold leaf, antique fabrics, canvas, bits of calligraphic material both borrowed and made. All these she combines freely with inks, watercolors, and the exotic papers she manufactures herself from cotton, papyrus, banana leaf fibers, and various local tropical grasses.

In their personal combination of the old and new, Villet's collages form a bridge between the traditional aesthetic of found papers and the deliberate cultivation of the exquisite handmade. Often she uses a contrast of the two in her collage compositions. In a different sense she also uses the contrast of her papers in their own right as textured background for collages. In this particular style she centers a collage directly on the wet pulp of a mold-made sheet, spot pasting it with PVA. Then the two layers – collage and backing sheet – are pressed together so that, in drying, the collage bonds to the cast paper forming a single piece.

In her papermaking, as in her traditional collage, she is interested in reforming and recycling materials – often with a history. Influenced by the atmosphere and light of the West Indies, her collages reflect the nuances of bleached tropical colors given to mysterious shadows. The works are small yet highly constructed and meticulously complete.

Villet uses a variety of adhesives: acrylic media and PVA. She presses her work under heavy plate glass and seals the top surface with diluted acrylic matte medium, which she sometimes paints. Thus her bleached colors and old papers are securely stabilized. The completed collage is drymounted to linen-covered matboard and framed in a window mat which opens onto her miniature island world. *Color illustration XX.*

SUSANA WALD (*see* Ludwig Zeller)

MARILYN MAGALIFF WEISS

Marilyn Magaliff Weiss has been working in collage since 1965. Her technique has evolved from originally integrating figure drawings from the model with opaque, found patterned papers. These early works have metamorphosed into extremely large collage paintings still based on life drawing but now combined with thin, transparent papers and cloth that swathe the nudes in a kind of faceless brooding.

Even the compositions originate in a collage pattern of thought. For six months Weiss works from a model, doing individual line drawings. Then, as she prepares for a painting, she selects figure drawings that might be integrated to a single composition. Projecting them from negatives onto a canvas, she enlarges the small sketches, setting them into the new relationship by drawing each in place from the sharp white lines of the negative image.

Once she has laid down a color ground, the figures are collaged and painted simultaneously, as if the two were a single technique governed by emotional spontaneity. She uses acrylic gloss medium to set down her papers and fabric,

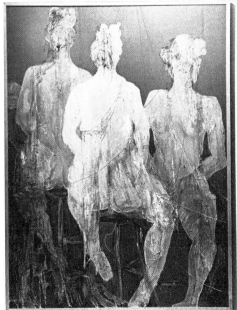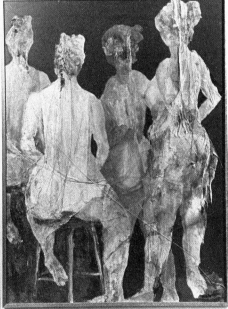

97 Marilyn Magaliff Weiss: *Waiting* (1982). Mixed media on canvas, 60 × 90 in. Collection of the artist.

working the medium also with her color. The matte medium, she finds, serves a secondary purpose in covering over pieces without leaving visible marks.

Even the thinnest tissues, packing materials, string, yarn and gauze she breaks down further by washing, bleeding, bleaching, and tinting. Many of the materials are drawn from her life – sewing patterns (she began in fashion design), blueprints, computer printouts, bandages. But the memories are forgotten and the artifacts faded and colored by the time they become the fabric of her large, classical figures. "I do not want the collage material to have its own identity or integrity – but that which I give it."

Even the identity and integrity of the figures are, in a sense, withheld. The august nudes are generally without faces and the wrappings often bind them mysteriously. The application of collage to classical figure painting is itself an exceedingly personal statement unique to these works.

MICK WOOTEN

Mick Wooten was born in the San Joaquin Valley, California, in 1950 and raised in Los Angeles. A self-taught artist, he was introduced to collage through an art class in high school. After studying art for a short time, he became dissatisfied and turned to photography, finally leaving school altogether in order to develop and define his personal style of collage.

He has been making collages full time since 1966, and several have appeared in limited fine art editions. Wooten's work evokes a certain air of mystery in which the unexpected lures us out of complacence. We are fascinated, intrigued, and simultaneously frustrated by his suggestive combinations of imagery: a doll's face balanced against a cathedral dome, a madonna in peacock's feathers. The more we attempt to comprehend their relationships, the more we find that simple repetitions of gesture and form seduce us by their recurrences.

Wooten's material sources are many and varied: newspapers, magazine photos, advertisements, and art reproductions. The adhesives used are non-water base and his hand press method creates the illusion that the final image is united in a single plane.

Wooten's mysterious effects are achieved by his expressive techniques. His collages appear at first glance to be a hybrid of abstract and figurative styles, but a closer examination reveals a conscious balance of the two. This is mirrored in the arresting contrast of his edges. Because he tears, cuts, and burns his edges, he catches the viewer in shifting, ambiguous planes of reality. Even when Wooten gives us a complete framework that we recognize, like a map of the United States, his distortions of scale and imagery form a compositional balance that shakes us out of our separate allusions. In his "Ultra Mundane" world, the imaginative play of contrasts revives the idea of novelty. Wooten's collages invite comparison between the inner voyage and the world at large.

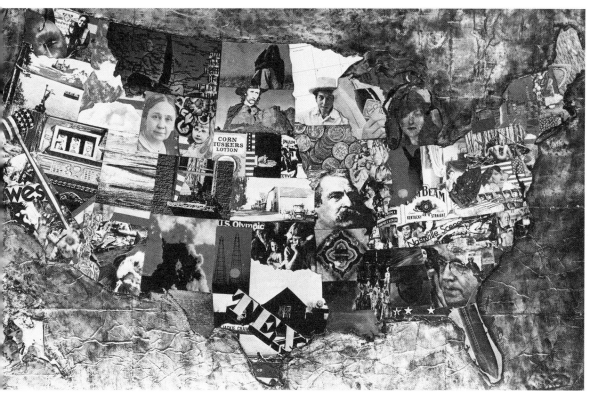

98 Mick Wooten: *Main Street* (1968). Magazine pictures, foil, india ink, 24 × 36 in.

FAITH-DORIAN WRIGHT

The work of Faith-dorian Wright goes back to the roots of collage in tribal expression. Heavily influenced by primitive art, she frequently chooses to employ its materials with deliberate allusion. The example of Bokongo people, who set their statues with mirrors, led her to evolve her own mirror series. In other pieces she employs leather, fibers, glass, sequins, decals, bark, leaves, and most dramatically, leaf silver and gold. These have a stunning impact in the "Moroccan Series," constructed in the radiating, floral geometries of Arabic tile designs. Lifted carefully on a brush, the leaf is set into wet pigment and allowed to dry, floating on the paint medium which acts as an adhesive.

The use of gold leaf in collage is an inspired application of a material Wright employs in bookbinding. Her bindings are themselves collages, in the tradition of Sonia Delaunay. They are composed of leather onlays applied to leather surfaces, over which she also draws in pen and ink or paints in oil. Binding takes her back to twelfth-century tools and methods, and it is not surprising that she frequently chooses to bind her treasured books about primitive art. She makes and paints her own papers, both to bind books and to make collage. And in making collages she often uses her bookbinding tools, as well as a variety of shears, nail scissors, and X-acto knives.

Influenced by the natural earth colors of tribal art, her papers (many handmade) are hand painted, making frequent use of powdered pigments – the latest of which is eye shadow! For a heavy paper, she sometimes uses large rolls of Arches, painting with water-based medium or acrylic, or coloring with Caran d'Ache pencils. She also uses Japanese papers, including the fretted Baika Lace. For her Chinese calligraphy series, she produced special batiked and dyed papers to accentuate the poetry of the delicately stitched and torn letter shapes.

Poetry has been a conscious influence on some of her collages, particularly the verse of A. R. Ammons, who writes about inner growth in relation to organic nature. This, too, is Wright's concern as a collagist, most visibly in her commitment to organic shapes, materials, and primitive allusions. Even in modern materials she finds a poetry that is tribal. Shattered pieces of a windshield she sets like totem crystal into one design; others are built on a graph-paper grid, stitched with needlepoint. Her most unusual discovery is Polaroid "Thermograms," pictures of muscle structure that register in red, yellow, and green like African textiles. These she cuts up and uses as overlays. Finally, influenced by textiles, her latest collages are a series of three-dimensional hangings and fans that suggest the shed garments of ritual magic.

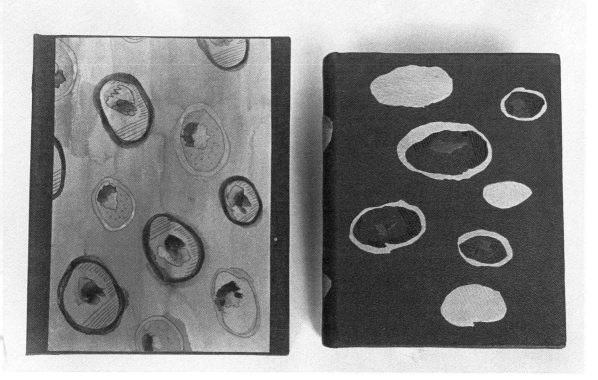

99 Faith-dorian Wright: Two collage leather bindings. *Left*, 12 × 9½ in., *right*, 10½ × 9½ in. Collection of the artist.

TADANORI YOKOO

Born in 1936 in Nishiwaki, Japan, Tadanori Yokoo is known internationally as a graphic designer. His posters, books, and record album covers respond to modern ambiguity with Zen calm. Since 1964 he has pursued collage as a route to reality – not the world we see, but the world of his mind's eye. He imagines and dreams a spectacle of self-knowledge and everlasting spirit that he sometimes calls paradise.

Desire that leads to paradise implies a rejection of all that is wasteful in modern material culture. And if he sometimes depicts the ugliness of materialism, he does so to emphasize what he considers the dead-end of this world and to rekindle the quest for eternity. It is his unique vision to apply this spiritual purpose even to commercial design. Thus he meets ambiguity on its own terms.

Cutting his images from magazine sources, he constructs a new and complex photographic reality that shows the dramatic contrast between the world as it is – overcrowded, violent, competitive, sexual, atomic – and the ideal world of placid space that is ordered and harmonic. Indeed, Yokoo's advertisements are laced with subliminal appeals for political vision. One apocalyptic ad for Dartimon cognac is constructed like gates of paradise. In the lower panels are crowded scenes of human turmoil. They flow upward to a sky torn by lightning and atomic clouds, which lead through religious altars into a cosmic eternity.

Yokoo's symmetry takes us there. In all his work symmetry is the structural expression of an ideal society. It is easy to see how Rodchenko's constructivist photomontages have had as decisive an influence on him as the dadaists' aggressive rejection of war and material values.

Like both, he is committed to political realism best expressed by the photographic image. While each photographic element stands as a single decisive moment of the real world, collage, in combining a multitude of such moments, becomes a force for expressing the simultaneity of time. Past, present, and future in harmonic balance represent Yokoo's eternity. "There is no balance in today's society," he argues, but collage can reconstruct a balance and present a vision that is missing, that we long for, and that is real.

Yokoo sometimes works as a traditional collagist, cutting his images from direct pictorial sources. Working in this style he builds a vocabulary of images from magazines, first without preconception of the final poster image. Arranged on a white background, themes and contrasts begin to assert themselves. In the first layout Yokoo fills all the blank spaces until the ideas manifest themselves clearly and the images solidify. He thinks symbolically, working to music and using the fire of incense to stabilize his mind and compose the order of the work. For him, the most difficult stage is filling the last space, like positioning the keystone of a building.

Once the composition is complete, he traces the final image as a template for pasting. Working from the back layer out, he still may make some slight shifts in imagery during the pasting process.

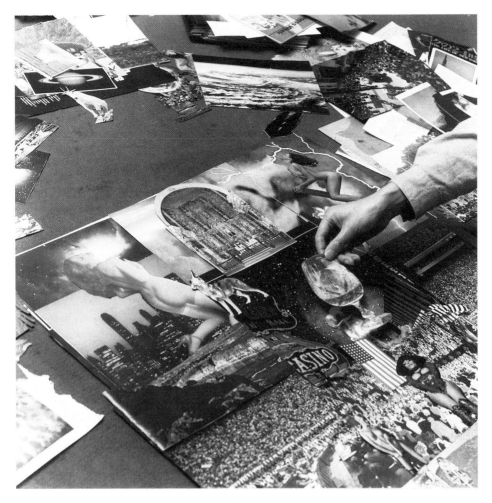

100 Tadanori Yokoo making the *Dartimon Collage*.

Not all of Yokoo's collages are made directly by cutting and pasting. Other photographic collages are essentially produced in camera. From original sources he traces the outlines of shapes he intends to use and composes from the tracings a final composition. Then a photographer shoots the separate images, makes four color separations, and prints them in place according to Yokoo's design.

He also uses copper plate printing of photographic images – both negative and positive – often linked with startling colors to produce bright green or purple figures that accentuate the heightened reality of dreams.

Yokoo's poster style is global. Into Japanese borders and landscapes intrude Indian gods, Ingres and Goya nudes, Adam, Eve, and rock bands. Theirs is a floating world watched over by the eternal eye.

LUDWIG ZELLER

"History and the superimposition of its events are the essence
of collage" in the eyes of Ludwig Zeller. "We live in quite
Byzantine times; wasn't Cairo built with the stones of
Memphis, and isn't it true that the streets of Egypt are paved
with the pyramids' hieroglyphs?"

In a sense Ludwig Zeller plays seriously at being a creator, an ancient god from a past culture. The impulse derives from his attachment to the void, the Atacama desert of northern Chile, where he was born in the town of Rio Loa in 1927. The barrenness left a deep impression on him as a child; it was so immense that in order to "people" it with men and objects, he had to go deep into his imagination. Zeller maintains that he could not even see the wind blowing, as there was nothing for it to touch or move.

Instead, the wind played upon him, as on an aeolian harp, and he became the instrument of poetry and vision. Zeller tells a remarkable story in which his father, an adventurous German-émigré engineer, fired his imagination by building large cardboard wheels. Placed in the desert at morning, the wheels would blow away towards a seemingly infinite horizon, yet on the following day, however mysteriously, they would blow back again to their original place of departure.

In Zeller's collages wheeling patterns and images subconsciously revive the mystery. Like the tidal flow of his father's cutouts, his own forms occupy a space surrounded by the void of the blank page. Often the collage itself suggests a circle, only partly completed by the shape and movement of the image. A pointing hand or figure, even a glance, appears to grasp at an object out of reach, like a carousel ring; and the energy of implied movement crosses the synapse to complete the circle. In this way, negative space plays dynamic effects in Zeller's compositions, just as the effect of the Chilean desert played upon his hunger to fill space.

No wonder this "hunger artist" pays homage to Kafka; no wonder he found refuge in a small group of surrealists harbored in Santiago, where he later moved until his 1971 emigration to Canada. Through the impact of surrealism, the circle back to the Europe abandoned by his father turned once again in his circle of imagery. Like Ernst, who originated the surreal application of nineteenth-century engravings, Zeller took his fragments from these European texts. But he built from them in a way that refers more to his father's engineered mechanisms than to the narratives of Ernst. Like machines shedding parts in rotation, his images spin off suggestive fragments from their central axis – his bones on the desert floor scattered by centrifugal force.

Zeller's collages, rarely rectangular or filled to the frame of a book plate, float suspended on the white page. The images, compounds of organic and mechanical parts, flow into a shapely whole that is of no species but includes all. In a sense, all his collages compose an alphabet of signs and structures, which he more deliberately works out in his *Alphacollage* (Erin, Ontario: The Porcupine's Quill, 1982).

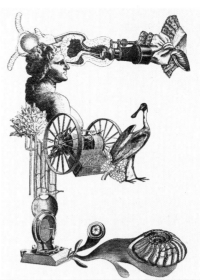

101 Ludwig Zeller: *"E" in the Alphacollage* (1979). Book illustration reproduced from paper collage, $6\frac{5}{8} \times 4\frac{3}{4}$ in. Collection of the artist.

Because we recognize the literal meaning of his design elements, we follow the flow with some reference to the meaning of his juxtaposed symbols. At the same time, we are conscious of their new contexts and new embodiment in baroque forms that cancel their origins. In two recent series, illustrations for Eugenio F. Granell's *Estela de Presagios* (Toronto: Oasis, 1981) and Edouard Jaguer's *La Poutre Creuse* (Toronto: Oasis, 1982), he sets ornate cuttings in black paper against the cold edges of severed machines and organic forms to fine effect, achieving a balance between images and templates of thought. Though he builds no narrative sequences, even in his books of collage, *50 Collages* (Oakville, Ontario: Mosaic Press, 1981), his imagery prompts the viewer to search for an allegory like the paintings of Arcimboldi.

In all his work, despite the brutality of anatomical and mechanical parts, there is a rococo delicacy which he achieves through fine cutting with scissors and knives. These tools also appear as recurrent imagery suggestive of his mental operations. His rare use of torn paper edges is calculated to startle by contrast against his dominant curves. For all his work he uses acrylic matte medium adhesive, occasionally varnishing over when the collage is part of a larger composition. These are sometimes undertaken in collaboration with his wife, Susana Wald.

"Perhaps the most transcendent aspect of the evolution of my collages is not so much the techniques or the media that I have used but rather the fact that I have been able to establish a collaboration as equals with my wife, creating a new reality. The work is not quite hers or mine but of a sort of third persona that is this *us*. The images that we have made we call 'mirages' because in doing them a changing and hallucinating phantasmagoria evolves. We have decided as our 'modus operandi' that I first make a collage, leaving it at a point where it seems complete. It then hangs on the wall in Susana's studio for some time, days, weeks, often months. There is an element of contemplation and daydreaming involved. Then the delicate drawing starts, like invisible wings or swarms that move in the negative spaces or even directly on top of the collage; at other times color is applied, directly around and glazing over the collage, transforming it into a painting."

Working in black and white, Susana Wald uses pen and waterproof India ink (Pelikan); the support materials for these mirages is illustration board in various off-white colors or 400 lb Arches rag. She also paints in various dilutions of acrylic color the mirages intended to give the appearance of paintings. These pieces are supported on wood, canvas or rag paper.

The essential aspect of their united work is that they start from a given image and arrive at a different one. The collage remains in it, but there is a superimposition, "the work of the unconscious that explodes in scales, bodies, and improbable machines." Much of their collage work illustrates poetry – Zeller's and others. Like his press, Oasis, the work itself stands in relief against spiritual dryness.

KATHLEEN ZIMMERMAN

Kathleen Zimmerman has been working in collage since the early 1970s. Trained in painting at the Art Students League and the National Academy School of Fine Arts in New York, she shifted her medium to collage in order to concentrate on abstract design.

Though abstraction still plays a role – especially in her smaller series – much of her current work investigates the formal composition of landscape. "I grew up in Floral Park, Long Island, when it was still country. Living in the city, I like to think about spaces – coves, marshes, fields." She has traveled West and the vistas of canyons and mountains inspire her collages. She does no preliminary drawing but prefers to imagine and feel the sense of autumn fields or red rock walls.

Feeling evokes colors, which she associates with moods. In color, texture, and tone she acknowledges the influence of Bonnard and Vuillard, for whom she has done a series in homage. Combining the textures of many papers, she builds her images in bold patterns that draw the eye toward an intricate horizon composed of small pieces. Space is her essential theme, negative space playing consciously against the positive. Her "interstices" allow the viewer to see between pieces into a further, elusive distance.

To achieve this complicated layering of space, she works with Oriental papers, tissues, lettering, and papers that she paints with acrylic. Each landscape has a dominant color range, and because it may take several months for a large landscape to become complete, she works on four or five at a time, each on a separate table, rearranging papers until the final composition is established.

Her paste-up technique is precise and elaborate. First she traces the composition accurately. Then she numbers each layer from the top down as she removes the pieces, starting with #1 and arriving at the bottom layer, often as high as #20. Working with a brush and PVA, she then pastes the collage onto canvasboard. She starts with the highest number, trimming the edges in order to avoid lumps from overlays. Thus when the top #1 layer is put into place the completed collage is still perfectly flat. Finally, the tracing, now liberated from its practical purpose, becomes the outline of a drawing, which she completes in its own right.

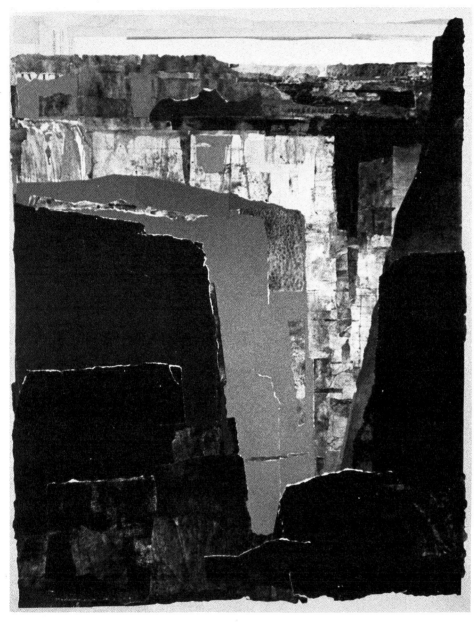

102 Kathleen Zimmerman: *Colorado Canyon* (1978). Paper collage, 24 × 30 in. Collection of the artist.

JIM ZVER

Born in Chicago, Jim Zver received his B.F.A. from the Art Institute of Chicago in 1957. After taking an M.F.A. at Cornell (1969), he moved to New York, where he has since lived and worked.

Zver's large, seemingly floating collages express the most basic cellular structures of life. In muted tones, subdued by gray striations, his "vocabulary of shapes" gather in mounting clusters like immense crystals, hovering boulders, or a budding hydra. It is not surprising that Zver takes inspiration from minerals and gems, or that he is influenced by music, the stratified soaring of Wagner, the broken "shards" of Bartok. Like Bartok's music, his collages gather momentum from abrupt thematic changes.

Only the formal element, the movement, the accretion of growing shapes, occupies Zver in making the pieces. His paper collages, begun in 1974, evolved from the debris of proof sheets done for photo silkscreen paintings. These were hard-edged and controlled, allowing no room for the chance element of the hand. The torn pieces broke the edge, and he discovered the liberating process of collage, which became and still remains for him a fast, intense medium for the construction of imageless ideas.

Zver's freedom in collage makes him resist the boundary of rectilinear form. This begins in his handling of paper. In conceiving a paper piece, he first prepares a large number of paper sheets in a particular color range, which he achieves by washes of acrylic color overlaid with lacquer spray paint and India inks. With the exception of the *Portrero Hill Series*, a chromatic response to California light, the color range predominant in earth tones is often veiled in strong lines of gray and blacks.

His principal collage method is to tear a collection of these painted papers into a lexicon of subconsciously arrived-at shapes and compose from them on the floor – often working on two to six collages at a time. The initial compositions, taped together, he mounts on corrugated board painted the color of linen. When at leisure he has arrived at the final revision, he fixes the pieces to each other with "Yes" dextrine paste, dotted at strategic points allowing the edges to curl slightly – like the scales of a mammoth dragon or the edges of mica schist. With the same adhesive he mounts the piece on linen attached to a chipboard backing that has been sealed with gesso. Thus the piece comes to float in its frame.

His desire to release the large work from rectilinear confinement led to his successful development of fiberglass collages. Industrial fiberglass (available in large rolls), he discovered, looked like matte finish Oriental paper and could be torn to achieve the same edges. With the help of a plastics engineer, he achieved a resin that could serve as a pigment medium and an adhesive. Diluted with acetone, his color resin washes penetrate the fiberglass and become totally bonded to it, giving the appearance of painted paper. In the new medium he is able to make large, durable, free-floating collages. The resin used as an adhesive allows him to reinforce the

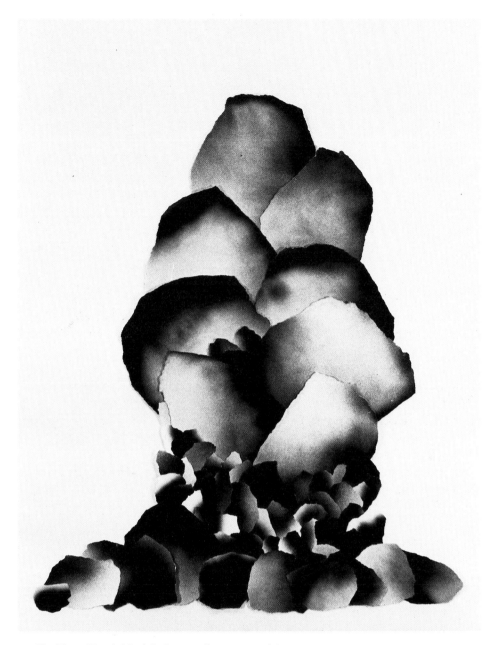

103 Jim Zver: *Untitled* (1982). Paper collage, 45 × 38 in.

painted piece with a second layer of fiberglass cut to shape, and he mounts the work directly on the wall with Velcro.

In their immediacy, these collages are most impressive. "I want them to be seen simultaneously as abstract forms implying three dimensional space and to have an openness to be read as a specific image." Organic catalysts for the viewer's imagination, they communicate the power of form from the violent flow of lava to the reality of the DNA helix.

Notes

CHAPTER ONE   **A Short History of Collage**

[1]Herta Wescher, *Collage*, trans. Robert E. Wolf (New York: Harry N. Abrams, n. d.), p. 7. Much of this brief history is indebted to her research and to Eddie Wolfram's *History of Collage* (New York: Macmillan Publishing Co., 1975).
[2]Wescher, p. 40.
[3]Ibid., p. 59.
[4]Cited in English by Wolfram, p. 80.
[5]Dawn Ades, *Photomontage* (London: Thames and Hudson, 1976), plates 29 and 38.
[6]Cited in English by Wolfram, p. 88.
[7]Lucy R. Lippard, *Surrealists on Art* (Englewood Cliffs, New Jersey: Prentice-Hall, 1970), pp. 79–85.

[8]Charmion von Wiegand, "The Oriental Tradition and Abstract Art," *The World of Abstract Art*, The American Abstract Artists, ed. Wittenborn (New York, 1957), p. 56.
[9]Charles E. Martin, "Appalachian House Beautiful," *Natural History*, February 1982, 4–16.
[10]Donald Windham, "Anne Ryan and her Collages," *Art News* 73: 76, May 1974.
[11]Born in 1906, working currently in Riverhead, New York.

CHAPTER TWO   **Paper: The Fiber of Collage**

[1]W. J. Barrow Research Laboratory, *Physical and Chemical Properties of Book Papers, 1507–1949*. Permanence/Durability of the Book VII, Richmond, Virginia 1974, p. 13.

Photographic Acknowledgments

Photographs courtesy of the artists: II, IX, XII, XIV, XV, XVI, 43, 63, 65, 67, 69, 71, 73, 88, 89, 103; Mario Cal: 90; Cavendish Photographic Co. 59; Geoffrey Clements: 84; D. James Dee: 91; Joan Digby: VII; eeva-inkeri: 45; Leigh Photographic Group: 81; Eric Pollitzer: XI; Porter-Wiener Studio: 87; Yoshiomi Tachibana: 100; Malcolm Varon: IV.

All work by John Digby is reproduced by courtesy of the Francis Kyle Gallery, London.

Acknowledgments

In the preparation of this book we have been privileged to encounter the generosity of a great many people. First we wish to thank all those collagists who have shared their time and the intimacy of their working methods with us so that we might come to see the whole process that brings collage to life. We also wish to thank the host of galleries that have offered us their assistance and graciously permitted us to reproduce work in their collections. Each separate photo credit is an acknowledgment of their participation. Among those who have offered continuous support in this project, we wish to thank particularly Mrs. Margaret Kilik of the Key Gallery, New York; Mr. Takis Efstathiou of the Ericson Gallery, New York; and Mr. Tim Walsh of the Andrew Crispo Gallery, New York.

One very personal note of thanks must go to Mr. and Mrs. Richard Feld, who have given us great encouragement and permitted us to reproduce work in their private collection.

Gathering information has led us also to a number of special people – chemists and paper conservators – whose expert knowledge has guided us through the chapters on materials and archival considerations. We wish especially to thank Professor Paul N. Banks, Director of the Conservation and Preservation Program, School of Library Service, Columbia University, for his scrutiny of the manuscript and patience in helping us to understand difficult problems; Professor Norbert S. Baer of the New York University Institute of Fine Arts for permitting us to credit his work on adhesives; Anne F. Clapp for providing us with her most current formula for paper deacidification; Dr. Richard D. Smith for answering particular questions about his Wei T'o products; and Betty Fiske of the Metropolitan Museum of Art in New York for spending her valuable time in heightening our awareness of paper conservation issues.

We also wish to thank Dr. Joan Shields, Professor of Chemistry, C. W. Post College, Long Island University, for adapting chemical procedures to studio use and serving as technical adviser on this book; and Professor James Dwyer of the same department for his light-box design. Among the chemists a special note of thanks must go to Dr. Irma T. Weiss, Professor Emerita, New York University, and Dr. Louis Weiss who offered their joint expertise as readers of the manuscript.

Several translators have helped us bridge the gaps in communicating with foreign artists. We would like to thank Professor Masako Yukawa, C. W. Post College, for her translation of Japanese material; Mrs. Hanna Konig for her assistance in correspondence and translations from Czech; Mr. Horst Fischer and Mr. Detlef Schmidt for communicating with the German artists and rendering the translations that we required.

These people and a great many others are responsible for our completion of this book. We wish to thank our patient typist, Mrs. Nancy Meyer, and the C. W. Post Faculty Research Committee for its assistance toward manuscript expenses, along with the librarians, gallery assistants, curators, and manufacturers who have supplied us with catalogs and technical information. To everyone who has been so generous and open we offer our acknowledgment of thanks.

Some British Suppliers of Archival Quality Collage Materials

Key
A   Adhesives
B   Mounting cards
C*   Catalogue available
D   Deacidification materials
MT   Artist's materials and tools
pH   pH testing materials
P   Paper
S   Storage materials
SF   Support fabrics
T   Tapes

Ademco (Archival Aids)	A	
Coronation Road	C*	
Cressex Estate	D	
High Wycombe	MT	
Bucks. HP12 3TA	SF	
(0494) 448661		
Atlantis Paper Company	A	
E2 Warehouse New Crane Wharf	B	
Garnet Street	C*	
London E1	D	
01-481-3784	MT	
	S	
	SF	
Dryad	A	
P. O. Box 38	C*	
Northgates	MT	for papermaking and marbling
Leics. LE1 9BU		
(0533) 50405		
Falkiner Fine Papers Ltd	A	starches, methyl cellulose, PVA
117 Long Acre	B	
London WC2E 9PA	C*	
01-240-2339	D	
	MT	including conservation products and books
	P	Western and Oriental, wide selection of papers from small private mills
	T	
J. Barcham Green Ltd	P	
Hayle Mill		
Maidstone		
Kent ME15 6XQ		
(0622) 674343		

Hercules Powder Company 20 Red Lion Street London WC1R 4PB 01-404-4000	A	methyl cellulose
Samuel Jones & Company St. Neots Mill St. Neots Hunts. (0480) 75351	T	linen
T. N. Lawrence Ltd 2–4 Bleeding Heart Yard Greville Street Hatton Garden London EC1 01-242-3534	C* MT P	including craft books Western and Oriental
Picreator Enterprises Ltd 44 Park View Gardens Hendon London NW4 2PN 01-202-8972	A C* pH SF	fungicides
Russell Bookcrafts Hitchin Herts. (0462) 59711	A C* D MT P T	

Note: Aclé spring binders (see p. 129) are available from Aclé, 50 rue Charenton, 75012 Paris, France.

Some United States Suppliers of Archival Quality Collage Materials

Andrews/Nelson/Whitehead
31–10 48th Avenue
Long Island City, New York 11101
(212) 937-7100

P
B
C*

Western and Oriental

Aiko's Art Materials Import
714 No. Wabash Avenue
Chicago, Illinois 60611
(312) 943-0745

P
MT

Oriental

Applied Science Laboratory
218 No. Adams Street
Richmond, Virginia 23220
(703) 231-9386

D
pH

Barrow spot test kit for paper analysis

C. T. Bainbridge's Sons, Inc.
50 Northfield Avenue
Edison, New Jersey 08817
(201) 225-9100

B
C*

Conservation Materials, Ltd
Box 2884
340 Freeport Boulevard
Sparks, Nevada 89431
(702) 331-0582
Telex 377405
Answerback SALOMONNA SPKS

A
C*
D
MT
P
pH
S
SF
T

full selection for archival work

80 Papers (Wendy Stewart)
80 Thompson Street
New York, New York 10012
(212) 966-1491

C*
P

Western and Oriental including a large selection from small handmills and paper-making kits

Fine Art Materials, Inc.
539 LaGuardia Place
New York, New York 10012
(212) 982-7100

P
C*

Western and Oriental, including Chinese

The Hollinger Corporation
P. O. Box 6185
Arlington, Virginia 22206
(703) 671-6600

C*
D
P
S

New York Central Art Supply 62 Third Avenue New York, New York 10003 (212) 473-7705	A B C* MT pH P	including fine paper catalogue Western, Oriental, paper-making kits and a wide selection of papers from small handmills
Process Materials Corp. (Archivart) 30 Veterans Boulevard Rutherford, New Jersey 07070 (201) 935-2900 Cable PROMATCO, Rutherford, N. J. TWX 710 989 0293 (LIND RTFD)	A B C* P SF T	including heavy and unusual mounting boards (Promatco)
Rohm & Haas Company Independence Mall West Philadelphia, Pennsylvania 19105 (215) 582-3000	A S	water-soluble resins (UF-3 ultraviolet filtering plexiglass)
Talas 213 West 35th Street 9th Floor New York, New York 10036 (212) 736-7744	A B C* D MT P pH S SF T	full selection for archival work Western and Oriental
University Products, Inc. P. O. Box 101 South Canal Street Holyoke, Massachusetts 01041 (413) 532-9431 800-628-9431	A B C* D MT P pH S SF T	
Wei T'o Associates, Inc. P. O. Drawer 40 Matteson, Illinois 60443 (312) 747-6660	C* D MT pH	
Zora's 11961 Santa Monica Boulevard Los Angeles, California 90025 (213) 477-0451	A P	

Selected Bibliography

Books on Collage History and Collagists

Ades, Dawn. *Photomontage*. London: Thames and Hudson, 1976.

Arnason, H. H. *Robert Motherwell*. New York: Harry N. Abrams, 1977.

Ashton, Dore. *A Joseph Cornell Album*. New York: Viking Press, 1974.

Bann, Stephen, ed. *The Tradition of Constructivism*. New York: Viking Press, 1974.

Bush, Martin. *Goodnough*. New York: Abbeville Press, 1981.

Forge, Andrew. *Robert Rauschenberg*. New York: Harry N. Abrams, 1970.

Friedman, B. H. *Alphonso Ossorio*. New York: Harry N. Abrams, 1965.

Haecker, Hans-Joachim. *Friedrich Meckseper*. Braunschweig: Westermann, 1982.

Janis, Harriet, and Blesh, Rudy. *Collage Personalities, Concepts and Techniques*. Philadelphia: Chilton Book Company, 1967.

Jean, Marcel, ed. *The Autobiography of Surrealism*. New York: Viking Press, 1980.

Lippard, Lucy R. *Surrealists on Art*. Englewood Cliffs, N. J.: Prentice-Hall, 1970.

Martin, Marianne W. *Futurist Art and Theory 1909–1915*. Oxford: Clarendon Press, 1968.

Matthews, J. H. *The Imagery of Surrealism*. Syracuse: Syracuse University Press, 1977.

Neumann, Eckhard, ed. *Bauhaus and Bauhaus People*. New York: Von Nostrand Reinhold, 1970.

Pomeroy, Ralph. *Stamos*. New York: Harry N. Abrams, n. d.

Rotzler, Willy. *Constructive Concepts*. Zurich: ABC Edition, 1977.

Rubin, William S. *Dada and Surrealist Art*. New York: Harry N. Abrams, n. d.

Schmalenbach, Werner. *Kurt Schwitters*. New York: Harry N. Abrams, n. d.

Waldman, Diane. *Joseph Cornell*. New York: George Braziller, 1977.

Washington, M. Bunch. *The Art of Romare Bearden: The Prevalence of Ritual*. New York: Harry N. Abrams, n. d.

Wescher, Herta. *Collage*. trans. Robert E. Wolf. New York: Harry N. Abrams, 1968.

Wolfram, Eddie. *History of Collage*. New York: Macmillan Publishing Company, 1975.

Zeller, Ludwig. *50 Collages*. intro. Edouard Jager. Oakville, Ontario: Mosaic Press, 1981.

Exhibition Catalogs

The Birmingham Museum of Art: Birmingham, Michigan. *Irwin Kremen*, 27 September–1 November 1981.

Castelli Feigen Corcoran Gallery: New York. *Joseph Cornell: Collages, 1931–1972*, 6 May–3 June 1978. Catalog text by Donald Windham and Howard Hussey.

Contemporary Arts Museum: Houston, Texas. *Collage International from Picasso to the Present*, 27 February–6 April 1958. Catalog text by Jermayne MacAgy.

——. *The Americans: The Collage*, 11 July–3 October 1982. Catalog text by Linda L. Cathcart.

The College of Wooster: Wooster, Ohio. *Miriam Schapiro: A Retrospective, 1953–1980*, 10 September–25 October 1980. Essays by Thalia Gouma-Peterson, Linda Nochlin, Norma Brouxe, John Perreault, and interviews with the artist by Paula Bradley and Ruth A. Appelhof.

The Andrew Crispo Gallery: New York, 1979. *Robert Courtright: Recent Works—Collages 1972–1977*. Catalog text by Calvin Tomkins.

——, 1981. *Robert Courtright: Collage Masks 1976–1981*.

——, 1977. *Masters of Collage: Twelve Americans*. Catalog text by Gene Baro.

The Solomon R. Guggenheim Museum: New York, 1975. *Max Ernst: A Retrospective*.

——, 1975. *Jiří Kolář*. Catalogue text by Thomas M. Messer, compiled from the writing of Jindřich Chalupecky, Raoul-Jean Moulin, Wieland Schmied, and Jiří Kolář.

Institute für Auslandsbeziehungen: Stuttgart, 1977. *Max Ernst Books and Graphic Work*. Catalog text by Werner Spies.

The Jewish Museum: New York. *Robert Rauschenberg*, 30 March–30 April 1963. Catalog text by Alan R. Solomon.

Marlborough Fine Art (London) Ltd. *Kurt Schwitters in Exile: The Late Work 1937–1948*, 2–31 October 1981.

Marlborough Gallery: New York. *Anne Ryan: Collages*, 16 November–4 December 1974.

Miami-Dade Community College, Frances Wolfson Art Gallery: Miami. *The Art of Robert Courtright*, 3 March–15 April 1983. Catalog texts by Calvin Tomkins and John and Joan Digby. Traveling exhibition.

The Mississippi Museum of Art: Jackson, Mississippi. *Collage and Assemblage*, 17 September–15 November 1981. Catalog text by Francis Naumann. Traveling exhibition.

Municipal Art Gallery of Los Angeles. *William Dole Retrospective 1960–1975*, 14 April–16 May 1976. Catalog text by Gerald Nordland. Traveling exhibition.

The Museum of Modern Art: New York. *The Art of Assemblage*, 2 October–12 November 1961. Catalog text by William C. Seitz. Traveling exhibition.

——. *Joseph Cornell*, 17 November 1980–20 January 1981. ed. Kynaston McShine with essays by Dawn Ades, Carter Ratcliff, P. Adams Sitney, and Lynda Roscoe Hartigan.

——. *Robert Motherwell*, 30 September–28 November 1965. Catalog text by Frank O'Hara.

National Collection of Fine Art, Washington, D. C., 1978. *Collages by Irwin Kremen*. Catalog text by Joshua C. Taylor, Ted Potter, John Cage, M. C. Richard, Merce Cunningham, Irwin Kremen and Janet Flint.

——. *Robert Rauschenberg*, 30 October 1976–2 January 1977. Catalog text by Lawrence Alloway.

SITES: Washington, D. C. 1981. *Collages: Selections from the Hirshorn Museum and Sculpture Garden*.

Staempfli Gallery: New York. *William Dole: A Retrospective Exhibition of Collages 1958–1978*, 14 November–9 December 1978. Traveling exhibition.

Whitechapel Art Gallery: London, 1964. *Robert Rauschenberg: Paintings, Drawings, and Combines 1949–1964*.

Wicheta State University: Wicheta, Kansas, 1973. *Goodnough*. Catalog text by Martin H. Bush and Moffett Kenward.

Articles

Berman, Avis, "Romare Bearden," *Art News*, December 1980, 79: 60–67.

Bultman, Fritz, "A Statement on Collage," *Cornell Review* 6 (Summer 1979): 43.

Bush, M. H., "Robert Goodnough's Collages," *Arts*, April 1982, 56: 89–91.

De Kooning, Elaine, "Vincente Paints a Collage," *Art News*, September 1953, 52: 38–41.

Firestone, E. R., "Fritz Bultman's Collages," *Arts*, December 1981, 56: 63–65.

Hess, Thomas B., "Collage as an Historical Method," *Art News*, November 1961, 60: 30–33, 69–71.

Jensen, Lawrence, "Acrylic and Collage," *American Artist*, June 1974, pp. 48–51.

Kotz, Mary Lynn, "Robert Rauschenberg's State of the Universe Message," *Art News*, February 1983, 82: 54–61.

Kramer, Hilton, "Rauschenberg and the Materialized Image," *Artforum*, December 1974, pp. 36–43.

Larson, Kay, "Rauschenberg's Renaissance," *New York Magazine*, 27 December 1982–3 January 1983, pp. 48–56.

Martin, H., "Mashed Potatoes: The Collages of Ray Johnson," *Art and Artists*, May 1972, 7: 22–25.

Wilson, William, "Ray Johnson: New York Correspondence School," *Art and Artists*, April 1966, 1: 54–57.

Technical References on Materials and Conservation

Barrow, W. J., Research Laboratory. *Permanence/Durability of the Book*. 7 vols. 1963–1974.
"Spray Deacidification," vol. 3, 1964.
"Polyvinyl Acetate (PVA) Adhesives for Use in Library Binding," vol. 4, 1965.
"Strength and Other Characteristics of Book Papers 1800–1899," vol. 5, 1967.
"Spot Testing for Unstable Modern Book and Record Papers," vol. 6, 1969.
"Physical and Chemical Properties of Book Papers, 1509–1949," vol. 7, 1974.

Barrow, W. J., *Manuscripts and Documents, Their Deterioration and Restoration*. Charlottesville: University of Virginia Press, 1976.

Baer, N. S., N. Indictor, and W. H. Phelan, "An Evaluation of Adhesives for Use in Paper Conservation," *The Bulletin* IIC-AG, Vol. II, No. 2 (April, 1971).

——. "An Evaluation of Poly(vinyl Acetate) Adhesives for Use in Paper Conservation," *Restaurator* 2 (1975): 121–137.

Baer, N. S., N. Indictor, T. I. Schwartzman, and T. L. Rosenberg, "Chemical and Physical Properties of Poly(vinyl Acetate) Copolymer Emulsions," ICOM Committee for Conservation, 4th Triennial Meeting Proceedings, Venice 1975. 75/22/5–1.

Banks, P. N., "Paper Cleaning," *Restaurator* 1 (1969): 52–66.

——. *A Selective Bibliography of Materials in English on the Conservation of Research Library Materials.* Chicago: The Newberry Library, 1978.

Bokman, W. "The Care of Photographic Colour Materials, Restoration Aspects and Archival Processing in General." Ottawa: Canadian Conservation Institute, April 1974. Manuscript.

Byrne, J. and J. Weiner. *Permanence.* Appleton, Wisconsin: Institute of Paper Chemistry, 1964. Bibliographic Series, No. 213.

Clapp, Anne F. *Curatorial Care of Works of Art on Paper*, 2nd. rev. ed. Oberlin, Ohio: Intermuseum Conservation Association, 1974.

Clydesdale, Amanda. *Chemicals in Conservation: A Guide to Possible Hazards and Safe Use.* Edinburgh: Conservation Bureau, Scottish Society for Conservation and Restoration, 1982.

Cunha, George Martin and Dorothy Grant Cunha. *Conservation of Library Materials.* 2nd ed. 2 vols. Metuchen, New Jersey: The Scarecrow Press, 1972.

Dolloff, F. W. and R. Perkinson. *How to Care for Works of Art on Paper.* Boston: Museum of Fine Arts, 1971.

Eastman Kodak Company. *Copying.* Rochester, New York: Eastman Kodak Company, 1974. Kodak Publication M-1.

——. *Black/White Processing for Permanence.* Rochester, New York: Eastman Kodak Company, 1976. Kodak Publication J-19.

Hunter, Dard. *Papermaking: The History and Technique of an Ancient Craft.* 2nd ed. New York: Knopf, 1947.

Indictor, N., N. S. Baer, and W. H. Phelan. "Evaluation of Pastes for Use in Paper Conservation." *Restaurator* 2 (1975): 139–149.

Langwell, W. H. *The Conservation of Books and Documents.* London: Sir Isaac Pitman and Sons, 1958.

——. "Methods of Deacidifying Paper." *Journal of the Society of Archivists* 3 (April 1969): 491–494.

Langwell, W. H. "Accelerated Aging Tests for Paper." *Journal of the Society of Archivists* 3 (April 1967): 245–248.

Norris, F. H. *Paper and Paper Making.* London: Oxford University Press, 1952.

Smith, Marrily A. *Matting and Hinging of Works of Art on Paper.* Washington D. C.: Preservation Office, Library of Congress, 1981.

Turner, Silvie and Brigit Skiöld, *Handmade Paper Today*, London: Lund Humphries, 1983.

Williams, John C., ed. *Preservation of Paper and Textiles of Historic and Artistic Value.* Washington D. C.: American Chemical Society, 1977.

Conservation Periodicals of Interest to Collagists

Paper Conservator. Institute of Paper Conservation. P. O. Box 17, London WC1N 2PE.

Restaurator. Munksgaard International Publishers. 35 Nörre Sögado. Di-1370. Copenhagen, Denmark.

Instruction Books

Ashurst, Elizabeth. *Collage.* London and New York: Marshall Cavendish, 1976.

Borja, Corinne and Robert Borja. *Making Collages.* Chicago: Albert Whitman, 1972.

Brigadier, Anne. *Collage: A Complete Guide for Artists.* New York: Watson-Guptil Publications, 1970.

Connor, Margaret. *Introducing Fabric Collage.* New York: Watson-Guptil Publications, 1960.

Firpo, Patrick, Lester Alexander, Claudia Katayangi, Steve Ditlea. *Copyart: The First Complete Guide to the Copy Machine.* New York: Richard Marek, 1978.

French, Brian. *Principles of Collage.* London: Mills and Boon, 1969.

Hutton, Helen. *The Techniques of Collage.* London: Batsford, New York: Watson-Guptil Publications, 1968.

Laliberte, Norman, and Alex Mogelon. *Collage, Montage, Assemblage.* New York: Van Nostrand Reinhold, n. d.

Lynch, John. *How to Make Collages.* New York: Viking Press, 1961.

Meilach, Dona and Ten Hoor, Elvie. *Collage and Found Art.* London: Studio Vista, 1965.

Portchmouth, John. *Working in Collage.* London: Studio Vista, 1973.

Priolo, Joan B. *Ideas for Collage*. New York: Sterling, 1972.

Share, Marjorie. *Collages: How To . . . .* Washington, D. C.: Smithsonian Institution Traveling Exhibition Service, 1981.

Stribling, Mary Lous. *Art From Found Materials*. New York: Crown, 8th printing, 1973.

Vanderbilt, Gloria with Alfred Allen Lewis. *Gloria Vanderbilt Book of Collage*. New York: Van Nostrand Reinhold, 1970.

Yokoo, Tadanori. *Collage Design*. Art Technique Now +18. Tokyo: Kawade Shobo Shin Sha, 1977.

Index